Values at Work

EMPLOYEE PARTICIPATION MEETS

MARKET PRESSURE AT MONDRAGÓN

Updated Edition

GEORGE CHENEY

ILR Press an Imprint of
Cornell University Press
ITHACA AND LONDON

This book is dedicated to the radical notion that
work ought to dignify rather than diminish
the human experience.

This book is published with the aid of a grant from the Program for Cultural Cooperation between Spain's Ministry of Education and Culture and United States Universities.

First published 1999 by Cornell University Press
First printing, Cornell Paperbacks, 2002

Printed in the United States of America

Library of Congress Cataloging-in-Publication Data

Cheney, George.
Values at work : employee participation meets market pressure at Mondragón / George Cheney.
p. cm.
Includes bibliographical references and index.
ISBN 0-8014-3325-8 (cloth : acid-free paper)
ISBN 0-8014-8816-8 (pbk. : acid-free paper)
1. Producer cooperatives—Spain—Mondragón. 2. Management—Employee participation—Spain—Mondragón. I. Title.
HD3218.M66C48   1999
331'.01'12094661—dc21   99-37026

Cloth printing   10 9 8 7 6 5 4 3 2 1
Paperback printing   10 9 8 7 6 5 4 3 2 1

CONTENTS

PREFACE TO THE
CORNELL PAPERBACKS EDITION

From the time I started working on this project in December 1991, I sought to balance an emphasis on a specific case study with a treatment of contemporary issues that would be broadly relevant to today's world. Three years after publication, I can say that I maintained that balance fairly well.

In the dozen or so reviews of the book that have appeared so far, an important tension has emerged between optimistic and pessimistic assessments of the case of Mondragón. While I was at Mondragón, other visitors would ask me "Have they sold out?" In contrast, interested readers have sought my take on and ultimately the answer to the future of the Mondragón worker cooperatives as a hopeful beacon of creative grassroots organizing. But I knew early on that I wanted to chart a course somewhere between upbeat accounts of Mondragón's exceptionalism and the skeptical, or even cynical, critiques that saw nothing but a veneer of democracy over the co-ops.

Although neither my book nor anyone else's could offer a definitive answer to the question of Mondragón's selling out, I did want to provide some practical recommendations for "cooperators" in business and in other sectors for dealing with the demands and pressures on value-based enterprises today. Since publication, I have been delighted to hear that some worker co-ops and social-movement organizations have found the recommendations discussed in chapter 4 to be useful.

This year, 2002, marks the tenth anniversary of my first trip to Mondragón. Since then I have continued to follow some of the co-ops' developments through e-mails and reports. I believe that most, if not all, of the trends I identified in the 1999 book are still in place and, if anything, the co-ops are moving further along the path toward becoming stable transnational corporations. What is somewhat less clear to me is how well new employee participation programs are working—in terms of both organizational effectiveness and individual satisfaction, and I would urge others to explore that issue in depth. The social question—"Can Mondragón keep its soul?"—is more difficult for me to *re*assess without conducting a new round of probing interviews and visiting Mondragón for a fourth time. However, based on the reports of several colleagues who have been there recently, I sense that there are no qualitative changes in what I reported in 1999.

What has commanded my attention in the time since *Values at Work* was first published has been the appearance of an array of *other* cases of workplace democracy and grassroots economic development around the world, seen against larger backdrops of the business for social responsibility movement and market globalization. Such cases may often seem isolated, but if they survive more than a few years, they quickly gain relevance for people trying to visualize and find guidance in doing business differently. While I have no space for detail here, I wish to cite several interesting cases of Mondragón-inspired organizing:

- In San Francisco, Mike Miller, now editor of *Social Policy*, uses the example of Mondragón widely, both to illustrate possibilities of alternative economics and to argue that even cooperatives need independent representation of rank-and-file worker-owners (which Mondragón lacks).
- Also in San Francisco, Dave Karoly and Tim Huet in the Network of Bay Area Collectives are facilitating small business start-ups such as the Arizmendi bakeries and pizza shops, as well as connecting them with well-established co-ops like Rainbow Grocery.
- In Missoula, Montana, Dean Ritz and the Jeannette Rankin Peace Center are sponsoring a series of discussions on "Defining Democracy," which consider ways to counter the concentration of corporate control in the United States through a variety of citizen actions, including al-

ternative local economies. These discussions include in-depth critiques of businesses claiming to be value-based or socially conscious.

- Chuck Sperry and his friends at the Rocky Mountain Center for Economic Democracy are exploring Mondragón-like options for co-ops in the wood products and rural sectors in the central and northern Rockies, including small businesses to be focused on persons with disabilities and low-income persons.
- In Cape Breton, Nova Scotia, Greg McLeod and his collaborators are hosting pan–North American conferences on promoting community economic development using Mondragón's successes and lessons. Greg's own book, *From Mondragón to America: Experiments in Community Economic Development* (Sydney, N.S., Canada: University College of Cape Breton Press, 1997), broadens the application of the Mondragón experience to visions of whole communities.
- Similarly, in Auckland, New Zealand, Manase Lua and the Working Council of the Tongan Vision Project are trying to unite New Zealand's Tongan people by bootstrapping their local economy with a home investment plan, a small business incubator, homework centers for school kids, and a computer networking academy for students in secondary and higher education.

All of these projects borrow heavily from the Mondragón experience, offering powerful testimony to the enduring relevance of the case. I am pleased to be in contact with all of these people and especially to be working closely with a few of them.

My greatest hope is that this book, especially in a less expensive paperback form, can contribute in some small way to discussions of the pressing issues of our time. Since *Values at Work* was first issued in November 1999, we have all heard a heightened debate over market globalization, especially with protests at Seattle, Genoa, and Quebec City. This is but one of many contemporary trends that cast the Mondragón case in a new and perhaps more urgent light. The other themes I see as most salient in the book and most relevant to discussions of economy and society today are:

- To what extent is this case of workplace democracy applicable to others?
- Can cooperativism enjoy a higher status and a wider success given today's market requirements?
- Can we reasonably expect top-down employee-participation programs to achieve the kind of vibrancy found in grassroots organizing?

- What does the Mondragón case say about the authenticity and viability of socially responsible business models?
- Does Mondragón offer any clues to avenues of resistance to market globalization?
- What sorts of values, practices, and demands can we expect from employees and consumers?
- What possibilities exist for economic justice within the current structure of multinational capitalism and consumerist culture?

I would like to close with a few words about pedagogy. From the beginning, I hoped this book would serve both as a case study supplement and as one in a series of topical books in upper-division undergraduate and graduate-level courses. I have not been disappointed. The book has been used in general courses on organizational communication, organizational sociology, industrial and labor relations, and management and organizational behavior, and in more specific ("special topics") seminars on workplace democracy, market globalization, organizational rhetoric and discourse, organizational decision making, alternative organizations, and quality of work life. I've received provocative and helpful feedback from many student-readers, and in several cases I've conducted conference calls with entire classes. This has been particularly rewarding, and I'm now incorporating the "interview with the author" exercise into several of my own courses. This strategy brings a book alive for students, allowing them and the author to challenge and extend parts of a book and even to inspire new research and writing.

At the request of readers, I have set up a website at http://www.hum. utah.edu/communication/general/faculty/cheney/html. The following items, along with other related documents, can be found there:

- A map of Mondragón and the larger area around it
- A chart of the organizational structure of a Mondragón co-op
- A list of meanings of *solidaridad* revealed at Mondragón
- A list of paradoxes and contradictions of workplace democracy and employee participation

I can be reached by e-mail at cheney@admin.comm.utah.edu.

GEORGE CHENEY

Salt Lake City

PREFACE

Co-operators have always been inspired by the ancient doctrine of human fellowship, by the new spirit of social service, by a firm faith that the day would come when each man and woman would work, not for personal subsistence or personal gain, but for the whole community.
—Beatrice Potter, *The Co-operative Movement in Great Britain*, 1891

At the close of the nineteenth century, important questions were being raised about the values of business organizations and the proper roles of business in society. In a series of massive studies, spanning publicly held corporations, labor unions, and employee-owned cooperatives, Beatrice Potter Webb and Sydney Webb examined not only the factors contributing to the longevity and growth of organizations but also the tensions between economic pressures and social commitments. In today's market environment we are compelled to return to the same set of issues, as we contemplate the future of work, productivity, and consumption.

In planning this book, I was searching for an exemplary organization: a profitable large business that adhered strongly to certain social values and, above all, held an enduring commitment to democratic participation. My driving question was: "To what extent is it possible for a business to maintain a core of social values—such as participatory democracy—while growing, becoming more complex, and being financially successful?" In a way, this practical question echoes the fundamental theoretical concerns of Max Weber, Robert Michels, Emile Durkheim, Karl Marx, and other early analysts of modern society.

The central question about the *social* potential and obligations of business remains with us, and we find it expressed today in various public debates, including discussions of the concept of business for social responsibility in countries around the world. In fact, during the time I was writing this book, such debates became more visible and more urgent. Efficient as the market is for achieving certain specified goals, in its current form, the critics are saying, it can't address inequality and it shouldn't set our social priorities for us. Given the huge roles played by major corporations in shaping policies throughout the world, it is crucial that we look closely at their activities with respect to the future of democracy.

While sharp questions are being raised about corporate capitalism in the "post-socialist" era, we find ourselves wondering aloud about the nature of the social contract between individual employees and employing organizations. Reengineering, downsizing, and outsourcing have significantly changed the character of many organizations in the public, private, and third sectors. Amid the rush toward heightened efficiency and competitiveness is a sense that most organizations don't care a great deal about their employees, however. In fact, worker insecurity and social dissatisfaction are on the rise at the very same time that the U.S. stock market is setting new records, suggesting that certain indicators of economic or market health are largely decoupled from other signs of social well-being. In newly "flattened" organizations, where teamwork is all the rage, it often seems that employees are under as much pressure as ever. Such business trends both reflect and contribute to developments in the larger society, as unexamined slogans such as "quality customer service" are shouted in all sectors.

In my teaching and research about organizations for nearly twenty years, I have focused on two distinct arenas, treating the internal and external affairs of the organization largely as separate universes. I've been observing and trying to improve the dynamics of communication, of human relations, inside the modern organization, and analyzing the various forms of communication (marketing, advertising, and public relations) outside the organization—that is, between the organization and its "environment." As I have continued to explore the expressions of social values and the programs of employee participation in organizations from major corporations to major universities, however, it has become clear to me that these two domains of activity are necessarily interrelated. It would be a mistake, speaking analytically or practically, to discuss one without keeping in mind the other. This broad view is just what the founders of modern organizational studies intended us to have.

Today, the image of the market unites the internal and external forces of the organization, even though people scarcely reflect on what actually comprises the market itself. Consultants speak of the interior of the organization as consisting of nothing but "internal markets," where employees and departments act as customers for one another. The work of the large organization is increasingly tied to what the consumer wants—or at least to what the organization *thinks or says* the consumer wants. Today the citizen has become the consumer, and the employee has become the consumer's supplier.

Much of this emphasis on the customer, as the career of the U.S. consumer advocate Ralph Nader attests, is well placed: it results in information for the customer and protection from abuses of large organizations in every sector; in some cases it even grants the consumer avenues for shaping governmental or corporate policy. However, when we probe more deeply, we find that much of the transformation of the citizen into the consumer that has come to preoccupy our factories, hospitals, agencies, and schools really involves only a type of pseudo-democracy. That is to say, what often seems like genuine employee involvement and citizen participation is actually quite shallow and routine—a process directed merely at producing and satisfying more and more momentary material wants and generating ever more production. Moving beyond the boundaries of the workplace, we find that consumption, at least in its common forms of expression, is no effective substitute for a rich notion of citizenship.

Further, what does employee participation or workplace democracy mean if it is directed *exclusively* at the presumed whims of the consumer, with complete subordination of other sources of employee motivation? To put it another way, when we're shopping at the mall we are all apparently "sovereign," but when we're at work we may be expected to do little else than try our best and fastest to make those other sovereigns happy. All the while we're at work, whether in factories or department stores, we may be simply looking forward to moments when we can rightfully wear the crown again.

Complicating matters further, an organization's relationship with its environment and especially the market isn't simply a matter of the market's exerting pressure on the organization. External pressures are also formulated by the organization itself in its own desired discourses of strategy, performance, and policy, as it strives to become what it thinks the world wants it to be, in synch with the "inevitable" trends of the marketplace. Ironically, it has been shown that corporations are remarkably adept at *projecting* their own experiences and images onto their actual and potential consumers. The organization often engages in *self*-persuasion about what's out there and how best to respond to it. Even one of the principal architects of corporate reengineering, Michael Hammer, has bemoaned the ways many managers jump on the bandwagon without knowing where the parade is headed.

This book takes a close, critical look at how one business is dealing simultaneously with its external pressures to compete in the global market and its efforts to revive its long-held democratic values within the new configuration of the customer-centered or market-driven firm. This multinational corporation is worker-owned, employee-managed, and is famous in some circles for its tradition of solidarity—both within the system and with the larger community. The Mondragón worker cooperatives, in the Basque Country of Spain, are now over forty years old and represent one of the most economically successful cases of a truly democratic workplace in the world. This is an organization of organizations. It includes, under the corporate umbrella of the Mondragón Cooperative Corporation (MCC), industrial, service, financial, and educational cooperatives. Also, there are several nearby co-ops that have broken administrative ties with the Mondragón Corporation to establish their own separate firm, the ULMA Group. But these co-ops are more than just an economic phenomenon, important as that aspect of their performance is. The co-ops have a lively and complex social dimension, which helps to explain how it is that they work to maintain values such as democracy, equality, and solidarity. The co-ops employ a blend of direct and representative democracy. They are in many ways people-centered while also trying to do a job and make money.

Mondragón is no Utopia; it is both more and less than that. Mondragón has its problems; it faces obstacles; it has changed over the decades. This book shows how employee-member-owners ("associates") and the organization as a whole are struggling with basic values such as participation, solidarity, and equality, at a time when the co-ops are undergoing internal transformation and experiencing great outside pressure. Cooperative and corporate values are unquestionably in conflict with one another, in a variety of ways.

A general manager of one of the co-ops told me in the summer of 1997, "Our greatest challenges can be summarized as two: responding to the client and involving all employees in the development of the firm so as to respond best to the client. These two objectives are strongly interdependent and tied to our very survival as a business."

The values of Mondragón themselves are discussed and to certain degrees enacted or lived. So it's important to consider how a value such as democracy is preserved through *both* the talk about it and the arrangements to make it happen. How we conceive of and discuss democracy is just as important as any particular institution we create to express it or put it into action. At Mondragón today, people *are* discussing their changing values, and the outcome of these discussions will shape how democracy is practiced there in the years ahead.

Value-related terms such as "participation" and "solidarity" refer in part to the ways people communicate with one another in certain situations: for example, in making collective decisions. However, like all terms for values, these are necessarily ambiguous and subject to change over time. One person's vision of dynamic and self-sacrificing teamwork, for example, is someone else's mask for the domination by a coach or a few star players. Terms such as "democracy," then, become key points of reference and key sources of inspiration for people. Words such as "efficiency," "productivity," and "competitiveness" are important loci where different interpretations and meanings come together or come into conflict. Some of our most frequently used terms are also some of our least examined, and that lack of reflection leads to both illusions of consensus and bandwagon effects—not to mention manipulation.

A close look at how an organization manifests its basic values or tries to achieve democracy leads us to pay attention to how value-related terms are expressed, debated, suppressed, or altered over time. After all, what is described as social solidarity today may be different from that of yesterday, and may be differently understood by various organizational members. In addition, an organization's official stance on values—as expressed in its mission statement, for instance—may be quite distant from how most members see the matter for their work lives. Answering the question of who represents the "real" organization and its values is crucial to understanding and improving it.

We can consider democracy (within an organization or in the larger society) to be practiced on at least two broad levels. One concerns the practices such as participation in key decisions that *count* as democratic, and the other concerns the ways "democracy" and related values themselves are *discussed* by the group. In this book I deal with organizational democracy on both of these levels, arguing that how we talk about democracy and other basic values in organizations really makes a difference in how responsive an organization is to its members as well as the extent to which the organization is effective in what it sets out to do—for example, to make a profit in a global marketplace or to provide employment for still more workers. An organization cannot *be* democratic without certain kinds of communication patterns and certain sorts of discussions. And the values and ideals of democracy itself must, in some way, be part of those discussions in order for democracy truly to thrive.

Above all, then, this book is about an organization at once struggling to serve its presumed customers and trying to arrange its activities in a way that is *both* democratic and productive. The case of Mondragón is important not so much for its peculiarities as a story of Basque co-ops but rather as a lesson about what's happening and what's doable in organizations of all types. Mondragón is no isolated or quaint case. As is evident in many others parts of the world, the culture of the customer is reshaping both work life and nonwork life there, often in ironic ways.

By carefully analyzing in-depth interviews (all of which I conducted in Spanish), informal conversations and interactions, meetings, and key documents, I try to present a vivid picture of the activities of the co-ops and at the same time address one of the most enduring and vexing questions in the study of organizations: "Can an organization dedicated to serving people really maintain its social values and its basic integrity, despite growth, bureaucratization, and market competition?" More specifically: "What does employee participation look like in the customer-driven firm of today?"

I have been fortunate to visit Mondragón three times. First, in March of 1992, I was part of an intensive ten-day tour, during which participants could observe the question of values arising in many discussions with representatives of the co-ops. Already in the late 1980s, a debate raged over the cooperatives' "selling out" versus "saving their soul" (as I hope to show, the issue is far more complex for Mondragón and for other organizations than this either-or formulation would suggest). The bulk of my time at Mondragón was spent doing fieldwork from February through June of 1994. I had total geographic and intellectual freedom, exploring what I wanted and talking with whom I wanted. Ultimately, I decided to focus my attention on three mid-sized industrial cooperatives, each in a different town, each with a distinctive history, and each with a specific kind of linkage to the MCC. I returned to Mondragón in July of 1997, mainly to conduct follow-up interviews and focus on the cooperatives' experimentation with semiautonomous work teams, Total Participative Management, and Continuous Improvement—programs to increase productivity and enhance employee participation.

This project itself has been in some important senses a cooperative one. I have many people to thank for their assistance, their openness and their ideas. Pilar Abad and Mac Johnson were generous and helpful during the Mondragón tour of March 1992. Over the course of the 1990s, discussions about workplace democracy with the following colleagues, friends, and students have been stimulating and valuable: Cliff Allen, Dave Atkins, Mohammad Auwal, Jim Barker, Gaye Barton, Rebecca Bauen, Nancy Bernius, Walt Blackford, Denise Bostdorff, Carolyn Bninski, Allan Bull, Connie Bullis, David Carlone, Craig Carroll, Paul Casey, Dana Cloud, Laurie Collins-Jarvis, Cathy Comstock, Charley Conrad, Steve Corman, Alayne Courtney, Kathy Crego, Stan Deetz, Dan DeGooyer, Sue DeWine, David Diamant, Susan Eicher, Gail Fairhurst, Fred Freundlich, Kathy Garvin-Doxas, Roseann Gedye, Thomas Gerber, Andrew Gilla, Hollis Glaser, Steve Goldzwig, Bill Gorden, Deb Gray, Nina Gregg, Don Habbe, Susan Hafen, Sandra Harding, Teri Harrison, Tim Huet, Maria Humphries, Bob Husband, Joann Keyton, Sally Klingel, Kathy Krone, Shirley Leitch, Mike Long, Laura López-Fernández, Antonio Lucas, Brian Mahan, Bob Marshall, Terry Martin, Steve May, David McKie, Jill McMillan, María Victoria Mejía, Mike Miller, LeRoy Moore, Tom Moore, Brendan Morris, Judy Motion, Dennis Mumby, Debashish Munshi, Antonio Noguero, Jeff Orrey, Michael Papa, David Purviance, Linda Putnam, the late Charles Redding, Fred Rice, Raymond Russell, Susan Schact, Laird Schaub, Craig Scott, Dave Seibold, Graham Sewell, Greg Shepherd, Nader Shoostari, Al Sillars, Mary Simpson, Laura Speirs-Glebe, Francisco Soto, Joe Straub, Nancy Sullo,

Beverly Sypher, Bryan Taylor, Lynn Tennefoss, Phil Tompkins, Sarah Tracy, Sheila Turpin, Teun van Dijk, Gail Verlanic, Barbara Vincent, María Helena Vivas, Juanie Walker, Ann Westenholz, Susan Whalen, Morgan Wilhelmsson, Peter Wissoker, Bill Whyte, and Francisco Zuluaga. I thank especially Cynthia Stohl, a dear friend and colleague at Purdue University, for extensive collaboration and for reminding me of the reasons for writing this book.

Both the University of Montana–Missoula and the University of Colorado at Boulder provided me with research grants at crucial times to make ongoing fieldwork at Mondragón possible. Also, Odense Universitet in Denmark indirectly supported my research on the cooperatives through grants for teaching and research. I give special thanks to a dear friend and colleague there, Lars Thøger Christensen, especially for his insight and generous help. Thanks also to another dear friend, Jürgen Denk, for lending me his car during my five months at Mondragón in 1994.

I have been blessed with opportunities to present this work in numerous forums during its development: at public events in Boulder, Denver, Memphis, Missoula, and Mondragón; in university lectures at Ohio University, Wake Forest University, the University of Utah, Flathead Valley Community College, the University of Amsterdam, Odense Universitet, and the Universidad de Antioquia of Medellín, Colombia; during meetings of the National Communication Association and the International Communication Association; at special conferences of the Federation of Egalitarian Communities in Colorado and the Northwest Cooperative Federation in Oregon; at CETLALIC Language School in Cuernavaca, Mexico; and in the form of a graduate seminar at the University of Waikato, in Hamilton, New Zealand. At Waikato, research support for final work on this book was generously provided by Ted Zorn and the Department of Management Communication. I thank them not only for their help but also for a delightful stay there during the second semester of 1998. The work has been enriched by all these discussions, just as my arguments have been refined through presenting the work to my regular classes.

At Mondragón itself, the kind and open people who have made this work possible are far too numerous to mention here; many of them I now consider friends and colleagues. For me, one of the extraordinary aspects of this research has been the almost unlimited access I had to the co-ops without the slightest pressure on the shaping of my results. At the Otalora Training Center and at MCC headquarters, José María Larrañaga, Mikel Lezamiz, Itziar Bazanbide, and Jesús Goienetxe each spent many hours assisting me, by setting up interviews, discussing the present and future of the cooperatives, and collecting documents. They were my hosts for five months in 1994. At Grupo ULMA, in neighboring Oñati, José Manuel Biain, José Antonio Ugarte, Fernando Recalde, and Iñigo Agirre made me feel more than welcome in July 1997, and invited my critical commentaries on their policies. Mila and Mertxe in the central offices of ULMA took time out of their busy schedules to help me with the many details of working at ULMA. Fran Etxaniz provided me with office space there. In the two MCC cooperatives I studied intensively, people were especially giving of their energies and insights. At MAPSA in Pamplona: Isidro Gárate, Javier Lecumberri, Juan Ramón Iñurria, Mari Jesús Zabaleta, Mikel Pueyo, Elias Pagalday, Francisco Javier Egea, and Neli. At MAIER in Gernika: Mikel Zaldegui, Julen Iturbe, and Carlos Zubero. Rafael Leturia and Felix Ormaetxea of MCC also deserve special mention. Rafael was especially helpful in answering my last-minute questions as this book went to press. Also I am grateful to several representatives of KT, an informal labor union in the FAGOR Group, for spending hours with me and for sharing their documents—especially Mila Larrañaga and Yoseba Ugalde.

In and around the cooperatives many people helped me and my wife, Sally Planalp, facilitated my work, and made us feel at home. In particular, I thank Pilar Zubillaga, Manuel Quintas and family, Bar Gurea, Cloti and Mari Carmen, and "The Sweet Ladies" at Muruamendiaraz, all in the village of Aretxabaleta; and Felix Barrena and Mari Carmen Arriaran in the town of Oñati. At the University of Deusto in Bilbao, Aitziber Mugarra and Miguel Ayerbe were gracious hosts. Koldo Azkoitia of the Alto Deba Economic Development Office in Mondragón was very generous with information.

At the University of Colorado, Manuel García and Margarita Olivas did some painstaking translation and coding work, and Chris Courtade Hirsch assisted me in gathering important reference materials. At the University of Montana, Jeff Berry helped me with tedious work on references. Three of my cherished colleagues at Montana, Sara Hayden, Betsy Bach, and Bill Wilmot, read complete drafts with great care; in various ways they helped me to improve the book. François Cooren, now of SUNY-Albany, offered provocative theoretical observations that have helped to propel my thinking toward extensions of this book. Juliet Roper, of the University of Waikato, did some careful proofreading at the final stage. Jan Perrin at the University of Montana, Christina Langkilde at Odense Universitet, and Jean Beaton at the University of Waikato provided generous office support. Mark Watkins at Freddy's Feed and Read and Garth Whitson of Garth's Books, both of Missoula, helped me obtain valuable resources, often on short notice.

Yudit Buitrago, my primary research assistant in 1996–97, became, in fact, much more than that: because of her excellent scholarship and spirited involvement in the project, she is the coauthor of Chapter 3. She is a good friend and collaborator.

My editor at Cornell University Press, Fran Benson, has negotiated the development of a book we would all be pleased with. Alis Valencia, editor of *At Work* magazine, challenged me to focus my ideas during the later stages of this project. I am grateful as well to the three anonymous reviewers for Cornell who offered helpful criticism. Joel Ray did exceptionally fine work in copy editing the manuscript.

Finally, I thank Sally Planalp, for spending so much time with me at Mondragón, in 1994 and again in 1997, often in ways that limited her ability to pursue her own research. Her love and unselfishness set a quiet and steady model for me.

GEORGE CHENEY

Missoula, Montana

Tensions over Democratic Values in Today's Business Market

We obviously do not yet have the conceptual tools for developing an integrated analytical framework that would allow the investigation of participation in its broadest sense.
—H. Peter Dachler and Bernhard Wilpert, "Conceptual Dimensions and Boundaries of Participation in Organizations: A Critical Evaluation," 1978

The notion of the customer is fundamental to current management paradigms. . . . departments now behave as if they were actors in a market, workers treat each other as if they were customers, and customers are treated as if they were managers.
—Paul du Gay and Graeme Salaman, "The Cult(ure) of the Customer," 1992

The New Old Workplace

The twentieth century has witnessed many trends to make management more effective, to improve work processes, and to transform businesses and other institutions into productive and efficient enterprises. Scientific Management, the Human Relations Approach, Systems Theory, Organizational Culture Management, and Team-based Restructuring of Work Processes are just a few of the trends that have been heralded in management texts and that have given birth to whole bodies of social scientific research. The chief proponents of such approaches to work, especially since the advent of the Human Relations Movement in the early 1930s, have "claimed that there is no conflict between the pursuits of productivity, efficiency, and competitiveness on the one hand and the 'humanization' of work on the other" (Rose 1990: 56). This assumption, underlying many programs to engage employees' job commitment and identification with the organization, has led to the insistence that workers' interests, goals, and values are integral with the financial success and growth of the organization. Within this framework of understanding, broad slogans with positive value connotations have served for both the sincere and the less socially inspired leaders of business. One Sears executive observed more than forty years ago that such slogans as "human relations" could be so compelling as to divert criticism by labor unions and other potential critics (Worthy 1957). "Efficiency," "quality," "customer satisfaction," and "employee empowerment" are a few of today's organizational mantras.

"Employee empowerment" for one, is a double-edged sword. The employee with increased responsibility for determining his or her own work activities may also be an employee with much more than one job to do. Observers of California's New United Motors Manufacturing, Inc. (NUMMI) plant, a celebrated joint venture between General Motors and Toyota, have reached differing conclusions about the merits of new programs of teamwork and employee participation (compare Adler and Cole 1993; Berggren 1994; Wilms 1996). Though employees' involvement in the work process has grown, so has their stress. Laborers at the NUMMI plant are required to make suggestions regularly for the improvement of production, engage frequently in problem-solving meetings, and immediately signal management about the slightest problem with production. One researcher reports high levels of job satisfaction under this form of "democratic Taylorism" (Adler 1992), while another describes the system as "management by stress" (Parker 1993). All observers agree that work has greatly intensified under the new system, but they differ in their assessments of the physical, psychological, and social impacts on workers.

In a number of popular Dilbert cartoons, created by a former employee of a Silicon Valley high-tech firm, subordinates raise sharp questions every time the boss announces a new program of teamwork or empowerment. "Employee empowerment," says Dilbert, effectively means that "you're the monarch of unimportant decisions" (Adams 1995). The brief but potent General Motors strike in September 1994, beginning in Detroit and spreading to other cities, represented one of the first widely publicized objections in the United States to the norms of the new workplace: increased responsibility, participation, and self-monitoring, but longer hours, more stress, and more frequent injuries. This tension troubled Levi Strauss & Co. in

1998, after the company, long known for its commitment to employees, restructured its work processes in terms of teams (King 1998). Self-directed or semiautonomous work teams, now the rage worldwide as a means of greater productivity, can be downright oppressive where the demands on employees become overwhelming and rigid and where surveillance of their labor remains a chief means of securing compliance. In these respects the more organizations seem to change, the more control over work processes seems the same (Cheney et al. 1998; Sewell 1998). Yet "what *is* different about [today's] lean methods is the *continuous search for marginal improvements* in costs by constantly stressing and readjusting the production system and, above all, the labor process" (Moody 1997: 87, emphasis mine).

A multiplant strike at General Motors in the summer of 1998 effectively paralyzed the corporation's North American operations. The event was one of the most important strikes to date over the issue of economic globalization. The conflict centered on GM's plans to further downsize its work force and heighten production efficiency, not because profits were down but rather in response to a new efficiency campaign by Ford and Chrysler's merger with Daimler-Benz. The confrontation was the sharpest in recent years between the United Auto Workers, which had by then been losing membership for two decades, and the giant auto maker. The UAW drew "a line in the sand" over what it saw as unnecessary cutbacks in personnel in the United States, Canada, and Mexico; the transfer of jobs to cheaper labor markets abroad; and undue pressures on the employees remaining at North American facilities (G. White 1998). In the end GM agreed to several of the union's terms, including a promise not to make strategic decisions completely outside the context of worker representation.

It is not surprising, then, that some observers these days speak of "the end of company loyalty" (Bennett 1990) or "getting not just a job but also a life" (Edmondson 1991). Moreover, Charles Heckscher, a labor and industrial relations researcher, concludes that faith in efforts at employee empowerment is waning because many organizations that have implemented such programs are neither more democratic nor more effective: they do business as usual, except that they do it with fewer employees and perhaps with fewer hierarchical levels (as cited in Yates 1996; see also K. Smith 1995). Chris Argyris, writer on human resources management, is even more specific in his critique of typical empowerment programs in suggesting that they tend to involve heavy monitoring of employees' behaviors at work and relatively few opportunities for creativity on the job (1998). Finally, social critic Richard Sennett charges that the type of teamwork typically promoted today lacks depth and vision: "it is the group practice of demeaning superficiality" (1998: 99).

Swedish organizational analyst Christian Berggren (1992) urges us to look carefully at what exactly is meant by "teamwork" and "participation." A work team in Canada may not be the same thing as one in Japan or Sweden or Israel. In fact, some applications of "team" or "teamwork" are not very democratic at all, involving undue constraints on the individual (though the control may be more horizontal or peer-based than vertical or top-down). In the name of team-based organization, some corporations simply try to engineer a new kind of superloyalty to the firm via the work group, giving little attention to increased worker freedoms or initiatives. What, precisely, is the role of the employee in newly reorganized work systems? Also, how is the description or "framing" of a new program likely to influence its specific application, and how are parameters for meaning set?

Business, the Market, and People

Multinational corporate capitalism is coming under increased criticism, even as the Dow Jones Industrial Average surpasses the 11,000 mark. Charles Derber (1998) questions the huge role now ceded to the corporation and finds the corporate concentration of power to be excessive. Holly Sklar (1995) attacks the growing disparity between the rich and the poor in the United States and other industrialized nations. Kim Moody (1997) charges that under the banner of globalization, workers in many countries are being subjected to harsh working conditions and are treated as disposable. William Greider (1997a) and Robert Kuttner (1997) argue that economic competition is now commonly used as an excuse for industries to ignore ethical concerns (as captured by the phrase, "just business"). Richard Sennett (1998) charts the erosion of individual moral character in an age when organizations devalue stability, loyalty, and ongoing relationships. The Hungarian American billionaire George Soros (1997) and former British political adviser John Gray (1998) question whether the rush

to "free trade" worldwide now needs to be checked by institutions
other than capital and values other than profit and power. And David
Korten (1998) calls for measures such as grassroots economic empowerment and reform of industrial policy to humanize the economy.

We have created the business culture in which we live, even
though we commonly describe major corporations and the sovereign
market as if they were something simply "out there," well beyond
our human hands (McMillan and Cheney 1996). "Insofar as there is a
dominant belief in our society today, it is a belief in the magic of the
marketplace" (Soros 1997: 48). Highly restrictive notions of the bottom line have encouraged us to forget about or overlook one of the
basic reasons we do business in the first place—to improve the
human condition (see Estes 1996). As David Korten insists, "Neither
a society nor a market economy can function effectively without a
moral foundation" (1995: 90), and the market in its current form cannot fully provide for that. Adam Smith's treatise on free enterprise
([1776] 1986) is commonly invoked today to support unbridled corporate maneuvering, though he himself envisioned a private sector of
tightly interconnected organizations balanced by compassion as well
as governed by self-interest (see Werhane 1991).

The everyday concepts and language we use in describing business
are revealing. We discuss organizations and bureaucracies as if *they*
were the social agents and not people and we speak of organizational
efficiency almost as if people were neither involved in making such
calculations nor affected by them. High unemployment is sometimes framed as a good thing by financial analysts who myopically
focus on single indicators of market performance, seemingly oblivi-
ous to the people behind the numbers (see, e.g., Holloway 1998). Productivity is touted as the answer to all of our economic and social
limitations and as a value in itself (Cheney and Frenette 1993). In the
popular book *Corporate Renaissance*, Cross, Feather, and Lynch
(1994) spend most of their time describing an organization that essentially runs like a machine and must get "back on track." Despite
the metaphor of (human) renaissance in the title, most of the book
deals with topics such as "administering the machine" and "over-
coming resistance to change," and is based on the assumption that
the machine/organization moves everything and everyone in its
path. Even when the authors discuss topics related to human resources, individual persons play very minor roles in this show. The
view of organizational change as sweeping and inevitable (like an

ocean's tide or the weather) has come to be common currency today, even for organizations that are working hard to anticipate changes in their market environment (Christensen 1996).

In overemphasizing the dictates of the market, we seem to forget our own roles in shaping organizations, maintaining them, and, occasionally, transforming them into bastions of excellence, creativity, trust, and joy. More important, when we talk in terms of inevitability in the marketplace (see Aune 1996), we surrender our capacities as social agents to "make a difference" and alter the system we describe (Polanyi [1944] 1957). We seem to forget that a market can best be defined as a network of people, or more accurately today, as a network of organizations—"self-producing social structures among specific cliques of firms who evolve roles from observations of each others' behavior" (H. White 1981: 518). Institutions imitate one another to a far greater extent than is often realized (Meyer and Rowan 1977). We need to demystify the market by highlighting the people, companies, and industries behind the decisions that make the market what it is (Daly and Cobb 1994).

Unusual companies such as Mondragón, Ben and Jerry's Ice Cream of Vermont, California's Patagonia Inc., the London-based Body Shop, the Grameen (Rural People's) Bank of Bangladesh, or New Zealand's Hubbard Foods encourage us to ponder what is possible. None of these organizations is perfect, of course. But because a social ideal is unachievable in its entirety doesn't mean that it cannot serve as an inspiring point of reference in our step-by-step realization of important values and goals. We can walk down a path even though we may never quite arrive at our intended destination.

Getting the Organizations We Ask for

In chronicling the rise of the modern organization, sociologist James Coleman (1974) explains that the original corporation in the late Middle Ages, such as a guild of cobblers, was designed to give craftsmen a voice in the market and to enhance their individual efficacy and power. A group of craftsmen, by pooling resources and knowledge, could gain leverage in an economic and political environment dominated by the medieval church and the feudal state. It is not overly romantic to observe that the emergence of capitalism was, in this respect, democratic. The early guilds enhanced the economic and social possibilities for a new middle class, freeing craftsmen from the constraints of a centralized and oppressive society. Guild membership enabled individual craftsmen or traders to do more than they could accomplish alone in setting standards of quality, determining fair prices, and protecting their common interests. But these associations and their descendants—that is, both the literal, legal corporation and many other types of organizations—became entities in their own right. That shift was both an opportunity and a potential trap, however. For example, despite all the emphasis on the individual person in U.S. public discourse today, it is the large organization and especially the major corporation that has been granted more and more persuasive and material influence (Scott and Hart 1979).

In one sense, a "corporation" is any association that transcends individual members in time, space, and resources. (The term is derived from the Latin word *corpus* and means "the body social.") The literal, legal corporation diffuses responsibility and shields the individual owner or member from various forms of liability. It was instituted as a "juristic" or legal person throughout the Western industrialized world in the late nineteenth and early twentieth centuries, and was thereby afforded much more recognition and power than partnerships or associations. Before the 1880s, a corporation was understood to be a political creation without significant and enduring rights of its own. But a corporation, in both the literal, legal sense and in terms of a general category, also deemphasizes personal roles, responsibilities, and relationships. The French and Spanish parallels to Inc. and Ltd., *société anonyme* or *sociedad anónima* (anonymous society), make this characteristic explicit.

According to Coleman, until relatively recently the proportion of power held by individual citizens (or "natural persons") was far greater than that held by corporate or legal persons. He warns of the ever-growing power of organizations of all types vis-à-vis human beings as individual, unaffiliated persons, and he is especially concerned about the growth in size and power of legal corporations. In growing, organizations tend to become detached from their original purposes, and they tend to alienate their own members (sometimes even their founders). The expansion of opportunities for corporate free speech in our day tends to reinforce the idea of the corporate person; granted the right to speak through a variety of media on important sociopolitical issues, organizations tend to cloak their intentions in such hybrid forms as the "advertorial" (Bailey 1996). In a variety of ways, corporations and other large organizations speak to us as persons with apparently coherent identities, offering unified expressions of preference that are, in effect, "votes" for certain public policies (Cheney 1992). The legal corporation has in fact accrued a set of rights formerly associated only with natural persons, and its resources and reach far exceed those of any natural person.

One might ask about the prospects for democracy when most public discussions are dominated by organized groups and corporations. For instance corporations often make deals with the largest environmental associations so as to make dialogue more predictable (Livesey 1999). A society where the loudest voices are those of large organizations is a society of corporatism (Held 1996), where private and parochial interests seem to dominate the public sphere and where the "unorganized" have no real voice (compare Habermas 1989; Leitch and Neilson in press; Roper 1998). Such a pattern may tend toward "taking the risk out of democracy" (Carey 1995) by creating a stable decision-making environment for the controlling institutions of society, especially corporations, and preventing challenges from groups and individuals with comparatively fewer resources.

An insightful analysis of organizational goals and activities comes to us from Chester I. Barnard, CEO of New Jersey Bell (then part of AT&T) during the 1930s and author of the classic book ([1938] 1968) on management theory, *The Functions of the Executive*. Both a philosopher and a practical manager, Barnard began with very basic questions about why people join organizations, what organizations do, and what sort of relationship one ought to have with his or her employing organization. Though neoroyalist in his belief in the need for strong individual allegiance to corporate enterprises, Barnard offered useful general concepts for reflection on the meaning of organizational life and especially on the essential elements of maintenance and success. In Barnard's own view, effectiveness is measured by the organization's success in pursuing its fundamental and collective goals, such as making a high-quality product, offering a valuable public service, or promoting sound health care. Efficiency, on the other hand, refers to the domain of everything else that happens—both intentionally and unintentionally—while an organization is pursuing its basic goals. Efficiency may be treated as the entire set of intended and unintended consequences surrounding pursuit of a goal. Speed, production of waste and by-products, environmental impact, and so forth are all relevant to efficiency. But especially interesting is that

Barnard considered the satisfaction of individual motives as foremost among such effects. Acknowledging that organizations are of, about, and for people, he saw correctly that inattention to efficiency could actually jeopardize effectiveness over the long haul, as when poor motivation and morale adversely affect production and diminish quality.

To survive, organizations such as cooperatives that maintain a strong social commitment must define organizational success and deal with the practical matter of organizational maintenance. An organization that maintains democracy, equality, and unshakable bonds of solidarity yet does not prosper economically will appear as a footnote in a history of cooperatives and so-called Utopian enterprises. Yet of what value is continuance if the organization's essential features become indistinguishable from those of a noncooperative? This is the fundamental dilemma facing many organizations that seek simultaneously to be distinct from and yet engage the larger market.

Democracy, the Market, and Organizations

In his provocative and popular book about the relationship of business to the environment, *The Ecology of Commerce*, Paul Hawken adopts an unusual and somewhat surprising stance. Taking the market for granted but looking for ways to improve it, he envisions a situation in which it recognizes that its own survival depends upon a larger physical, social, and biological system. The market needs the world, and the market should therefore be *for* the world. For the market to serve only itself would lead to its undoing because, for example, there would no longer be resources to provide inputs into it. The market, Hawken believes, should be a means to achieving certain social "goods" and not an end in itself, following short-term goals that are ultimately self-destructive. The U.S. timber industry, for instance, which now treats one year as "long-term planning," may indeed soon find itself with no more trees to fell. Hawken's gloomiest scenario is a cataclysm of runaway consumption whereby modern business shortsightedly swallows up the very things it needs for sustenance, but his more hopeful vision describes a market that serves the earth and its people and fully accounts for its own practices.

The present study tries to address the inner workings of the organization, especially the business enterprise, as Hawken has addressed the impact of the organization on its external environment. Hawken begins with organizations' use of resources and the products and services they offer to the human community, and he ends up looking at their internal dynamics and their purposes. My story proceeds in reverse fashion, from a focus on the internal affairs of organizations to an insistence that organizations ultimately ought to improve the human condition.

Political scientist Robert Dahl (1985) considers what "economic democracy" would mean for the work organization as well as for the society in general. He asks, if the principle of equality applies to all individuals, shouldn't the ownership and structure of organizations in which they spend so much time also reflect this principle? For Dahl as for many other contemporary observers, worker ownership and governance offers one source of hope.

Another recent source of inspiration for my book is political scientist Robert Putnam's *Making Democracy Work*. That book, which has spawned a wide-ranging debate in the 1990s over the nature and future of democracy in Western industrialized societies, shows how the "dense webs" of civic associations in contemporary northern Italy—including groups in the workplace and even such nonpolitical groups as sports leagues—can give both vitality and stability to democracy in the society as a whole. For Putnam, democracy is not limited to organized political parties; it is related to our nonpolitical pursuits as well. Perhaps his central point is that the vitality of democratic institutions depends on people, their values, and their relationships with one another. Putnam's is a deeply social vision of democracy that offers a good starting point for the examination of values, democracy, and participation in organizations (see also Pateman 1970).

But in analyzing democratic forms of organization we must be specific about what democracy or participation means in practice. For example, in a famous 1976 article in *The Journal of Economic Issues*, Paul Bernstein outlines what he sees as "essential elements for effective worker participation in decision making." Above all, Bernstein insists, we need to distinguish among different types of participation. He does not deal with the various popular programs such as quality circles, quality of worklife compacts, and self-directed work teams, but rather with the fundamental criteria that should be used to assess *any* effort at increasing employee participation.

Bernstein's first standard is the degree of control employees exert in decision making. For example, though a suggestion box may be visible at work, it may be that contributions to it are never implemented. Second, what are the issues over which employees' control is exercised? For instance, in the quality circle movement in the 1970s and '80s, problem-solving groups were typically not allowed to discuss issues of compensation or organizational structure, and as a result many employees felt a contradiction between the imperative to participate more and the limitation on discussion (Stohl 1986, 1995). Bernstein's third criterion is the level of the organization's hierarchy that employees can influence. Here again, we find many organizations sending conflicting messages to employees. In implementing self-directed work teams, for example, teams are often not used at the highest executive levels, and top management can thus retain an autocratic, top-down mode of directing policy and work. This practice effectively puts a ceiling on democratic practice and it is seldom fully explained or even understood by the parties involved.

The real meaning of democracy for organizations, then, is to be found both in how it is conceived and in how it is practiced in specific cases.

Revisiting Mondragón

One set of organizations that has become keenly aware of itself in its larger environment is the Mondragón Cooperative Corporation (MCC) of the Basque Country (Euskadi). These hundred and fifty or so cooperatives, which now comprise the tenth largest private firm in the Spanish economy and have annual sales exceeding seven billion U.S. dollars, celebrated their fortieth anniversary in 1996 (see MCC 1998). At the end of 1998, they employed a total of 42,000 persons. Though quite successful within the Basque and Spanish economies, the corporation now faces new competition in the European Union and a rapidly globalizing marketplace. And, as revealed in recent issues of the Mondragón cooperatives' magazine, *Trabajo y Unión* (Work and Union), the challenge of maintaining cooperative values in a corporate context is one of its greatest preoccupations.

In certain academic and economic circles Mondragón is one of the most famous cases of workplace democracy in the world. It is regularly applauded for its size, longevity, and vitality (Dauncey 1998).

The headquarters of the Mondragón Cooperative Corporation is in the town of the same name, a city of 35,000 in the heart of the Spanish Basque Country, in north-central Spain, where the provinces of Gipuzkoa, Araba, and Bizkaia (Guipúzcoa, Álava, Vizcaya) meet.

The Mondragón system has witnessed a remarkable process of organizational transformation. Starting as a small manufacturer of gas stoves in 1956, the system now includes dozens of manufacturing firms, the most important tool-and-die makers in Spain, the largest refrigerator manufacturer in the country, a prosperous bank, various service providers, a training center, its own social security system, and an educational system extending from kindergarten through the master's degree (see MCC 1994; 1997b).

The co-ops of Mondragón are under the umbrellas of two corporate heads and share basic principles that prescribe employee ownership and employee governance. Every worker-owner (*socio* or associate) holds an equal share in the co-ops, and decision making is handled through a complex system of direct and representative democracy. José María Sarasua, a middle-level manager, told me in 1994, "The maximum authority is with the *socios*, which all of us are." However, the character of democracy at Mondragón is changing, especially in light of external market pressures and shifts in corporate policy itself.

The cooperatives of Mondragón have been studied before, but largely in terms of their origin and history (Ormaechea 1991); their economic performance and efficiency (Thomas and Logan 1982); their decision-making and leadership structures (Whyte and Whyte 1991); the organizational culture of one of the largest and oldest co-ops (Greenwood and González 1989, 1992); and with respect to Basque and Spanish labor movements (Kasmir 1996). Little has been written about either day-to-day work in the co-ops or about the many forms of informal and formal communication that breathe life into the cooperative system. These forms of communication are especially important in understanding the cooperatives' current struggle with both internal transformation and external pressure.

Today the cooperatives are experimenting with new methods of asserting their presence in the marketplace, such as centralizing strategic planning, and contemporary techniques for restructuring work processes, including self-directed work teams. The new strategies, though not unlike those being pursued in many large businesses, are in Mondragón necessarily set against a background of visible and enduring value commitments, of which perhaps *solidaridad* (solidarity) is most important and has the greatest range of application. But real tension exists over the extent to which the Mondragón co-ops can, in the words of several people there, "hold on to their soul" (see Cheney 1995, 1997, 1998, in press-a). "Solidarity is hard, especially these days," said María Luisa Orueta, former president of ULMA-Forja co-op, in 1994. Could it be that the cooperatives would succeed in the market yet fail to be what they were originally intended?

How Does an Organization Keep Its Soul?

The heart of the matter is what I call *organizational integrity*: the extent to which an explicitly value-based organization such as Mondragón can keep to its humane and democratic commitments over time, even while growing, enjoying financial success, and becoming more centralized and even bureaucratized. This application of the term "integrity" doesn't imply that the values of a complex organization can ever be completely coherent or internally consistent. Rather, I ask, *Can a values-based organization be true to its original standards for decision making and behavior while allowing for organizational restructuring and new means of engaging in a dynamic market*? An organization may not itself be a "natural person," but it is a collection of natural persons' efforts. In using the term "integrity," which we commonly associate with individual persons, I want to focus attention especially on how organizations treat individuals. José Manuel Biain, director of Personnel in ULMA-Forja, one of the industrial co-ops, insisted to me in 1997: "Whether a particular organizational practice is just or is not just is often hard to say, but people will ask that question; and the answer they find will determine whether there is sufficient trust in the organization for it to work well."

The answer to the question of organizational integrity must be determined by a "conversation" between members of the organization and various groups of outsiders. For the Mondragón cooperatives, important stated values include solidarity, participation, and equality. These values are literally part of the constitution or charter of the cooperatives, and they are discussed widely and frequently. For example, as I discovered in my interviews there, a community-and-land-based understanding of social solidarity was a pivotal issue in the 1992 decision of five cooperatives to secede from the Mondragón Cooperative Corporation. In the spring of 1994 the president of this group, called ULMA, told me: "We did not want our group to be divided, with one cooperative being linked to a group somewhere else. We derive our strength from one another and we maintain a commitment to the *local* community."

Changes in the co-ops' structure, the economy, and the larger society threaten traditional cooperative values. The co-ops are becoming somewhat more bureaucratic and centralized; there is much more talk today about being competitive in the market; and there is great fear among the old-timers that young professionals are more career-minded than dedicated to the common good. Many old hands lamented to me that "the new *socios* are more concerned with advancing their careers than they are with the life of the cooperatives." These cultural shifts, in addition to the market pressures already profiled here, pose urgent challenges to the maintenance of core social values in the cooperatives and to the shape that employee participation will take in the future.

What Does It Mean for an Organization to *Have* Values?

The question of organizational integrity at Mondragón and elsewhere harks back to one of Max Weber's ([1968] 1978) greatest fears with respect to large bureaucratic organizations: the tendency to depart from fundamental human goals. Weber described three types of organizations, each based on a different type of legitimate authority. Charismatic authority, founded in the personal characteristics of a dynamic leader, is perhaps best exemplified in an energetic new religious sect or the early stages of an entrepreneurial company. Traditional authority has its prototype in a monarchical order, where biological lineage dictates the transfer of power and status, but it can also be seen in organizations where the overriding rationale for decisions and actions is "That's the way we do things around here." What Weber termed "rational-legal" authority, a system of prescribed rules and regulations that minimize arbitrariness and diffuse control, is best shown in a rule-governed bureaucracy. Writing from the perspective of the first two decades of the twentieth century, Weber saw bureaucracy as dominant in the future. Bureaucratic development was, for Weber, inevitable in all economic systems; in his view, the march of rationality would sweep the world as all employees and organizations submitted to systems of production and standards of performance.

Weber's metaphor of the "iron cage" was intended to represent how bureaucracy simultaneously protects and confines us (du Gay 1996b). Bureaucracy is maddening precisely because it is *both* enabling and constraining (see, e.g., Adler and Borys 1996). It happens to be a very logical, efficient, and noncapricious way of organizing work. It works slowly but reliably. It can be fair, but at the expense of individuality and "personalness." Moreover, bureaucratic methods can be used to structure organizations as large and as far-flung as the Roman Catholic Church, IBM, and agencies of the United Nations. Bureaucracy also happens to be the most familiar model around, a point demonstrated vividly when I ask my students to imagine other types of organizational structures and draw them. Often the only model they can imagine is a complex and fairly rigid bureaucratic organization, even as they condemn such a system. Today, more and more observers are speculating about the widespread emergence of a truly post-bureaucratic type of organization (see Donnellon and Scully 1994; Drucker 1992), one based more on ad hoc and flexible coordination among team members than on specified rules, regulations, and guidelines.

Though his premature death in 1920 prevented him from writing much about it, Weber may have had in mind a fourth type of organization, organization dedicated to higher human values and committed to periodic reflection on them. Two insightful scholars, Joyce Rothschild-Whitt (1979) and Roberta Satow (1975), have argued that there is a gap in Weber's own typology; that his discussion of organizational types or categories was incomplete; that there are hints of a value-driven organization scattered throughout his works and notes. Whether these scholars are right is largely an academic point, but Weber's own doubts about the long-term soundness of modern organizations, when they fall into bureaucratic myopia, are undeniable.

What does it mean to be a truly value-based organization, especially in an age when everyone's talking values but also doubting them? Can an organization really be expected to maintain its values over time and in the midst of change all around it? If so, certainly, we expect an explicit value-based orientation in religious organizations, social-service agencies, certain social movements, and many largely or completely volunteer organizations in the third or independent sector, yet we know from experience that these organizations can go off track and become obsessed with their own power, wealth, and continuance (Simon 1976). For instance, a public-relations crisis of United Way in the United States a few years ago was exacerbated by the fact that the head of *that kind* of organization would receive a half-million-dollar salary.

In the Mondragón cooperatives some vocal members say that regardless of competitive market pressures the co-ops should not be "just like any corporation" that does not privilege social concerns.

Why is it so difficult for organizations to maintain basic value commitments, especially those concerning the well-being of their members and the betterment of the society? One difficulty comes with growth, in that being bigger makes it harder for an organization to be homogeneous with respect to values (Mansbridge 1983). Thus small political parties find it easier to stay unified around certain values and ideologies than do larger parties (Hansmann 1990). Another risk to the maintenance of values is the concentration of power in the hands of a few (Michels [1915] 1962). Bureaucracy may begin with the democratic impulse toward all organizational members, but as patterns of power concentration become entrenched it often moves toward oligarchy. Still another problem is goal displacement. Many an organization has drifted away from its original goals, such as service, high-quality products, social betterment, and become reduced to maintenance of power, satisfaction of greed, and pursuit of personal ambition. Bureaucratization can also lead individuals in an organization to focus exclusively on quantity ("How many forms processed?" "How many hamburgers made?" "How many students enrolled?") and neglect quality, both of the product and work life. Such an organization can lose social energy or dynamism and degenerate into a more authoritarian and traditional model of doing business. Finally, market forces can transform an organization that was relatively unconcerned with its profit margin into a fiercely competitive enterprise.

Some organizations are not much concerned about values in the first place. A few radical organizational critics go so far as to say that no organization really has any goals other than its own survival, growth, and enhancement (Georgiou 1981). Also, discussions of values can devolve into nothing more than a cynical language game, disconnected from anything of substance going on inside the organization (Christensen and Cheney in press). What do we make of nearly every organization announcing core values that sound almost the same as those of their competitors? Where is the organization today that is not for "quality"? But then what does that word really mean?

Rothschild and Whitt's in-depth case studies of California cooperatives (1986)—an alternative high school, a newspaper, a legal clinic, a health clinic, and a food co-op—show that while organizations are tempted to change in accordance with the demands of their environment, continued devotion to democratic principles is also possible. The free legal clinic, however, voted to go out of existence after a certain time. This rare instance of organizational suicide resulted chiefly from the members' perception that the organization was drifting too far from basic goals and being coopted by outside forces—especially by organizations that the firm was dependent upon for financial resources. The members of the clinic saw themselves as becoming more hierarchically organized, more market-driven, and less autonomous. This case reminds us that democracy ought to incorporate deep reflection, and that most organizations do not wish to contemplate this.

In the lore of worker cooperatives, there is something called "the degeneration thesis." The proposition is that over time a democratic, worker-owned firm will tend to fall into decay, chiefly because of declining economic efficiency but also because of a loss of social dynamism. The latter may come about as a result of diminished group cohesion around important goals. This thesis, advanced at the turn of the twentieth century through studies of British co-ops by the Webbs (Potter [1891] 1987; Webb and Webb 1897), is important because it throws down a gauntlet to all who would try to maintain a radically democratic and economically egalitarian firm. Although this proposition is appealing, particularly when expressed in terms of the deterioration in economic efficiency that often occurs in a worker cooperative, it also has its skeptics. Co-op specialist Chris Cornforth (1995), for instance, argues strongly that degeneration of a democratic firm is *not* inevitable; that renewal can occur in both economic efficiency and democratic arrangements. The key to such revitalization, though, is in openness to new ideas, periodic reflection, and the will to adapt the arrangements of the organization to changing times and people. From the standpoint of open systems theory, we might say that an importation of new energy is necessary in this kind of social organization in order to counteract the natural atrophy of cohesion that comes with time (what is called in many contexts entropy). Whether an organization such as a co-op, which is typically grounded in commitments to important values, can reinvent itself (to use a phrase currently popular in Washington, D.C. and in corporate boardrooms) remains debatable (compare Ellerman 1990; T. Harrison 1994; Stryjan 1994).

Why Values and Discourse about Values Are Important

As the Mondragón cooperative system faces a host of challenges, how key values are discussed and practiced demands our attention. What does it mean for an organization to be democratic? What does it mean for an organization to have human values? What is the "good" organization, the organization of integrity? To what extent can an organization's values be anything more than empty promotional slogans? How far should an organization bend in the direction of serving individuals—its own members or others, such as customers?

How we express basic values is terribly important. We may say that talk is cheap, but deep down we know and behave otherwise. Whether the U.S. Congress calls taxes "revolting," "an unfair burden," "civic responsibility," or "revenue enhancement" determines to a great extent where discussion over reform will lead. Whether or not the term "corporate welfare" becomes an enduring label in popular discourse will influence the relationship between big business and government (see Barlett and Steele 1998). The outcome of the U.S. Justice Department's antitrust suits against Microsoft, still in the news as this book goes to press, will be determined in part by whose interpretation of "fair competition" prevails. The proliferation of euphemisms for what used to be called simply "layoffs" and "firings" approaching the number of expressions we have for death, reveals how the more brutal aspects of economic life are often shrouded or treated as being natural (Deetz 1992). (Why *would* a CEO refer to those unlucky recipients of pink slips as "unassigned employees"? See Uchitelle et al. 1996.) When we speak of "getting a real job," we are saying a lot, implicitly, about what levels of work, status, and income count as legitimate in our culture (see Clair 1996).

Democracy does not exist in nature. Neither do values. "No one has ever seen an 'equality' strutting up the driveway, so if 'equality' exists at all, it has meaning through its specific application" (McGee 1980: 10). Humans create these things called values, in part as points of reference in their own affairs; in part to structure their lives; in part, to be sure, to control the behavior of others. Values such as freedom, justice, and democracy are abstract—and vague. But, they're also very powerful, commanding both our rational attention and our emotional energy. Values are abstractions that nevertheless concentrate meaning. We know deep down that they are important, even when we can't say exactly what they mean or come to a consensus among ourselves about how they are best practiced.

Values *talk*, so much so that merely mentioning to someone in the United States these days that "the federal government is trying to curb your freedom" may produce a vocal or even a violent reaction—even though no one in the situation specifies what is meant by freedom. Similarly, we can incite a rally simply by shouting, "We love our freedom!"

Value-related terms unify us, but they also conceal differences. Though we seem to come together around a value such as freedom, huge differences in interpretation can become apparent upon probing into the presumed consensus (see Bakhtin 1981). Communication processes are built upon such ambiguities and polysemy, though we often assume otherwise. We mostly all agree that world peace is a desirable goal; but on the specific routes to achieving that end, we differ greatly. When we speak of the value of competition, we seldom notice how it is simultaneously seen as "natural" and yet needing systematic promotion in Western industrialized societies (Kohn 1986). With a fairly high level of abstraction we make it more likely that a working consensus can be achieved.

Numerous contemporary commentators have observed that Thomas Jefferson knew well the peculiar powers of language when he drafted the U.S. Declaration of Independence. By speaking of abstract values such as "liberty," "equality," and "the pursuit of happiness," Jefferson tried rhetorically to inspire his audience and transport them to a state of mind in which they wouldn't necessarily notice the unavoidable tensions between liberty and equality; in the process he helped to delay for decades a political confrontation over slavery.

Organizations help to shape situations with their mission statements, too, by stressing "service," "innovation," or "quality." The LEGO corporation of Denmark speaks of itself as both a bearer of tradition *and* a source of constant innovation. General Dynamics, a major U.S. defense contractor, explains in ads that it "pins its hopes on peace." And R. J. R./Nabisco and Philip Morris announce their commitments to "liberty" and "individual rights" as part of a campaign to advance their interests as cigarette makers. GM-owned Saturn Corporation of Tennessee speaks of the "community" of its car buyers, as it tries to incorporate consumers into its marketing function and instill pride in being part of the company.

In almost *any* organization in the United States today, getting the label "efficient" to stick to a proposal can win the argument and win the day (Cheney and Brancato 1992). So powerful is the idea of efficiency that it usually goes unexamined, used like a child's new hammer on everything in sight. When a value-related term enters the domain of unquestioned "common sense," it can easily be employed in propaganda (see Gramsci [1929–30] 1971). For example, so loud is the chorus of "privatization" and "restructuring" in New Zealand's public sector that oppositional voices and even questioning ones are often labeled as "reactionary," or worse, as "terrorists" (Galloway 1998). One New Zealand business scholar observes that many of the market-driven changes in that country, which have in some ways been even more dramatic than those of the United Kingdom or the United States in the past two decades, were pushed through using the slogan of "quality management," which was seen as sacred in the private and then later in the public sector (Humphries 1998).

A value term can cue listeners to a whole familiar set of words, images, and expectations. The sheer suggestiveness of value-based terms can simultaneously provoke thought and constrain discussion (Foucault 1984). The mere assertion of "justice" as a governing value may suppress the question of "whose justice?" The term "socialism" is a vivid illustration of a *devil-term* (Burke 1966), evoking little but an overwhelmingly negative dismissal. In my classes, bureaucracy receives the same angry reception. (I ask the students, "Can you imagine someone running for public office on the 'pro-bureaucracy' platform?") For students to accept the positive aspects of bureaucracy or understand why it developed as an organizational form, first in ancient China and now all over the world—in part to eliminate whim and the arbitrary treatment of personnel (see Riggs 1979)—takes real work.

For their users, value-related terms can be powerfully meaningful or almost devoid of meaning. In explaining how the almost indisputable term "quality" has become a favorite slogan of today's organizations, Wilkinson and Willmott say: "Arguably, its vague, but nonetheless positive associations make the appeal of 'quality' immediate and extensive" (1995a: 2). They continue by explaining how the pursuit of quality becomes one of the self-confirming practices of the organization: "From the quality 'expert' perspective, any good or service can legitimately receive the seductive sobriquet of 'quality' so long as it consistently meets the standards—however 'inferior' these may be—that beat the competition within its market niche" (3). Finally, these organizational analysts suggest how the idea of quality is typically applied to work processes themselves: " 'Quality' does not necessarily mean the attainment of exceptionally high standards with regard to employees' terms and conditions of work. Instead, it means the development of 'uniform and dependable' work practices that are congruent with delivering products or services at a low cost with a quality suited to the market" (3). Similarly, organizational critics Steingard and Fitzgibbons (1993) explain how "quality" is at once a broad-ranging term and a strictly defined imperative as applied to work systems—in practice emphasizing customer responsiveness much more than employee initiative. "Quality" in many cases becomes another means of controlling work processes rather than encouraging employee creativity (Tuckman 1995).

Realizing that many organizational policies seemingly directed toward the consumer are actually the organization "talking to itself," one can see just how tricky is the business of assessing an organization's relationship to its environment. Lars Thøger Christensen's marketing research (1994, 1995) shows that many business efforts at being "proactive" with respect to the customer actually consist of much self-persuasion. Many organizations engage in rituals of self-confirmation as they adopt and promote the slogans of the day. Through surveys, focus groups, and periodic forecasts, organizations are in part seeing what they wish to see with respect to "doing the right thing for the customer" (Feldman and March 1981). Businesses are quick to adopt the language they think will put them at the forefront of their industry, while at the same time striving to maintain as much predictability as possible internally. They are not just looking down the road ahead and over the shoulders of others but also at their own noses. The diffusion of information about new business trends often moves so that organizations in all sectors are quick to adopt the latest fad (such as "teamwork") without really questioning its applicability to them or considering its subtleties. This makes it especially difficult to sort out the internal and external affairs of organizations.

The image of having certain values can be just as appealing for a society or an organization as the values themselves. James Boyd White (1984) offers a fascinating account of ancient Athens in which he argues that terms like "justice" came to have several different functions in the public discourse of the city-state. It became evident to White that over time the governing elite became less interested in *being just* than in *speaking the language of justice* so as to be seen as behaving appropriately. Only by participating in discourse as defined by the elite group could other groups or individuals hope to have influence. In U.S. political discourse today, the term "family values" operates in much the same way. Both the Republican and Democratic parties now claim to *have* them, but neither is quick to explain what they are or what they mean. In fact, if either party gets too specific, it will hurt its own cause.

Many organizations today vie for control over the terms of discussion. Values enter the debate as malleable labels under which organizational actions are justified and support is sought. Value-related terms are used to fix the identities of organizations and position them in the discourses of advertising, marketing, and public relations (see Douglas 1986). Moreover, businesses in the same industry eye each other carefully to try make sure that their programs and labels are the most current, most advanced, and most on the "cutting edge." There's nothing so common today as an "innovative, market-driven firm." Businesses that announce themselves as "green" dot the economic landscape these days. But organizations strive toward predictability and the reduction of uncertainty, so the authenticity of their value-based slogans remains open to question.

In trying to get ahead by voicing the right corporate values, many organizations seem a bit cynical about the notion of a value in itself, and thus they may help to promote cynicism in the public. McDonald and Gandz (1992), for example, see the use of core values largely as a tool for profit making; no mention is made in their essay of values as social goods in themselves. The authors speak consistently of "managing," "manipulating," "shaping," and "fine tuning" corporate values, reporting that "nearly all of the organizations participating in our study were to some degree attempting to modify their traditional sets of shared values as a means of gaining competitive advantage" (73).

Finally, *values and value-related terms change over time and in a variety of ways.* Efficiency was not a central organizational or business concept until Frederick Taylor's Scientific Management program ([1911] 1967) became a household notion in the 1920s and 1930s, although a society preoccupied with progress and productivity certainly offered fertile ground for the growth of such trends (Banta 1993). Today in U.S. public discourse, the political word "liberal" can hardly be uttered; and at the same time, the term "radical" is now sometimes applied to extreme conservatives. Throughout the industrialized world today, almost anything done in the name of the customer or the consumer is seen as positive, even though the customer's *other* roles in society are seldom addressed. The term "citizen" has been almost wholly replaced by "consumer," and consumerism is indeed "the century's winning 'ism' " (Gopnik 1997).

In the word "consumer" we have a disturbing example of how terminology can be transformed over time. At the beginning of the twentieth century, "consumption" referred primarily to waste and to the disease of tuberculosis. With the rise of advertising and the greater availability of mass-produced goods from the 1920s through the 1950s, consumption became desirable and thus the notion of the consumer emerged (Ewen 1976, 1988). Still, as recently as the early 1960s, even after the modern institution of marketing had been born, people were only infrequently called consumers in the industrialized world (Williams 1980).

By the 1960s, with the rise of modern marketing, it was apparent that the term "consumer" was in ascendancy. Only one generation later the term "citizen" is viewed as archaic by many young people (Wexler 1990). We should therefore expect further permutations of "consumer," perhaps even including the revival of older or forgotten meanings such as "wastrel" or incorporating an activist sense of one who chooses based on principle and not only on personal whim. (See Belk, Wallendorf and Sherry 1991; de Certeau 1984; Gabriel and Lang 1995.)

The new emphasis on the consumer came partly from the campaigns of Ralph Nader and other consumer advocates, in which consumerism meant the rights to be properly informed and treated with honesty and respect. But infused with the ethos of marketing, consumerism has become self-centered and impulse-oriented—an ultimately shallow form of democracy. Thus the application of the ideal of the consumer to a wider range of activities such as education and religion ought to be viewed with some skepticism. The aggressive pursuit of the customer's satisfaction has led to some rather undemocratic results in colleges and universities, for instance (Cheney, McMillan, and R. Schwartzman 1997). Among other things, such a model effectively places the student-consumer outside the process of co-creating education, as if one were simply zipping by a fast-food drive-in window (see also McMillan and Cheney 1996). Today "consumption" means choice but it also means demand as a personal right. Thinking of themselves as consumers, alumni of universities and colleges may be unlikely to see their relationship with their *alma mater* in any terms other than those of a pure *exchange* relationship.

Such a transformation in the ideology and appeal of this key term not only instructs us in the impossibility of legislating terminology but also cautions us about advancing a campaign for social change under a rubric we might expect to control (Baudrillard 1966).

Analyzing Organizational Communication

In considering how democracy gets put into practice in the workplace or how values are maintained in an organization, we must look carefully at the role of communication, for language contributes greatly to shaping what we understand to be reality. Material forces do exist apart from language, and they often resist efforts to change them, as union rhetorical strategies fail to modify managerial plans or alter the conditions of work (Cloud 1994, 1996). But the power of language is dramatically evident in the workings of ideologies such as the Horatio Alger myth, where inequities among different social groupings are obscured by the appealing notion that anyone (and everyone?) can become rich through hard work.

Though certain interpretations may take hold at particular times and places, the meanings of "democracy" and "participation" are continually contested. Communication researcher Cynthia Stohl

(1993) found in a study of managers in European Union (EU) countries (Germany, the United Kingdom, Denmark, France, and the Netherlands) that the practical interpretations of "employee participation" ranged from very broad or open to highly specific and restrictive. Some managers thought of governmental policy; others focused on individual will; still others considered particular programs that they themselves had witnessed or implemented (compare Tsiganou 1991).

What "participation" means can only be understood by scrutinizing context: who's "in the loop," what people in meetings are saying, how much they're saying, how they're saying it, who's talking and who's not, what's not being said, what options are not being considered, and so on (see Clay 1994). This point is shown vividly in Helen Schwartzman's detailed study of a mental health clinic in Chicago (1989). For many of the professionals that worked there, staff meetings *themselves* came to symbolize the democratic nature of the organization. As an opportunity to gather, to catch up on the week's events, to offer mutual support, to reach new understandings, and to make decisions, the meeting *was* the organization.

When we say that someone practices what he preaches, we don't really mean that the preaching itself isn't a type of practice (see Searle 1969). After all, words constitute the ways we make promises, conduct negotiations, write contracts, debate important questions, give pep talks, honor the work of others, and so on. The announcement that "we have a democracy here" must be tested against other messages, other decisions, other actions. As all of us have no doubt witnessed, the assertion of democracy may be merely a code for "I want *my* way, but I'll get it nicely." To assert democracy is one thing; to enact it or to bring it to life is something else.

The distinction becomes clear and powerful where employee-participation systems such as work teams are mandated from the top, as though simply declaring that "henceforth, we will have grassroots democracy!" will create the reality. Though some outcomes may be beneficial, the contradiction of democracy by decree must be recognized and dealt with. Raymond Russell (1985) and Frances Viggiani (1997) find that in avowedly democratic organizations tensions over hierarchy, accountability, expertise, authority, and ownership (in its economic and/or social senses) are common. Such challenges constantly recur in the communication processes that constitute much of the experience of an organization. Even cooperatives that establish specific rituals in meetings to insure equal participation inevitably find that they have to be modified, or that they are insufficient to maintain the democratic character of the organization.

We usually think of the material world as solid and real, dependable and sure, but of our own created symbols as ephemeral, fuzzy, and even deceptive. And so we dismiss much of communication as "mere rhetoric." We can, after all, bump our heads on a tree, but not on democracy. But much of what we call "the world" is made up of symbols (Burke [1950] 1969). What is the thing we call "history," for instance, but a set of symbols that point to certain people, events, and forces? With our folk dismissal of the importance of language (as illustrated in the expression "put your money where your mouth is") we obscure the fact that what we call things is extremely important. Otherwise governments wouldn't so vigorously try to cast wars as "police actions" or "limited strikes" rather than "invasions" or "acts of war." As political scientist Murray Edelman insists, "Language is only one aspect of [a] material situation; but a critical one" (1985: 11).

Words for social matters such as relationships, values, and ideologies are especially interesting because of how they arrange our world. Though one might be tempted to dismiss terms like "democracy" as vague and imprecise, Burke urges us to examine them closely as "strategic points at which ambiguities necessarily arise" [1950] (1969). Through terms and concepts such as "freedom," "liberty," "free enterprise," "private property," "individual rights," "free trade," we work out issues such as what it means to be human, to do a job, or to have a government. These words stir emotions and evoke values, even though they are ambiguous. Moreover, they often take on a nearly material force when used propagandistically, in ways that prevent reflection (McGee 1980). In New Zealand's recent government ad campaign on "social responsibility," for example, attempts were made to lodge the idea solely in the home and at the level of individuals, so as to distract attention from government's reduction of certain social services (Campbell 1998).

In talking about values, organizations will often advocate precision while at the same time making use of "strategic ambiguity"—for example, in simultaneously empowering and controlling their employees (Eisenberg 1984). Consider how a shift in terms from "employee participation" to "employee involvement" can shift focus away from the idea of workers' rights to what an organization needs "to get workers to do" (compare Cotton 1993; Ewing 1977). And consider how the mantle of "entrepreneurship" can be used in restructuring an organization so as to disguise employees' lack of autonomy or power (Markham 1996) or the fact that electronic monitoring of performance is being rigidly employed (Alder and Tompkins 1997). However consciously or unconsciously such deceptive policies are pursued, they allow for a great deal of flexibility on the part of those in charge.

While most organizations use a mix of methods to control employees' behavior (including outright coercion), the use of values to motivate employees internally is generally on the rise. We see this in the growing emphasis on the organizational mission, as a rallying point for internal as well as external communications. Such efforts may be called "concertive control" (Tompkins and Cheney 1985), a term that highlights the ways organizations seek to motivate and direct their work force around a mission. Often coupled with such efforts are a high degree of coordination, elevated levels of training, and the implementation of the team concept. Management hopes thereby that employees will internalize the values of the organization, developing something of an "organizational conscience" and heightening dedication through active participation. But programs centered on employee empowerment and a common vision based in core values may also involve a high degree of monitoring by top management (see Alvesson 1992; Knights and Willmott 1987; Kunda 1992). In this way, a strong organizational culture, especially at the work group or team level, can be both a source of employee motivation and a means of managerial control. Thus there can develop a somewhat oppressive regime of organizational values, with attempts to extend managerial control to the prescription of employees' attitudes, identities, and behavior (Barker and Cheney 1994). The call for organizations to profess value commitments is not without risks.

Values are important to organizations in their external as well as internal communications. Interestingly, many large organizations are performing and transforming one of the functions of classical Greek rhetoric: to celebrate and promote certain abstract values in public discourse (see, e.g., Cheney and Vibbert 1987; Crable and Vibbert 1983). Organizations talk to us about values all the time. The regular advertorials of Mobil Oil Corporation, for example, speak not about oil but rather about such abstract matters as American common sense. These messages celebrate certain values, opinions, and

perspectives on public issues such as free trade. Businesses and other
concerns rush to craft mission statements, core principles, and codes
of ethics; they are expected to *have* values and be able to speak about
them loudly to the world. The term "quality," for example, is "one of
the latest weapons in the battle for corporate image and high-street
reputation, where every company seeks to become the corporate
leader in their sector" (Kerfoot and Knights 1995: 223). To be "competitive," organizations have to talk about values. And it is certainly
more acceptable anyway to promote customer service and quality
than profit and mass production.

In view of the foregoing observations, we must ask the following
questions, specifically in relation to Mondragón: What do value-
related terms such as participation, quality and customer service
mean, practically speaking? Do they have multiple senses? What
tensions exist between different values—say, between solidarity and
efficiency? Whose meanings for key values have the upper hand in
the day-to-day work of the co-ops? How are meanings molded in specific work practices? How have values changed, from the points of
view of various individuals and groups within the co-ops? Which values and meanings are dominant or on the ascendancy? How are the
central values of the co-ops demonstrated or practiced? What possibilities for further value transformation are evident? And what do
the answers mean for the future of workplace democracy worldwide?

Meanings of Democracy

The questions I am asking in this book about the nature of values
and value-related discourse within the organization apply as well to
the challenges that confront society in general. Some postmodernists
ask whether broad participation in meaningful debates is really possible in today's world (see Laufer and Paradeise 1990). If rational,
democratic dialogue is to have a future, we must come to terms with
how to restructure it, renew it, and relive it. Perhaps the most serious threat of the postmodern critique to Enlightenment values is
that democracy (as we typically idealize it) is dead and beyond resus-
citation (see Baudrillard 1983). Perhaps we are living in an age when
more communication is less; when different symbols are simply jux-
taposed (like ads that place a beautiful body next to a sleek car so
that the consumer will make the association); when most citizens

are anesthetized; when the democratic process has become a set of empty rituals; when politics has become nothing but a circus of the absurd; and when nonorchestrated collaborative discussion between people with honest differences is beyond reach. Thus, as we explore values, democracy, and communication in the modern organization, we should see the parallels for analyzing and perhaps improving the larger society. In the struggle over the meaning of our future, organizations are important players, yet we often fail to engage them for their genuine potential.

Among the most important changes at Mondragón, we can see the strong emergence of a form of "neocooperativism" which privileges an externally driven form of participation, in marked contrast with the more internally focused forms of participation that have long represented the Mondragón tradition—that is, forms of employee participation in which workplace democracy is justified primarily or significantly in terms of the benefits for the employees and the organization as a whole. By externally driven forms I mean the ways democracy inside the firm is justified chiefly by what it does for the consumer and the larger market. Of course, the distinction is complicated by the fact that some value-based organizations may see their mission as rooted in the larger society. In practice, neither form of employee participation can be pure. Nevertheless, there are important differences, as the organizational researchers Dachler and Wilpert (1978) have explained. Customer-oriented forms of employee participation include a strong rhetoric of efficiency, with priority to corporate performance as opposed to the traditional social concerns of the co-ops. The internal concerns of the organization, including its core values and its regard for democracy as having merit in itself, can be completely overridden by a race to serve the presumed consumer in the fastest, most efficient way possible.

All sorts of decisions today are referred to the market as the ultimate decision maker. "Thus what counts as a 'good' product is judged by reference to the wishes and preferences that consumers happen to have, whether or not these are consistent with the [organization's] own internal standards, and when the two conflict, the market dictates who will be victor" (Keat 1991: 223). By extension, the metaphor of the market is being applied internally to recast employees' relations to their work and with one another. "When constituted this way, employees are expected to think of themselves as suppliers of the next person in the supply chain; and to take on the role of this person when performing their work so that they experience a sense of fulfillment when their 'customer' is satisfied" (Wilkinson and Willmott 1995: 15). Though such "customer consciousness" has important advantages for the organization and represents a kind of democratic orientation toward the wishes of consumers, it can narrowly recast employee participation so that intrinsic reasons for democratizing work (for example, health, personal efficacy, job satisfaction, equality) are pushed entirely out of vision and practice.

One of my central purposes in this book is to identify changes in the prevailing understandings of "employee participation" in the Mondragón co-ops and link those changes to the culture of the consumer in the larger international market in which the co-ops increasingly operate. I believe that the answer to the oft-asked question, "Have the Mondragón co-ops sold out?" is not a simple one. My response would be "yes and no," as I will explain in the chapters that follow. Attending to a variety of data, including the diverse views from within the cooperatives, we can better understand not only the particular experiences of the cooperatives themselves but also learn important practical and theoretical lessons regarding various types of organizations in other parts of the world. At the same time, through the examination of three distinct and diverse cooperatives, each with a different relationship to the corporate entity MCC, I hope to show both patterns and exceptions with respect to cooperative development and transformation. Ultimately I argue that what's happening at Mondragón is strikingly relevant to organizations around the world in an increasingly global marketplace. We can see the "cult(ure) of the customer" (du Gay and Salaman 1992), with all its ironies, in just about every sector of life these days: business, government, education, health care, the environmental movement, and even religion.

The Social Question and the Economic Question

Of the Mondragón cooperatives and other "alternative" businesses, economists ask: "Is such a system financially viable over the long haul?" This bottom-line question is fundamental. A U.S. Catholic nun and CEO of a hospital chain puts it sharply: "no margin, no mission" (Langley 1998). But the question also suggests its own obverse: "Can an organization which has been economically successful also maintain a democratic order and its own professed humane values?" This is the social question that motivates my analysis. To address it, I take a close look at what makes an organization (of any type) possible on a day-to-day basis: communication. Open meetings, deep collaboration, access to power, opportunities to express minority opposition, a real measure of self-determination, a shared and expressed commitment to the collective, fair treatment of one another, consideration of the individual, and an ongoing process of exploration that is itself open to discussion and change—these are some of the key ingredients for a democratic work life (compare Gustavsen 1992; Tannenbaum 1986).

There are three key ways in which the social and the economic are interdependent, and these bear directly on the present study. First, the market is not nearly so rational as commonly assumed: its development may often undermine its presumed goals. According to Robert Lane (1991), the market should be evaluated primarily in terms of the extent to which it meets the fundamental social goals for which it has been designed, such as maximized happiness. Without detailing the mismatches which Lane finds between the current market economy and the basic sources of human well-being, I would say that the market's advance and the widespread allegiance to it should by no means be taken as a sign of collective, systematic reflection about the extent to which it satisfies fundamental human wants. Though it is unquestionably an efficient and dynamic system for the creation and distribution of goods, unbridled corporate multinational capitalism can be and often is profoundly undemocratic and even antidemocratic by restricting participation and competition but under the symbolic umbrella of "free trade" (see Gibson-Graham 1996; Rule 1998). Lane reveals, moreover, that many of the currently popular justifications for the market's form, while initially compelling, are really quite tautological: that is, the market is used to justify itself. Indeed, much pro-free-trade discourse resembles religious doctrine (Cox 1999; Vincent 1996; also as cited in Welch 1998) in advancing seemingly unchallengable articles of faith and obscuring certain facts: for example that governmental regulations were actually put in place to promote business competition (see Roper 1996).

Many appeals to the market as a locus of values and action simply serve to deny agency to the very individuals and organizations that the market is supposed to benefit. "The market made me do it" becomes an almost universal justification for action (Derber 1998). Few citizens, consumers, or workers (whether they are powerful policy-makers or not) seem to be reflecting on the nature of the market, its goals, or their roles in it. It is seldom recognized, for example, that many business leaders who extol the virtues of market competition are pursuing policies that will protect their own firms from the effects of competition, through joint ventures, strategic alliances, and de facto cartels (B. Harrison 1994; Mathews 1989).

A second way in which the social and the economic dimensions of work life are interrelated, in regard to scale and growth, pertains even more directly to worker cooperatives and other alternative organizations. In his ground-breaking research on Mondragón and other worker cooperatives, Jaroslav Vanek (1975, 1977) explains that in typical non-worker-owned capitalist firms the desire for growth may well be infinite, whereas in cooperatives an efficient level of equilibrium may be achieved beyond which substantial growth will not be pursued. Vanek writes, "The labor-managed firm will never grow beyond the [efficient scale of operation], whereas a capitalist firm often will, its growth being governed, even after the greatest technical efficiency is reached, by the desire for profit maximization" (1975: 9). If a worker-owned firm's goals for profit are strictly tied to the provision of benefits to members, there may be a natural limit on the impulse to expand the capital base. But the character of the worker-owned firm may change, thus raising the social question of whether it has ceased to be a worker cooperative. This question has been raised by the sharpest critics of Mondragón (e.g., Chomsky 1994; GEO 1996; Kasmir 1996). Vanek's research offers us a theoretical and empirical baseline from which to evaluate a worker cooperative's departure from its mission. On the social side, we must carefully examine the kinds of symbols and arguments that are invoked at Mondragón (or elsewhere) in favor of growth, centralization, and organizational change.

Finally, Deidre McCloskey (1985, 1994) points us to the fact that economic arguments, like all others, are unavoidably tied up with our use of symbols—that is, with *rhetoric* (see also Tompkins 1987). An economist needs symbols, metaphors, and graphs to describe how the economy works. But these same symbols help to shape what we "know" and should not therefore be seen as transparent. The unemployment rate, for instance, is not just a "fact" but in part a social construction—to the extent that determinations are made about what and whom to count in reporting the percentage.

As one of the defining institutions of our age, the market is not simply something "out there," beyond our grasp or even the sum of many individual transactions. For many observers and participants it is a sacred symbol, a mythology, an ideology, and an overarching perspective on the world. McCloskey asserts that "rhetoric provides a place to stand from which to admire and criticize radically different metaphors of economic life" (1994: 384). Our discourse about such things as the market and democracy does make a difference. If we see the market as "a rising tide that will lift all boats," then we are likely to envision its democratic potential and support all "free-trade reforms." If we term the market a "race to corporate global dominance," however, we may be led to a different conclusion about policy. The point is not that either of these slogan-like labels is correct but that we should be conscious of where our words "lead us" (Rosenthal 1984). Just as the market economy (or any economy, for that matter) relies mightily on the foundation of social trust among people, so it depends upon particular ways of thinking and talking about the world. That it would have been unthinkable fifty years ago to refer to the sum of a nation's people as "American consumers" or "the emerging Chinese market" should remind us that persuasion and social change are ongoing.

So, too, must be our analyses of high-minded organizations such as Mondragón. As William Whyte recognized when he first approached the cooperatives with his students in the late 1970s (see Whyte and Whyte 1991), the Mondragón case offers us a remarkably complete case with which to probe the broad issues raised in this chapter. Here we have a system built from the ground up, based on a foundation of social values, and dedicated simultaneously to the individual and the group. Moreover, that system has enjoyed tremendous economic success. Today it is contemplating further expansion; it is striving to be more productive and more competitive; and it is aiming to reorganize its internal activities around new forms of participation and the master symbol of the customer.

The ironies inherent in the customer-driven firm are as evident at Mondragón as anywhere, but the cooperatives there provide a specific instance of the how the culture of the customer affects a strong tradition of employee participation and workplace democracy. Amidst all the talk of increased competition, internationalization, and the need for an expanded capital base at Mondragón, the symbol and presence of The Consumer stand out. Over my three visits there

(1992, 1994, and 1997), I have found that idea increasingly a key subject of the formal and informal communications of the co-ops. Practically speaking, the growing prominence of a consumer orientation means that both productive activity and worker participation is being linked more and more directly to the real or perceived demands of the environment beyond the organization's boundaries. This phenomenon I call the "marketization of employee participation" (see Fairclough 1993). Outside the walls of the co-ops, citizens are talking about themselves more and more as consumers. As we shall see, these shifts in culture and terminology have significant disadvantages as well as advantages.

In Chapter 2 I offer a selective history of the Mondragón cooperatives, with special attention to their professed values and the challenges posed to the cooperatives' commitments to those values in recent years. Chapter 3 provides an in-depth look at communication within the Mondragón system, emphasizing tensions between cooperative and corporate values and considering especially the new ways that employee participation is coming to be redefined in the organizations. In Chapter 4 I present some practical lessons from the case, focused on the best ways for organizations to preserve commitments to core social values while engaging the larger market. Chapter 5 then considers the possible futures for democratic work practices in the consumer-driven society.

CHAPTER TWO

The Development of the Mondragón Cooperatives

The Mondragón cooperative tradition has many different parts to it, and we are a diverse bunch. And, there's a lot to learn from the differences as well as from the similarities. There's more than one "Mondragón," and they're changing in various ways.
—Felix Ormaechea, 1994

The One and Many Mondragóns

Though it is certainly meaningful to speak of the Mondragón cooperatives as having a coherent tradition, the fabric of the cooperatives is more of a patchwork quilt than a seamless cloth. Recognition of this fact can help us understand the sharply different views of Mondragón expressed in such books as Roy Morrison's *We Build the Road as We Travel* (1991) and Sharryn Kasmir's *The Myth of Mondragón* (1996). Morrison celebrates the co-ops as an example of "ecological postmodernism" and a hopeful beacon for many businesses of the future. Kasmir, by contrast, sharply criticizes Mondragón for not living up to its glowing public image, noting especially the conservative influences on the organizational structure of the co-ops vis-à-vis leftist labor unions and political parties in the Basque Country. Each of these accounts has an important empirical ground, but I would argue that neither reflects well the complexities of organizational life within the co-ops or the diverse perspectives from which the co-ops are understood, by their participants and by others in the surrounding communities.

Furthermore, scholars of organizational culture have usefully reminded us that most large organizations manifest multiple cultures (Young 1989). At Mondragón, for instance, individual co-ops as well as sectors of co-ops are pursuing distinct specialized programs such as Total Quality Management (TQM), Total Participative Management (TPM), and Continuous Improvement to heighten productivity and enhance participation. On the other hand, as I argue in the coming chapters, certain interpretations of key values such as participation, solidarity, and efficiency do prevail throughout the cooperatives. We must observe both prevailing trends at Mondragón and the distinctive, sometimes conflicting, expressions of workplace democracy there. Though the Mondragón experience is idiosyncratic, it can serve to help us understand double-edged global trends and how to support employees who ought to be appreciated not only as a means to providing service to others but also as something of value in themselves.

Key Moments in the Development of the Mondragón System

Excellent, detailed descriptions of the founding and development of the Mondragón co-ops appear in books by economists (Thomas and Logan 1982, Bradley and Gelb 1983), sociologists (Whyte and Whyte 1991), a founder and manager of the co-ops (Ormaechea 1991), anthropologists (Greenwood and González 1992 and Kasmir 1996), and a community economic development expert (MacLeod 1997). As a scholar of both communication and organizational studies, I differ in focus from each of these, yet I rely on some of their information and insights and I share many of their concerns.

My attention centers on how patterns of discourse reveal fundamental aspects of the organization, its character, its mission, and its direction. The published work on Mondragón that comes closest to the type of analysis I offer here is Peter Leigh Taylor's (1994) examination of the "rhetoric of efficiency" in the cooperatives' restructuring and internationalization since the late 1980s. I believe that Taylor is correct to highlight the ways in which somewhat narrow, production-and-profit-oriented conceptions of efficiency have come to overshadow the more people-oriented concerns for job satisfaction, participation, equality, and solidarity. Like other analysts of Mondragón (e.g., Freundlich 1996; Long 1996; Miller 1994) as well as many worker-members and local citizens, Taylor observes a gradual displacement of key defining values of the cooperatives. Taylor explains, "Most participants in debate in the Mondragón cooperatives agree that the firms must be efficient but differ on how the concept is to be understood" (467). The tension between what Taylor calls "the rhetoric of the businesslike firm" and the "rhetoric of the social firm" is the locus of my analysis. The debate over "how the co-ops should respond to the market" is also a debate over how the co-ops will function internally and thus over their identity. As I will show, this tension is solely a product of market forces but is to a significant extent shaped internally through management's initiation.

Taylor justifies his emphasis on the analysis of communication patterns this way: "Rhetoric does not by itself drive social change, yet neither is it a mere reflection of greater social forces. Rhetorical practices help shape the way the cooperatives handle external and internal structural change by influencing the public interpretation of their situation and the range of alternative strategies deemed to be plausible" (465). I'm especially concerned about how external aspects of the life of the organization, especially the market, are framed and discussed so as to shape internal practices such as employee participation. The movement of the Mondragón cooperatives toward being customer driven involves a heightened emphasis on certain interpretations of efficiency, which play out in internal decisions affecting participation. So my analysis of the cooperatives is an attempt to widen Taylor's frame of inquiry.

I was fortunate to visit the co-ops in 1992, 1994, and 1997, spending a total of six and a half months there. I participated in formal tours, attended in-house meetings, witnessed training sessions, conducted surveys, collected official and unofficial documents, and, most important, interviewed or conversed informally with over three hundred persons associated with the co-ops or living in the communities near them.[1] Early in my second visit (February through

---

[1] Because of the large number of personal interviews and corporate documents involved in this study, I have chosen to reference most of them within the text only. In the case of the three co-ops where I focused most of my research—MAPSA, ULMA-Forja, and MAIER—I interviewed a stratified random sample consisting of at least 10% of the *socios* (worker-owners). These interviews totaled nearly one hundred in 1994 alone.

In addition, general background interviews were conducted with select persons from across the cooperatives. There were nearly fifty formal interviews of this type. With both types of interviews, I selected all of the interviewees, using the assistance of personnel managers from the co-ops. In most cases I indicate the month and the year of the

June, 1994), I made the decision to focus on three specific mid-sized cooperatives, in order to capture a range of types of cooperatives, insure that my analysis was manageable, and examine relationships between production co-ops and the Mondragón Corporación Cooperativa (MCC) organization. In my third visit, for the month of July 1997, I analyzed the implementation of new programs of employee participation and productivity. What follows here is a description of the basic structure and practices of the Mondragón organizations, some key moments in their history, and the most plausible reasons given for their economic success and institutional longevity—all with sensitivity to tensions over values.

The Mondragón cooperatives began with the efforts of a socially committed but relatively uncharismatic Basque priest, José María Arizmendiarrieta (1915–1976), and five young engineers who gathered around him in a discussion group after his assignment to Mondragón in February 1941. "Arizmendi," as he is still called today, was by all accounts an intensely reflective but also supremely practical man. Though no captivating orator in the pulpit, he was able to inspire others through his example and his personal charm. His thoughts about business, labor, and organizations were to a great extent shaped by the horrendous experience of the Spanish Civil War (1936–39), from which he barely escaped with his life, and by World War II. These experiences led Arizmendi and his companions to ask: How can we create a better society, at least in part, through the way we do work together? The result was what he and the other founders called "a third way" between unbridled capitalism and centralized socialism: a worker-owned-and-governed company that elevated collective security and rewards while maintaining individual incentives. Benefits for one would be benefits for all. Seeing themselves as neither in the service of capital nor alienated from it, the coops

---

formal interviews. All interviews were conducted by me and completely in Spanish, except where occasional references to specialized terms in either English or Euskara/Euskera required translation by another person. Though only one interviewee asked for his name to be concealed in my research report (in response to my offer of confidentiality), in many cases I identify *socios* only with general designations ("a middle-level manager in the finance area"), in the interest of protecting nonmanagerial employees who may have offered comments critical of the cooperatives. A few published corporate documents are listed separately in Works Cited, but most, and especially issues of the corporate house organ or employee magazine *Trabajo y Unión* (*TU*), are identified only within the text. All other sources of data are indicated clearly within the text (as in the case of meetings I attended) or cited in the text with a reference to Works Cited.

aimed to subordinate the maintenance of capital to the interests of labor and human values. Arizmendi wrote: "Cooperation is an authentic integration of the person in the economic and social process, and it is central to a new social order; employees working cooperatively ought to unite around this ultimate objective, along with all who hunger and thirst for justice in the world of work" (Arizmendiarrieta 1983: 175, trans. mine).

Starting more or less from ground zero, Arizmendi sought democratic economic and social arrangements that might benefit all in the community and give a strong footing for postwar society. His readings took him across a wide range of theories and models in sociology, economics, politics, and religion. Adam Smith, Marx, Durkheim, Weber and many others played important roles in shaping his thinking about work organizations. In reflecting on the experiences of various "cooperativistas," Arizmendi gravitated to the famous ones established by Scottish industrialist Robert Owen in Britain and in the United States, such as New Harmony, Indiana, in 1829, and to England's Rochdale Pioneers, who in 1844 set up the forerunner of the International Cooperative Alliance (1996; see also Hartman 1997). Arizmendi was also quite aware of the traditions of agricultural co-ops in various regions of Spain, and he was inspired by the anarchist-leaning producer co-ops of Catalonia before and during the Civil War (Lucas 1992, 1994). Arizmendi noted that the Rochdale group and the co-ops inspired by Owen eventually dissolved or were converted into standard capitalist firms largely because of the pressure to expand their capital base by selling outside stock. Furthermore, in Owen's factories there was extensive over-the-shoulder monitoring of workers' behavior (Wren 1987). As absentee control of the co-ops increased, their autonomy and distinctiveness were lost. Gradually the co-ops became absorbed into the larger business market that they had so assiduously fought to keep at arm's length. In some cases, of course, factors of internal deterioration helped to bring about their demise.

From these and other historical instances, Don José María learned to value institutional autonomy and identity as two of the most important characteristics of alternative organizations. He realized that it would be important for any new system of cooperatives to strike a good balance between engagement with the larger society, especially the market, and protection of its integrity as an organization or set of organizations defined in large part as being outside the business

mainstream. A successful cooperative system would have to participate in yet be somewhat buffered from market forces. A parallel tension exists for the co-op in terms of the promulgation of its own values. It must be in tune with some dominant values of the society in
order to enlist sufficient support, and yet it must maintain something of a "social-movement orientation" in order to sustain energy
around its own ideals (see Rothschild and Whitt 1986). The organization's mission must be believed and promoted.

Through his studies and small-group discussions in Mondragón,
Arizmendi's faith in the cooperative model was forged. He wrote
later: "Cooperation is an authentic form of involvement of man in a
larger economic and social process—and it figures in a new social
order. . . . *Cooperativistas* ought to work together toward the development of [a new order], alongside all who hunger and thirst for justice around the world" (1983: 175). This perspective on work was un-
dergirded by Arizmendi's strong affinity with the Catholic social
justice tradition, especially as represented in papal encyclicals on
human dignity and workers' rights.

The founding of the Mondragón cooperatives occurred in three
steps: the gathering of a small group of engineers and managers
around Arizmendi in 1941; the opening of a small technical training
school in 1943; and finally the opening of the first cooperative business, a firm to make small paraffin-powered heaters and gas stoves,
in 1956. That first business was the forerunner of the present
FAGOR group, a cluster of cooperatives based in the Mondragón valley and the historic heart of the system. One of the surviving
founders told me in the summer of 1997, "Although there was much
talk about a 'third way,' we weren't entirely sure what exactly we
were embarking on. From the perspective of the 1990s, of course,
everything that came to pass in the past forty-some years all looks
much clearer." At the same time, this founder, Alfonso Gorroñogoitia, emphasized: "We *did* have strong value commitments, especially to creating employment and more generally benefiting our
community; that dedication made possible the great personal sacrifices that secured the position of cooperatives. That fact was crucial
and it is not fully appreciated by many younger worker-members
today."

ULGOR opened its doors in 1956 with just twenty-four workers;
within two years the work force had grown to 143. Several other cooperatives were founded in the Mondragón valley between 1956 and

1959, including an iron smelter, a foundry, a manufacturer of domestic appliance components, and a small consumer co-op. Each of these initial efforts has its representation in the system of today. ULGOR eventually evolved into the FAGOR regional group of industrial co-ops. Today, while retaining the FAGOR brand name, those co-ops have been linked to others in the new sectoral or functional reorganization plan.

Because of the rapid growth, the cooperatives had exceeded their capital sources by 1959 (Ellerman 1984). Recognizing the importance of the cooperatives' independent sources of capital, Arizmendi persuaded the other founders and many community members to create the Caja Laboral Popular ("Working People's Bank"). Pilar Zubillaga, an elderly citizen of the neighboring village of Aretxabaleta, recalls: "Don José María was very persistent. He literally went around town from door to door, asking us for investments to create his new bank. Although we of course had no idea what would happen with our money, we trusted Arizmendi completely. And we held in the same high regard the group of men he recruited."

One of the innovations of the Caja, besides its cumulative lending power, was its Empresarial Division. This division, created as part of the Caja soon after the bank's founding, eventually spun off as its own organization, LKS, in 1991. Initially devised as an arm of the bank to offer feasibility studies and support services for prospective or new cooperatives, LKS now includes financial, organizational, and technical consulting services and has great influence on MCC's policymaking.

Two of the founders, José María Ormaechea and Alfonso Gorroñogoitia, were particularly instrumental in the development of banking and financial management. Ormaechea became the first director of the Caja, and Gorroñogoitia the founding chief of the Empresarial Division, and they held these positions into the early 1980s. Largely as a result of the Caja and its Empresarial Division, the number of start-ups at Mondragón averaged between four and five co-ops per year between 1961 and 1976.

The year 1966 saw the first exports (machine tools) beyond the boundaries of Franco's Spain. Until the lifting of trade barriers throughout the European Union (EU) in 1992, the cooperatives enjoyed a protected economy. Tariffs on imports from other European countries into Spain ranged between 18 and 35 percent, while tariffs on exports were seldom more than 3 percent. Since that time, the cooperatives have become progressively more internationalized. Today MCC has representation or holdings in China, Mexico, Argentina, the Netherlands, and many other countries. The corporation antici- pates for 1999 that over 10 percent of its industrial sales will be out- side Spain.

In 1969 the consumer cooperative Eroski (which means "group buying" in the Basque language, Euskara/Euskera) was launched. It is now the largest single cooperative in both employment and sales, and it dominates the Distribution Group of the MCC. As of the sum- mer of 1997, the Eroski Group employed over twelve thousand work- ers, over one-half of whom are full worker-owners. (Two other cate- gories of employees are *socios temporales*, or time-limited owners, and contract-based nonowning employees.) Eroski had over two hun- dred thousand consumer-members in the Basque Country by the mid-1990s, with continuing expansion through joint-venture agree- ments with noncooperative supermarket chains in Spain and France. Including these collaborators, as of December 1997 Eroski consti- tuted the largest supermarket chain in Spain (*Trabajo y Unión*, or *TU*, Dec. 1997).

Thus the organization has spread well beyond the Spanish Basque Country, opening scores of stores since 1990 in a number of other au- tonomous communities or districts of Spain. At issue today, though, is that many of these are not fully cooperatives; few of their employ- ees are economic owners with voting rights in the organization.

As Whyte and Whyte (1991) explain in their detailed chronicle of the development of the Mondragón cooperatives, 1974 was a water- shed year, for two very different reasons. First, the research and de- velopment co-op, Ikerlan, began. That co-op has grown in size and importance, and includes among its clients a variety of firms from European Union (EU) member nations as well as EU agencies them- selves.

Second, 1974 saw the first and only strike in the history of the Mondragón cooperatives.[2] The official stance of MCC disallows

[2] The four principal labor unions with representation in the Basque Country, in order of current support, are the Basque Nationalist Union (ELA), at about 33%; the Spanish So- cialist Union (UGT), aligned with the Spanish Socialist Workers' Party (PSOE), at about 17%; the Workers Commissions (CCOO), a Communist union, at about 16%; and the Basque Radical Nationalist Union (LAB), with about 15%. There have been important changes in the positioning of these unions, along with political parties, in the 1990s. For example, the Spanish Socialist Workers' Party, with whom UGT is closely affiliated, was defeated nationwide by the more conservative Partido Popular (PP) in 1995. And LAB,

strikes, seeing them as nonsensical in that worker-owners cannot strike against themselves. Indeed, this was Arizmendi's own position, in that he saw the structure of the co-ops as transcending the usual class divisions between managers and workers. Still, Don José María did not take a stand during the strike itself. The conflict erupted when a new system of job evaluations was put into effect, resulting in 22 percent of the jobs being downgraded in ULGOR. The leaders of the revolt saw the changes in pay, which included the application of a new merit increment system to be used by supervisors, to be unreasonable and counter to the spirit of cooperativism. Ultimately more than four hundred workers struck ULGOR. The General Council of the ULGOR group expelled seventeen who were considered to be instigators and fined 397 others. Most of those expelled were women, and many of the grievances that were filed concerned charges of unfair treatment of women in matters of job classification and reevaluation. After a protracted period of conflict, the expelled workers were reinstated in 1977, three years after the strike.

---

which along with the radical Basque nationalist party, Herri Batasuna, is one of the few institutions regularly in contact with the Basque separatist and terrorist group ETA (meaning "Basque Homeland and Freedom"), began to suffer declining influence in some areas of the Basque Country in 1996–97, after large-scale protests against violence in many large cities of Spain and the Basque Country. Nevertheless, it was clear to me that all four of these unions have considerable influence in the economy and politics of the Basque Country and in the *comarca* ("country," roughly speaking) of Alto Deba, of which Mondragón is the seat. For example, a number of FAGOR group employees are quite open about their affiliations with CCOO, seeing it as an outside source of inspiration to help hold the cooperatives to their stated and traditional ideals. Representatives of all four unions agree that the co-ops would benefit from more formal unionization because it would strengthen worker control. Further, as Kasmir (1996) has stressed, there has been and continues to be a great deal of radical political activity in and around the town of Mondragón, including substantial support for ETA's push toward complete independence of the Basque Country from the Spanish State—through violent means, if necessary. As this book goes to press, government-level negotiations are being conducted with ETA to bring an end to the violence and to secure certain rights for the Basques—for example, that all Basque political prisoners be held in prisons within the Basque Country. Even with this knowledge, usage of the terms "liberal," "conservative," and "radical" with respect to the labor unions and political parties of the Basque Country should be made with great care. Clusters of beliefs are not easily predicted; what's more, they are often shifting. The dominant political party of the Basque Country, for instance, is the Basque Nationalist Party (PNV), whose membership, despite its name, is quite divided on the issue of total independence. The shifting and diverse terrain of Basque politics is nothing new, however, given the massive changes that took place in the political life of the Basques before, during, and after the Spanish Civil War, when pro-independence Basques, who had been aligned for almost a century with conservative Catholic loyalist forces, became linked to the leftist Republican government which held power for only a few years prior to and during the war.

The strike was and remains important for several reasons. As Whyte and Whyte (1991) explain in detail, the event called the attention of both cooperative members and the general citizenry to power relations within the cooperatives, as well as to organizational changes that had occurred with their rapid expansion. Soon after the dismissals, the violent Basque separatist organization ETA (in Euskara/Euskera, "Basque Homeland and Freedom") issued a statement condemning the actions of the General Council in firing the strike organizers. Arguing that the cooperatives were problematic in their very structure, ETA insisted that they were denying workers the avenue to destroy the larger capitalist enterprise. In ETA's view the cooperatives were victims of their own internal contradictions, as in the case of capitalism more generally, and they needed to break with the capitalist order completely if ever they were truly to cultivate worker self-governance.

Surprisingly, in this instance the Catholic Church implicitly aligned itself with the radical left by criticizing the cooperatives for a kind of managerial elitism that distanced the governing structure from the workers who were supposed to comprise it. A statement from the Social Secretariat of the Diocese of Vitoria (later to become the capital of the new Basque Autonomous Community under the 1978 Spanish constitution), was blistering in its attack on the management of the co-ops. The secretariat wrote that "the virulence and crudeness of the cooperative leaders greatly surpasses that of the firms that they disrespectfully call capitalist" (Azurmendi 1984: 633).

The cooperatives defended themselves with a statement co-authored by Jesús Larrañaga, one of the founders, and Javier Mongelos, who became president of MCC in the 1990s. They argued that the grievances of the workers had not been expressed through the proper channels: first to their management, then to the general (or governing) councils of the relevant co-ops, then to the general assemblies of those same co-ops.

Although he stayed out of the conflict, Arizmendi did reflect on the strike and its aftermath as an indication of the problems of bureaucracy that accompany the growth of the cooperatives into a large multifaceted organization of organizations. He lamented: "Any system of organization which attains a certain size runs the risk of being undermined, if within it flourishes a typical bureaucratic and functionary spirit, a fearful illness which degrades any achievement no matter what its nature, as it blocks the dynamic agents which strive to maintain efficiency in response to changing conditions" (as quoted in Whyte and Whyte 1991: 100). Whether by intention or not, Arizmendi's critique was noticeably Weberian in that he identified certain developmental patterns, specifically in the evolution of organizational roles, that could jeopardize the guiding values of an organization.

One of the most positive results of the strike and the ensuing conflict was the strengthening of the role of the co-ops' social councils as mechanisms for advocating employees' needs. It was widely perceived that the functions of the councils needed to be revisited in light of the fact that many of the strikers bypassed them in expressing their grievances. Eventually, a well-developed statement of the rights and responsibilities of the social councils was drafted and approved by the cooperatives (Caja Laboral Popular 1986).

Discussion following the strike also put a spotlight on the role of women in the cooperatives, which continues to be a sensitive issue for many members. The majority of strike organizers and vocal participants were women, and at Mondragón in the 1990s several of their complaints from the time of the strike persist: unequal job classifications, insufficient representation at upper levels of the co-ops (and now, also, in the Governing Council of MCC), and weak social councils.

It is important to realize that a women's cooperative existed from the late 1960s until the early 1990s. This co-op was called, in Euskera, Auzo Lagun,[3] meaning roughly "neighborhood helper." It

---

[3] In most cases throughout this book I have chosen to use the Spanish rather than Euskara/Euskera terms, despite the widespread reliance on the Basque language in the Mondragón area. I made this choice based on how the cooperatives have been presenting themselves to the larger world, which is through the more generally accessible Spanish terminology. Hence, while many of my contacts spoke regularly of "Arrasate," the Basque name for the town of Mondragón, they usually referred to the cooperatives as "Mondragón." In cases where there are commonly used English terms for places or institutions (e.g., Navarre for Navarra or Nafarroa) I used these for purposes of clarity.

Euskara/Euskera is unrelated to the Indo-European language family and has no clearly traceable origin. More germane to this study is that the speaking and writing of Euskara/Euskera are absolutely central to the identities of many Basques, particularly in the Mondragón area. Its revival in post-Franco Spain is evident in public as well as private life. For a majority of citizens in and around Mondragón, Euskara/Euskera is the language of choice in the home and to some extent at work, although public business meetings are often conducted in Spanish because of its currency as the world's third most spoken language. In the course of my research in the cooperatives, only one formal interview had to be canceled because the worker did not feel sufficiently fluent in Spanish to engage me in conversation.

was created in 1968, partly at Arizmendi's urging, "to provide a partial solution to the problem of women's employment in the co-ops" (Berger and Clamp 1983: 7). At the time, co-op law forbade women from working outside the home after marriage, even though the Spanish national law had dropped this restriction some years before. A reasonable solution was to provide women with temporary, usually half-time work through the coordinated efforts of a single cooperative, and so Auzo Lagun became something of a "temp" co-op, offering outsourcing services principally to the other cooperatives. The cooperative began with four areas of service: food, temporary workers, simple mechanical assembly, and a laundry for schools and hotels. Start-up was difficult, in part because women of the region generally saw no economic necessity for working outside the home. As Auzo Lagun's personnel manager put it in 1982, "Women had married precisely to liberate themselves from having to work" (quoted in Berger and Clamp 1983: 7). Eventually, however, the idea caught on, and in its later years the cooperative even took on the manufacturing of clothing. Later dissolved as unprofitable, Auzo Lagun can be characterized either as opportunity or tokenism. Some male leaders in MCC point to Auzo Lagun's history as evidence of the cooperatives' commitment to women, yet today women still hold relatively few top positions in MCC (Harding 1994). A recent issue of *Trabajo y Unión* (July 1998) celebrates the role of women in the development of the cooperatives, but it places greater emphasis on the "hidden" support of the founders' wives than it does on the leadership of contemporary female managers.

An additional realization in the wake of the strike concerned the overall structure of the organization. In 1981, researcher Agustín Uribe-Echebarria wrote *Bureaucracy or Participation: An Essay about Organization and the Cooperatives of Mondragón*, in which he noted that the vitality of employee participation varied according to the size of the individual co-op, the place in the organization that the individual occupied, and the nature of the work process. In industrial assembly lines, or where a *socio*'s work was otherwise governed largely by standardized procedures, Uribe-Echebarria found little opportunity or incentive for participation. He concluded that the personnel or human-resource policies of the co-ops needed to recognize the dignity and potential of the individual person in attempting to maximize productivity.

Another key moment in the development of the Mondragón cooperatives, especially from the standpoint of organizational structure, was their reconfiguration in 1984–85 as a centralized "Cooperative Group" with a corresponding Cooperative Congress. This transformation simultaneously weakened the autonomy of individual co-ops ("cooperativas de base") and allowed for a more corporate system of governance. An internal memo from the general management of the cooperatives offered the following rationale for the reorganization, in words that would be echoed in the 1990s as the cooperatives again restructured themselves in the direction of greater centralization and managerial coordination: "The configuration of the cooperative model, that has permitted us over the years to realize a rich human and social-industrial experience, is now demonstrably inadequate for responding adequately to the rapid change that implicates both technological and market-oriented activities" (MCC 1985: 44). The Cooperative Congress was charged with approving general documents on the policies of the cooperatives, resolving social problems within the coops, shaping relations with the exterior market and political entities, and establishing certain targets for productivity and profit. The General Council is elected by the Cooperative Congress, and though neither the council nor the congress can, generally speaking, impose their will on the cooperatives—for example, by insisting that *all* co-ops widen their wage indices—they do exercise strong voices. The Cooperative Congress, for example, adopted the Ten Basic Principles of the Mondragón cooperative system at the first meeting of the assembly in 1987. The same body supported moves toward further reorganization along sectoral lines at its third and perhaps most important meeting in December 1991.

Both supporters and critics within the Mondragón Cooperative Corporation point to the Third Cooperative Congress as a watershed event. First of all, the meeting occurred during the second economic recession in a decade. The cooperatives had more or less successfully weathered the previous recession, in the early to mid-1980s, through consolidating certain functions, placing a virtual halt on the creation of new cooperatives, making personnel transfers from struggling co-ops to better-positioned ones, and, for the first time, laying off some segments of their work force. Also, as crucial elements of the cooperatives' response to that earlier crisis, the Entrepreneurial Division of the Caja had been spun off and the Cooperative Congress itself was created (MCC 1991).

Second, the Third Cooperative Congress was held on the eve of the transformation of the European Union through the dropping of most barriers to the flow of goods, services, capital, and labor across international borders. Spain, which had joined the EU along with Portugal in 1986, was both enthusiastic and apprehensive about this important economic development.

Already in 1987–88, when the Mondragón Cooperative Congress was still forming, the system's leaders had worried openly about what course to chart in a future market where they might be subject to competition with major multinational corporations, especially in the industrial sector. At a special conference in Cuenca, Spain, in October 1988, MCC cofounder José María Ormaechea had argued essentially that cooperatives of all types would need to become more like their traditional capitalist competitors for the sake of survival. At the same time, he had wondered how cooperativism could survive as a broad movement within the European Union (then the European Community) without strong legal, financial, and institutional supports at the level of the EU as a whole (see MCC 1988).

Certainly the unification of EU nations and restructuring of their economies in 1992 have played an enormous role in the transformation of the Mondragón cooperatives, opening them to new forms of competition and encouraging new arguments by cooperative managers for changes in the system. Timothy Huet explains: by 1988, "the Mondragón managers concluded that most of their key industrial companies had 'passed ... the point of no return.' In other words, they had invested too much in their current products and plants to radically change course. Having committed themselves to competing with the multinationals [e.g., in auto parts manufacturing], the co-ops adopted characteristics of their rivals" (1997: 18).

Each of the first three Cooperative Congress assemblies (in 1987, 1989, and 1991) made important policy decisions, but it was the 1991 meeting that really put the organization on a new course. The first congress had voted to widen the permissible pay ratio or index from 1: 4.5 to 1: 6 (as a ratio of lowest-paid to highest-paid employees). The second congress had created the Fund for Education and Intercooperative Development, the most important aspect of which was the provision for financial assistance to smaller or financially weaker co-ops through the pooled resources (specifically called "Social Contributions") of the larger and more profitable ones (Grupo Cooperativo Mondragón 1989). But the formal restructuring of the co-ops, first recommended by the Caja in 1984, did not come into full view until the December 1991 meeting.

The key decisions of the Third Cooperative Congress were: (a) a move toward greater centralization through expansion of the managerial superstructure and pursuit of a univocal strategy regarding the cooperatives' presence in the market (including the renaming of the Mondragón Cooperative Group as the Mondragón Cooperative Corporation); (b) the beginning of a major structural reorganization of the cooperatives, away from the long-standing reliance on regional groupings (often in distinct valleys and municipal areas) and toward clustering according to business sector; and (c) the allowance for further widening of the wage index, by permitting salaries of top managers to rise to 70 percent of established market equivalents. (Salaries at lower levels of the hierarchy have tended to be very close to market averages.) As we shall see shortly, all three of these decisions proved to be significant not only materially but as symbolic departures from basic cooperative values.

In the months that followed the December 1991 meeting, most of the co-ops voted to be part of the newly reorganized Mondragón Cooperative Corporation, but a few voted to secede, most notably the ULMA group in the town of Oñati and its neighboring valley. Differing with the MCC management especially over sectoral restructuring and centralized control, the four ULMA industrial co-ops voted 80 percent to 20 percent in early 1992 to create their own autonomous group (in effect, a separate corporation). The ULMA group now has five cooperatives, a number of satellites and holdings in other countries including France, South Africa, and Brazil, and high profitability. Like its giant neighbor MCC, ULMA is pursuing strategies of capital expansion, internationalization, and strategic interfirm alliances. By itself, ULMA is among the two dozen largest private firms in the Basque Country, has about 1,200 employees, and its current balance sheets reveal a strong financial position.

ULMA's departure from MCC is especially interesting, as we will see, because it sharpened the debates over key values: autonomy, solidarity with the community or geographic area, and hierarchy versus relative equality. José Antonio Ugarte, president of the ULMA group from 1991 to 1997, explained to me in reflecting on ULMA's move toward independence: "The new structure of MCC put us in the position of choosing between their project and our own; as things stood, we couldn't have our own project within the new structure of MCC."

As one of the case examples for this book, ULMA-Forja forges pipe fittings and flanges principally for oil companies. Forging is a profession with a long and fabled history in the Basque Country, dating back to the earliest evidence of industrialization. Forja was created in 1962 as a worker cooperative, partly with the assistance of Arizmendi. Today it employs about 175 persons, approximately 70 percent of whom are *socios*. The cooperative is undergoing rapid change because of demands for increased output and the struggle to keep pace with new technological developments in production.

ULMA's break with MCC over issues of local control now allows it to pursue internationalization from its own base and according to its own plan. However, ULMA's very identity as a breakaway (and underdog) group of cooperatives is now being overtaken by its own consolidation and expansion. Thus, at the same time that the case of ULMA can be examined against the backdrop of the larger MCC, it should be seen as experiencing some of the same challenges and difficulties, though on a smaller scale.

A number of cooperatives have been added to MCC during the period of corporate reorganization. In the 1990s, the MCC's entrepreneurial strategy has emphasized conversions of existing S.A.'s or *sociedades anónimas* (that is, traditional capitalist firms)[4] over the creation of entirely new cooperatives.

One of the case examples I explore in depth in Chapter 3 is a converted firm. MAPSA (Manufacturers of Aluminum of Pamplona for the Automotive Sector), in the bull-running city of Pamplona, Navarre, is a manufacturer of aluminum wheels for automobiles and became a part of MCC in 1991–92, after several years of operating in the red while being owned by a British conglomerate. The firm began in 1956. The work-force has hovered between one hundred and two hundred employees in the 1990s, most of whom have been worker-

---

[4] The four principal legal and tax-related structures for corporations in Spain today include: *sociedades anónimas* (SAs), *sociedades limitadas* (SLs), *sociedades cooperativas* (SCoops), and *sociedades anónimas laborales* (SALs). The last two involve some degree of worker ownership, with the SAL structure requiring a minimum of 51% worker ownership and the SCoop, at least in principle, requiring 100% (see Lucas 1994). The Mondragón co-ops have always emphasized that their structure and tradition as employee-owned firms make for greater equality, more substantial rights to information, and more meaningful participation in decision making than would typically be found in SALs (see *TU*, Jan. 1998).

owners since the conversion of the plant in 1992. More recently, the recruitment of some contract-based employees has taken total employment of the firm to about three hundred. In 1997 the company reached its goal of producing and selling over one million wheels.

This former S.A. has a history of authoritarian management practices and bitter labor disputes. During a heated debate in 1991 over whether or not to join MCC, many of the most active union members opposed the acquisition and conversion. At issue were the likely nature of decision making in the converted firm and the fact that the unions would effectively be disbanded. An assistant department head, Javier Lecumberri, told me, "There was fear on the part of many workers as well as managers about the changes in work culture required by the transition to become a cooperative." A close look at this case strikes to the heart of what "cooperativism" or organized cooperation means in practice. "Now that we are a cooperative," said a staff assistant in 1997, "the responsibilities of work belong to everybody. That means that the possibilities for the cooperative are within each of us."

The third case in-depth example is of MAIER, a highly successful maker of plastic auto parts, located in the historic town of Gernika, just thirty-five kilometers from Bilbao, the Basque Country's largest city. Gernika is the ancient political and spiritual capital of the Basque Country which marks the place where the *fueros*, or regional laws of self-governance, were established. It is also the town made famous by the devastating bombing raid of Hitler's Luftwaffe in 1937, at General Francisco Franco's bidding. The horrors of that event are immortalized in Picasso's "Guernica," a painting that now symbolizes the pain and senselessness of war for the entire world. Today the town of Gernika, with about fifteen thousand inhabitants, remains a burning source of pride for many Basques.

MAIER is a key member of MCC's Automotive Division, yet the co-op retains a strong independent spirit. Despite the perhaps apocryphal stories about the origin of the cooperative's name (no one is sure of its actual source, and it has no real meaning), many employees there are pleased that the title is German-sounding and easily recognized and pronounced in the international market. MAIER prides itself on its cosmopolitan corporate culture (the main receptionist speaks five languages), which is stimulated by an expanding network of suppliers and purchasers abroad. The co-op displays its autonomy by pursuing its own distinct ventures, such as the creation of a new high-tech research and development center and the establishment of its own fairly direct relationships with clients and customers, while also being a part of MCC's general corporate strategy. MAIER's tremendous success—it more than doubled its employees to over six hundred between my 1994 and 1997 visits—carries with it a number of problems, including difficulties with the new complexities of communication, a rapidly accelerating pace of work, and tensions between service to the customer and employee autonomy. A machine technician there said to me in 1994, "The growth of our business has brought us many benefits, especially high profits and good benefits. But many of us that have been around here since the beginning or when the company was small miss the kind of intimate work climate we once had." With the rapid expansion of the work force, many people have been hired on a contract basis, and so tensions have emerged between owning and nonowning employees. In 1998 MAIER and its associates became a Cooperative Group, signaling their increased clout within MCC's corporate structure.

Contemporary changes, bringing challenges and opportunities of the Mondragón cooperatives, cannot be captured in their totality in any one study, but through the in-depth exploration of three specific mid-sized cases, each representing a different aspect on the Mondragón experience, we can better appreciate where the co-ops are now and where they might be headed. Before moving to an analysis of Mondragón today, however, we should review how major studies of the cooperatives account for their longevity, financial strength, and social viability.

Reasons for Mondragón's Success

Undeniably the Mondragón cooperatives have had tremendous success. Not only does MCC in itself constitute the tenth largest private firm in Spain, but the cooperatives in general account for about 30 percent of the economic activity in the Basque Country (Mancomunidad de Alto Deba 1994). Although the number of new co-op starts declined sharply in the early 1980s and has remained relatively low, there continue to be conversions of traditional capitalist firms as well as buy-outs and conversions of other capitalist firms. Also the cooperatives now see themselves as the premier generators of new employment in several different districts of the Basque Country (*TU,*

1 June 1997: 6). Furthermore, the internationalization of the Mondragón and ULMA co-ops is accelerating (though most of the firms acquired in other countries are noncooperatives and have no plans to convert). In 1997 alone, MCC concluded agreements to form delegations, establish new plants, or purchase existing firms in Morocco, India, Brazil, Colombia, and China. Many observers consider Mondragón to be a model system. Canadian futurist Guy Dauncey (1997: 2) declares: "Mondragón has proved beyond question that co-operative ownership, co-operative banking and co-operative networking between businesses bring a level of success, stability and employment that can be matched by very few privately owned companies."

Opinions vary widely on the reasons for Mondragón's longevity and success, yet three sets of important explanations can be posed as crucial. The first set is *cultural*. Several analyses of Mondragón have emphasized the system's uniqueness and how it drew its values and energy from Basque culture (see the summary of research in Whyte and Whyte 1991). Especially compelling is the concept of solidarity. As Roger Collins (1990) observes, Basque culture displays a simultaneous stress on self-reliance and collaboration (see de Azaola 1988). Thus Basques will often appear to outsiders as both staunchly independent—individually, as well as in their collective nationalistic pride—and highly interdependent. *Solidaridad* (in Spanish, or *elkartasun* in Euskara/Euskera) symbolizes Basques' commitment to one another as well as their connections to the land, especially the region in which they live.

The mountain valleys and coastal inlets in which most Basque towns are situated were quite separate until well into the twentieth century, because of the difficulties in transportation over the mountain passes. Before the standardization of spoken and written Euskera early in the century, two communities in very close proximity—say, even as short a distance as ten kilometers as the crow flies—might have had very different terms for common objects such as tools. Mondragón, a small city of 35,000, and Oñati, a town of 12,000, are just twelve kilometers from one another, but the barrier of a mountain ridge left them with comparatively distinct traditions until the latter half of the twentieth century. Even now, the people of Mondragón speak of those in Oñati as snobby and distant because of the town's five-hundred-year-old university (the first in the Basque Country) and the fact that it was ruled by a count until the mid-nineteenth century. To reduce the sense of distance, the people of Mon-

dragón enjoy joking about the sexual exploits of the counts and ru-
mors of incest in the community. To the people of Oñati, Mondragón
is less picturesque, and has less charm and sophistication.

Regional solidarity is thus a strongly evocative concept for many
Basques. One Basque engineer, who was working temporarily as a
quality and participation expert in ULMA-Forja in 1996–97, told me
that he could no longer feel good about his "long commute" or about
living during the week in the town of Oñati, where Forja is located.
"I need to return to my place" (a town just thirty kilometers away).
Although an interest in working in other regions of Spain or even in
other countries is growing among young professional workers, ties to
the land and people of one's community of birth remain very strong
among nearly everyone I met in and around Mondragón.

Solidaridad is written into the constitution of the co-ops as one of
the famous Ten Principles, all of which became fully articulated and
approved by the First Cooperative Congress of the Mondragón cooperatives in 1987. These principles were inspired by those of the
Rochdale Pioneers in England and they are largely consistent with the
recent Statement on the Co-operative Identity by the International
Cooperative Alliance (1996). MCC's (1994) ten official principles are:

Open Admission
Democratic Organization
Sovereignty of Labor
The Instrumental Character of Capital
Self-management
Pay Solidarity
Group Cooperation
Social Transformation
Universal Nature
Education

The last five principles all incorporate some notion of solidarity,
even though the term is mentioned explicitly only in respect to
salary and wages. The broadest meaning of solidarity includes: (1)
maintaining a relatively narrow salary range between highest-paid
and lowest-paid employees; (2) "intercooperation," or the sharing of
resources by cooperatives in the same groupings within the larger
corporation; (3) connection with the communities in which the cooperatives operate; (4) identification with social justice movements

elsewhere; and (5) training focused on the coming generations. In addition, solidarity of employee relations was emphasized in many interviews. These aspects of solidarity persist today, although they are threatened by the internationalization of the cooperatives and the sharper focus on efficiency.

Another aspect of the cultural explanation for Mondragón's success is the co-ops' long-standing opposition to Franco. Having been forged during the hard years of oppression under the fascist dictatorship and within a culture that to some extent had to go underground from 1939 to 1975, the co-ops of Mondragón benefited from their distinctive identity and their vitality. Although labor unions were strictly outlawed until 1958 and carefully controlled by vertical management-worker councils from that time until Franco's death in 1975, cooperatives were legal. An experienced union representative outside the cooperatives told me, "The co-ops derived a surprising double benefit from Franco's regime: first, they were allowed to and in some ways even encouraged to exist through beneficial tax laws (that continue today); second, they could use Franco as a target of criticism and hatred so as to fortify their own internal sense of mission." The co-ops benefited from what has been called "identification by antithesis" (Burke, 1969; compare Cheney 1983a), in that they derived cohesion from opposing outside threats and forces. A U.S. economist who has recently studied the cooperatives observes that even though it is now a powerful multinational corporation, Mondragón continues to make symbolic use of its former underdog position (Martin 1994).

Finally, I must mention the role of the Roman Catholic Church in the culture of the cooperatives. While the Church performed no formal function in establishing the cooperatives—despite Arizmendi's formative role in their creation—its twentieth-century concern for labor and social justice certainly served as one of the important backdrops for the cooperatives' emergence and development. Basque religious historian Patxi Ituarte (1994) explains that Pope Leo XIII's famous 1891 encyclical *Rerum Novarum* ("Of the New Things") was central in Arizmendi's thinking about the cooperatives. Among other things, *Rerum Novarum* explicitly asserts the rights of workers to organize and proclaims that their interests should not be subordinated to those of capital or property. This conception of the dignity and rights of the worker later appeared in the constitution of the cooperatives, as summarized in the Ten Principles above.

Some researchers insist that these cultural factors be given less weight now than in the initial research on the cooperatives. William Whyte (1991), perhaps the most prolific U.S. writer on the cooperatives, agrees that cultural distinctiveness has been overrated and chooses instead to feature the co-ops' key organizational structures. Ituarte stresses that the substitution of new values for long-held religious and cultural ideals shows that at least in recent years the cooperatives' success must be attributed to other factors. Such changes are revealed, for example, in the dramatic drop in regular attendance at Mass in the Basque Country, from about 75 percent in 1975 to less than 25 percent today. Now "there is more and more talk about money," says Ituarte.

Perhaps more important than the institutional solidarity are the "second-order" cooperatives such as the Caja Laboral bank, a social security system, and an educational system, which have allowed the cooperatives to achieve longevity and success in large part by "buffering" them from the ebbs and flows of the larger market and society.

Especially important in this respect has been the Caja Laboral. By the early 1980s, when the Caja was just twenty-five years old, it was already Spain's twenty-sixth largest bank, with over 120 branches, over a thousand workers, and nearly half a million customers. Today, the Caja is one of Spain's largest financial institutions, with reserves and projects that extend far beyond those linked to the cooperatives of Mondragón. In fact, Spain's central bank required the Caja to open its doors to clients and investments beyond the co-ops in the mid-1990s, although the Caja still offers low-interest loans to the cooperatives. With respect to MCC, the Caja Laboral is a special type of second-order cooperative in that it serves both individual members (all worker-owners in the co-ops plus many outside holders of accounts) and institutional members, in the form of individual cooperatives.

From the time of its creation in 1959, the Caja Laboral has provided not only low-interest loans for the development of new cooperatives but also an array of support services. Economists Thomas and Logan (1982) explain that the Bank is important not only in the protection it affords fledgling cooperatives and the system in general but also in its structure. Jaroslav Vanek's theory of labor-managed firms (1975, 1977) cautions that pure self-financing by worker cooperatives can lead to tremendous inefficiencies; but Thomas and Logan observe that Mondragón has been largely able to avoid such problems through a complex and interdependent relationship between the producing co-ops and the Caja.

As already noted, the Empresarial (Entrepreneurial) Division of the Caja Laboral, which in 1991 became LKS, has functioned since 1959 as the internal consulting arm of the co-ops. Ellerman (1982) described this division as "a factory factory" largely responsible for the huge expansion of the number of the cooperatives within the system: during 1959–82 over a hundred new co-op starts, only one of which failed. Since 1986 the record is more difficult to assess because of acquisitions and sell-offs, and there have been practically no new co-op starts. LKS and its organizational forerunner have served the larger cooperative system in terms of what Ellerman calls "the socialization of entrepreneurship," through the development of mechanisms for consolidating expertise and bringing it to bear on existing and potential cooperative ventures. Beginning in the late 1970s, the Entrepreneurial Division replaced certain managers, altered product lines, and enabled the transfer of worker-members among cooperatives (Morris 1992). As a key part of the superstructure of the co-ops, this unit increasingly took on managerial functions with respect to the whole system. In 1991–92, for example, the LKS was instrumental in converting a failing capitalist firm, MAPSA of Pamplona, into a part of the Automotive Components Group of MCC; its contributions included specification of management plans and programs for retraining.

Thus the Caja Laboral and LKS have helped to protect the co-ops from many of the ebbs and flows of the larger market, granted them economic opportunities, offered social security (literally and figuratively), and provided cooperative management.

Another factor in Mondragón's success story is the internal dynamism and adaptability that have resulted from a complex system of direct and representative democracy. Although these mechanisms are changing—indeed, this is one of the important points of my analysis—their long-term contribution to Mondragón's achievement are crucial to discuss in some detail. Further, by way of this discussion, we can consider exactly how the individual co-ops are structured and how they fit together under two corporate umbrellas.

Within each cooperative, whether it be the Otalora Training Center with thirteen members or the Eroski supermarket chain with thousands, there are several governing bodies. First and foremost is the general assembly, which includes all worker-members. In principle this is the highest governing body of each cooperative, and by statute it must meet at least once a year (usually in the spring). Data collected by the Otalora Training Center in 1994 indicate that attendance has been averaging around 70 percent across the co-ops. Absences from general assembly meetings are negatively sanctioned in most co-ops. A *socio* who misses a single meeting is "advised"; a second unexcused absence results in loss of vote (which may become permanent); and a third leads to a fine. Members who must miss a meeting can give their proxy votes to others that attend, but each person in attendance can carry only one proxy vote per meeting.

Assemblies operate on a one-person, one-vote principle, but position papers and business plans are prepared in advance by key members who form a panel for presenting their recommendations to the assembly. In the spring of 1994, I attended four assemblies and found each to be rather formal, largely scripted, and relatively controlled. Given the liveliness of the debating culture among Basques—evident in bars as well as in boardrooms—I was surprised at the lack of spontaneity. Even oppositional voices were expressed through planned statements at key points in the proceedings. After a call for comments from the assembly by the conductor of the meeting (or one of the panelists) the *socio* would read a prepared *intervención*. This process was all the more surprising given how intensely oral Basque culture remains, even with industrialization, modernization, and internationalization. In most business situations, as on the street, face-to-face communication and one's word are considered more reliable than letters, memos, or written reports. (This cultural fact has important implications for research: interviews are more easily arranged than are surveys—the exact opposite of what we typically find in U.S. organizations.) Prior to the general assembly meeting for a large cooperative, *charlas* or preparatory chats are held for groups of thirty to forty socios, during which time the policies, plans, and strategies of the firm are reviewed and perhaps modified.

The *consejo rector*, or governing/directing council, is the principal governing body of each cooperative on a day-to-day basis. Members of the *consejo rector*, almost always elected to four-year terms, come from the general membership of the cooperative. Thus, the council may consist primarily of laborers as opposed to white-collar professionals (as was the case in the MAPSA co-op when I first visited in 1994). In each of the cooperatives I visited, the *consejo rector* was considered to be the most powerful organ in the co-op. *Socios* spoke with respect of the governing council even when they criticized its decisions.

One of the most important decisions made by the governing council is the selection of a general manager or *gerente*. The general manager of a co-op is often brought in from the outside, and many are even hired from traditional capitalist firms. Qualifications for this position include leadership ability, technical expertise, and faith in the cooperative vision of business. Most of the general managers I met were enthusiastic, dynamic, interpersonally adept, and ambitious. Fernando Recalde of ULMA-Forja, for example, was hired from a noncooperative company in 1993 and has helped to increase the sales of his co-op dramatically, particular by updating presses and other machinery and by an aggressive program of international marketing. Forja is now selling pipe fittings to petroleum companies in the United States, Mexico, and Southeast Asia. Especially impressive about Recalde's managerial style is his personal dynamism and caring relationships with employees all over the plant.

In moderately sized to large co-ops, there is also a *consejo de dirección*, or management council, chaired by the general manager and usually including key administrators such as the financial director, director of production, personnel director, and director of quality. Like the general manager himself, the other members of the management council are hired by the governing council, usually for unspecified terms. This organ, as in the case of smaller co-ops with only a general manager, recommends policies and plans to the governing council. Frequently the relationships between these two governing bodies are strong; in recent years the presumption that they will be in agreement has increasingly become the norm. While the recommendations of the *consejo de dirección* are in no way binding for a co-op, in practice they tend to guide the decisions of the *consejo rector* when it comes to purely business matters. The management council may meet as often as weekly.

The final important organ within each cooperative at Mondragón is the *consejo social* (social council). U.S. labor organizer Mike Miller explains, "It is recognized in Mondragón that managers are not the appropriate custodians of the interests of shop-floor workers, and that full participation on the part of all members requires more than formal participation in annual general assemblies. The social councils are the vehicles of two-way communication from the bottom up and the top down" (1994:8). The social councils are in fact designed to counterbalance the business orientation of the governing councils and the management councils with an explicit concern for safety, hygiene, remuneration, and personnel issues. Arizmendi commissioned the social councils envisioning that they would represent the individual and collective interests of all the *socios* of a cooperative, as related to but also distinct from the concerns of efficiency.

In practice, the performance and power of the social councils is highly variable across specific cooperatives, in part because they lack the clarity of purpose held by most governing councils. Also, in newer co-ops or conversions there is little tradition for the social councils to rely upon. And in some cases the governing council assumes a disproportionate amount of control because it has the statutory right to treat the recommendations of the social council as purely advisory. In two of the three co-ops I examined, for example, the social council was weak. The social council of MAPSA of Pamplona lacked direction because the co-op was a recent conversion from a traditional capitalist firm. In the case of ULMA-Forja, the social council had a long history of ineffectiveness, reinforced by very low interest in participating in the body. One worker-member at Forja told me, "It's like a trap from which we cannot escape: no one takes the social council seriously, so it never has the chance to get better. And so, things go on like this, year after year." At MAIER of Gernika, the immensely successful plastic auto parts manufacturer, the social council does play a very active role in the affairs of the firm. It is seen as both a complement to and a partner with the governing council, and these days it is raising important questions about the increasing pace and hours of work.

In addition to the general manager, each cooperative has a president, elected for a four-year term by the entire cooperative. The president is an ex-officio member of the governing council and the social council, and is invited to all meetings of the management council (where there is one). The general manager is occasionally invited to meetings of the governing council or the social council, usually to make informational presentations on the state of the co-op or to recommend future policy. Thus each co-op has a dual leadership structure. In most co-ops I visited, including Forja, MAPSA, and MAIER, both figures were powerful within the context of daily business, conducting important meetings and assuming leadership in the policies and management decisions of the firm. In many cases the two act as partners in the management of the co-op, the elected president being typically more conscious of his or her constituencies than is the selected general manager.

This dual governance-management structure gives vitality to the cooperatives, producing a fairly strong democratic awareness. Even as worker-members complained about the performance of *their* governing bodies or leaders, they recognized that the governing bodies' purposes were, among other things, to enlist significant participation, consult widely with the membership, and make informed decisions or at least offer credible recommendations. A middle-level manager in MAPSA was quite passionate when he said to me: "To participate in the governance of the business is a privilege that carries with it weighty responsibilities. The organs give us legitimate means for expressing ourselves, but it's up to us to take on the roles of true *socios* through vigorous involvement."

This comment, expressed by a thirty-year veteran of a recently converted firm, speaks to the critical issue of structure versus process. Vehicles for participation in decision making and other affairs have been present almost since the co-ops' founding in 1956, but the use, specific functioning, and vitality of these institutions are always open to question. In many co-ops the general assembly meetings have "become as predictable as Catholic Masses," as one dissatisfied worker-member of FAGOR-Electrodomésticos told me in 1994. And I have observed that many of the social councils are lacking in definition, vigor, and power. I would add that there is also a general perception of diminishing participation—especially in departmental or co-op meetings associated with information sharing and strategizing. As we will see in Chapters 3 and 4, a further question is whether new forms of participation at the level of the job and team are usurping some of the power of the social councils (just as they are supplanting traditional, decision-centered understandings of employee participation).

Interestingly, a recent master's thesis (Klingel 1993) found that neither past nor current membership in the governing bodies was a good predictor of *socio*'s desire to participate in decision making. Further, the study found it difficult to isolate personal characteristics such as education, tenure, or position as predictors. The study found, rather, that interest in and satisfaction with the current performance of the organ in question were the best predictors of an overall desire to participate. That is to say, one's sense of "how a governing body is doing" turned out to be the single most reliable indicator of whether or not a *socio* wanted to be more involved than he currently was. This conclusion is important not only because it confirms what emerged from my own interviews, but also because it reminds us of the circular nature of democratic participation. Simply put, per-ceived efficacy is likely to energize more participation, and if that participation is then seen as valuable, the perceived efficacy of the involvement will increase. This finding is generally in line with re-search by sociologists Derber and Schwartz (1983), who found that effective employee participation often results in the desire for even more participation. On the other hand, a negative spiral can easily take hold and may be quite difficult to reverse—as is the case with ULMA-Forja's social council. The question then becomes how and when to intervene so as to turn the council into a "club people want to join."

In sum, when I offer internal dynamism as one of the key factors in Mondragón's success, I am highlighting the *operation* of the system rather than its structures. A fact of organizational (or political) life is that institutions established to serve democratic interests and chan-nel democratic energies may become old, tired, stale, or simply un-used. The development and adaptation of the institutions must be supported by complex and vital means of communication that con-nect the governing bodies with one another and involve ordinary members with the activities of the councils. And, if it is to be truly democratic as well as flexible, such a system must be able to reflect upon and modify itself.

The Social Question as a Complement to the Economic Question

Concern for the social as well as the economic dimensions of Mon-dragón is the underlying motivation for this book. As I mentioned in Chapter 1, the two key questions about cooperatives and other orga-nizations that strive to be democratic or espouse values of social jus-tice are these: (1) Can the system survive economically, given the pressure for it to perform in a larger marketplace? (2) Can the system maintain its social values and commitments—that is, keep its soul?

These two questions emerged as overarching, interdependent themes in the discussions in the Otalora Training Center at the end of my group tour of Mondragón in March 1994, and the questions have been posed in various ways by a number of recent writers on the co-ops (see, e.g., Freundlich 1996; Harding 1998; Huet 1997; Miller 1994; Morris 1992). In an important article on the recent financial strategies of the cooperatives, Melissa Moye explains just how interdependent are the social and economic priorities of the Mondragón cooperatives. I quote her study at length:

> The interplay between social priorities and institutions developed by the group [of cooperatives] should be recognized in any attempt to understand its success. The original priorities of the group led members to develop institutions and practices of employment, finance and governance, which led to high employment, investment and participation. A sort of virtuous circle resulted which sustained an environment of high investment and productivity, and which produced problem-solving institutions such as intervention, social councils and a system of movement of excess workers which operationalized the social priorities. As the institutions built in the last two decades are revamped, one of the concerns voiced by co-op leaders is that the co-operatives must survive as businesses if they are to survive as co-operatives. The question that is raised here is whether they can succeed *without* being co-operatives, in the sense of maintaining their social priorities. If we see their social priorities as guiding the development of institutions that contributed to economic success, what happens as these institutions, and maybe even the underlying priorities, change? Then they cannot be seen as businesses first, but co-operation must be viewed as central to the business. (1993: 273)

Moye identifies one of the two reasons why my exploration of the social dimensions of the Mondragón cooperatives includes an explicit consideration of the market and especially an examination of the trend of "marketization" in discourse. The other reason, as explained in Chapter 1, was my recognition of the increasing interdependence of the internal affairs of organizations, such as employee participation, with external concerns, such as how to serve the customer better.

The Importance of Being Mondragón

Some current developments at Mondragón represent significant departures from its traditions, and go far beyond the obvious secularization of Basque society. The breadth of the changes is hardly surprising, given how much the cooperatives have been internationalized in the 1990s, the degree to which they now admit outside influences in the form of worldwide management trends such as TQM and *Kaizen*, and their romance with technology and modernization in general. In many of my interviews and conversations I found a disturbing degree of resignation to and sometimes full acceptance of organizational restructuring and the advice of the most celebrated management gurus. Talking of being in a technological "race" was common. Young people are thinking a lot about the development of their personal careers. And both *socios* and people on the street were describing themselves and others more and more as "consumers" and less as citizens or as community members. The co-op member may be as interested as anyone in accumulating goods and getting more and better service "for my peseta" at the store.

This study of Mondragón is above all about the capacity of the cooperatives to "keep their soul." This question is not new, but it comes to us with fresh importance as we consider not only how organizations of the future will meet the "needs" of consumers, but also how larger social problems are going to be addressed. The new global market has been proclaimed to be the key form of international activity for the twenty-first century, and is promoted as the primary vehicle of democratization in both industrialized and developing societies. But it is becoming increasingly clear that the wholesale substitution of market functions for social ones not only produces a rash of inequities (Sklar 1995) and yields a number of irrational outcomes such as overcapacity (Uchitelle 1997) but also leaves even many of the well-off strangely dissatisfied, with a sense of "Is this *all* there is?" (Samuelson 1996).

Considering the relevance of these changes to employee participation, we must note the increasing pressures on the worker through new regimes of efficiency, quality, and customer service. Many of these developments have occurred in the name of market reforms and customer orientation, but popular labels like "the customer-driven" firm are inadequate in helping us understand fully the diverse and often contradictory influences on businesses and other organizations today. For example how do we account for increased monitoring of employees' work at the same time they are being asked to be more "entrepreneurial"? Thus I wish to focus on the role of the employee and the meanings of participation at work.

I offer this case study, as well as the larger analysis of what might be called "problems of democracy" in contemporary organizational life, toward a more general discussion of individual and organizational futures. Rather than presenting Mondragón as either a quaint historical footnote or as a peculiar blip on the screen of business in the twentieth century, I suggest that it deserves special attention for what its dynamics reveal for the prospects of other organizations and institutions. The study of Mondragón is relevant to other organizations precisely because it represents an especially vigorous, unusually long-lived, and perhaps fairly "pure" attempt to guide a profit-making enterprise according to social values. So, followers of the case might ask: "Well, if Mondragón can't maintain its social commitments in the face of the international market, just who can?"

Key Value Debates at Mondragón

With Yudit Buitrago

We have to participate for reasons of competitiveness and the expansion of the market. And, the kind of participation we most need is not something up in the clouds, dealing with abstract issues, but something continuous and concentrated in one's job.
—Jesús Larrañaga, 1994

The Transformation of Values at Mondragón

S orting through the conflicts and areas of overlap between the traditional cooperative values and the more recently evolved corporate ones at Mondragón is not an easy matter, especially given the ambiguities and changes in meaning within the co-ops' various constituencies. As the magazine of the Mondragón Cooperation, *Trabajo y Unión* (*TU*), put it in a February 1996 cover story on "the corporate values," corporate and cooperative values are *not* completely incompatible. The list of ranked values in that issue includes "people" (second), "cooperation" (third), and "social commitment" (sixth), along with "satisfaction of the customer" (first), "products and services" (fourth), and "continuous improvement" (fifth). Though formal communications heavily emphasize modeling the activities of noncooperative multinational corporations (with the possible exception of MCC's strategy of increased centralization), debates and discussions over the "social side" of work at Mondragón persist in general assemblies, corporate documents, orientation and training programs, and informal departmental "chats." My own questions of workers and citizens about the "values that actually *do*" or "the values that really *ought* to represent the cooperatives" produced passionate and thoughtful monologues and exchanges. Few were at a loss for words about this subject.

In January 1999, MCC issued a new mission statement, which begins: "MCC is a socio-economic experience with an entrepreneurial character, created by and for persons, inspired by the cooperatives' basic principles, committed to competitiveness and customer satisfaction, in order to generate wealth in the society" (*TU*, Jan. 1999).

One of the founders of MCC, Jesús Larrañaga, argues that the "old" cooperative values such as participation and social solidarity must be recast or reframed to accommodate the globalization of the economy; the top priorities of profit and efficiency must be based in the direct engagement of the worker-owner in the management of the firm (TU, Jan. 1996). For Sharryn Kasmir, author of *The Myth of Mondragón*, the tension between old and new values has already been lopsidedly resolved in favor of the corporate culture. "In situating the Mondragón cooperatives within the global economy, one lesson becomes clear. Worker-owners are not shielded from the forces of the global market" (1996: 194). This view is consistent with what some representatives of the quasi-union KT ("Cooperative Groups") told me in April 1994: "The management of MCC is now very distant from our heritage; they have violated some of our most enduring principles, such as solidarity." Numerous informal conversations during 1997 in the street and in local bars supported this interpretation. But Javier Mongelos, former president of MCC, told me in an interview in May 1994, "Far from seeing employee participation on the decline, we are encouraging and witnessing its resurgence." Moreover, leaders and many workers in the ULMA group of coops that broke away from MCC in 1992 believe linkages to the local community can be maintained within the context of progress in the market. The former president of the ULMA group, José Antonio Ugarte, told me in early 1994: "We saw separation from MCC as the only way to preserve our commitment to the community, the land, and local autonomy." Some of the *socios* in the Otalora Training Center also think core values can be sustained during globalization. The house sociologist, Mikel Lezamiz, insisted in 1994 that there were many opportunities to revitalize the cooperative spirit of MCC.

The tensions at Mondragón between corporate and cooperative values have been present from the very beginning. MCC cofounder José María Ormaechea told me in a 1994 interview, "Don José María [Arizmendiarrieta] was as much a realist as an idealist: he knew that the cooperatives would have to make it financially and he knew they would have to adapt to the changing fortunes of the market. This idea is not new to our present day, though the globalization of the market certainly presents us with new challenges."

The tension between what Peter Leigh Taylor (1994) calls the "rhetoric of the business firm" and "the rhetoric of the social firm" can be understood to some extent in terms of one of the very operating principles of Mondragón: *equilibrio* (equilibrium). Although this principle is not explicitly enshrined in the Ten Principles that were adopted by the First Cooperative Congress in 1987, Whyte reported that "in discussions and in written reports we find frequent use of the term" (1991: 99). In a way the concept of equilibrium is a foundation for the Ten Principles, whose underlying theme is that the concerns of labor and of the community are means of achieving social ends. Whyte explains: "[*Equilibrio*] refers to the principle that the cooperatives must guide their growth in terms of balancing economic and technological requirements with social needs and the social vision" (1991: 99).

In their study of workplace democracy in the FAGOR group in the late 1980s, anthropologist Davydd Greenwood and his collaborator in the co-ops, José Luis González (1989, 1992), explained that the principle of equilibrium actually applies to several different dimensions of life inside the cooperatives, including especially the dialectics of efficiency-participation, dynamism-stability, and cooperation-conflict. In focus groups, *socios* spoke readily about each of the values and recognized the trade-offs with respect to those values that must be faced with each organizational decision. Perhaps the most important equilibrium is between efficiency and participation, because it crystallizes the potential conflict between organizationally centered reasons for policies and employee-focused ones.

Key concepts such as "the market," "the consumer," "democracy," "efficiency," and "solidarity" are being continuously redefined at Mondragón. For example, I found an almost supernatural conception of the market to be a common perception among *socios*, and accorded a measure of supreme social agency without reference to its constituent parts. Some of my contacts in the co-ops would insist simply that "the market means that we must grow or die," often without being able to pinpoint the signals from the market that led to such a certain conclusion.

"Customer service" has become a dominant value in many organizations today—a reason for being and a way of reconceptualizing every organizational activity and every employee (George 1990). Like "mom" and "quality," customer service is difficult to attack in debate. Yet it may not be what it first appears, in that "service" may be a narrowly conceived and mechanical sort of impulse rather than based in thoughtfulness, dedication, and creativity. Still, multiple interpretations within the diverse organizational cultures at Mondragón may sometimes stimulate resistance against the dominant or emergent values of the organization.

By offering a selective history of Mondragón within Chapter 2, I have previewed a number of the value-oriented tensions and challenges faced by the cooperatives. I have mentioned important changes in Basque and Spanish cultures: for instance, the decline of religiosity and the rise of careerism and consumerism. At the same time, we have seen the growing involvement of women in the work force and the emergence of environmentalism. Finally I have noted the most important internal changes in the co-ops, many of which have become especially pronounced in the 1990s: the consolidation of corporate functions and the further strengthening of a managerial superstructure; the restructuring of MCC's cooperatives along sectoral lines and away from reliance on regional groupings; the widening of the wage differential and the linkage of top managers' salaries to the market; the pursuit of corporate flexibility through the creation of new categories of employees that are not permanent *socios*; and particularly the introduction of new programs of quality, productivity, and participation. All of these changes, and a few others yet to be mentioned, will come more clearly into focus in this chapter, along with the patterns of discourse surrounding them.

Below, I consider in turn several clusters of interrelated values, all of which emerged as important in my five-year investigation of the cooperatives: first, growth, internationalization, and competitiveness; second, solidarity, equality, and autonomy; and third, efficiency, quality, and customer service. Also I consider what the changes at Mondragón mean for a fourth cluster of values: employee participation, communication, and information. The chapter concludes by elaborating on the advantages and disadvantages of casting employee participation chiefly in market terms, while drawing upon other relevant aspects of the preceding discussions.

Growth, Internationalization, and Competitiveness

Because growth is an almost unquestioned value in corporate and economic circles, organizations of all stripes can easily blind themselves to its unintended consequences. One such consequence, as Robert Michels ([1915] 1962) warned the world, was that even in the most egalitarian of organizations (such as the German Socialist Party just after the turn of the twentieth century), growth beyond a certain point would lead to concentration of power in the hands of a few.

With almost a century of further experience behind us, we can see not only the problems associated with organizational growth—such as goal displacement and organizational inflexibility—but also how remarkably persistent is the ideology of growth (Teune 1988). For example, in a systematic study of U.S. public corporate documents (annual reports and house organs or employee magazines) for 10 percent of the *Fortune* 500 corporations, growth was a prevailing value in *every* document and far exceeded all other values in both frequency of mention and in emphasis (Cheney and Frenette 1993). Indeed, some of the organizations examined talked about expansion as potentially "limitless."

Consistent with the analysis of organizational values throughout this book, the issue of growth should be understood on two levels. The first is the actual effects of increased size on such aspects of the organization as coordination, cohesion, and communication. The other is the nature of the discourse about growth—that is, the arguments advanced in favor of it. Both are important to an understanding of the dynamics of size, in mainstream organizations as in so-called alternative ones.

Clearly, each organization should decide why, when, and how it needs to grow, recognizing that growth may change the fundamental character of the organization and substantially alter its relationship to other organizations and institutions. Many an organization has been seduced by the illusion that there are no social costs to growth, only material benefits. But individuals' management of information, supervisory effectiveness, and full participation may all be jeopardized when growth exceeds a certain level. The cases in Rothschild and Whitt's *The Cooperative Workplace* show that some organizations, seeing their small size as constitutive of "who they are," choose caution and deliberation in considering growth. For instance, organizations of a democratic or egalitarian nature may choose to cap the overall size of the organization or place limits on the sizes of departments and committees.

The expansion of the Mondragón cooperatives has been dramatic. Once defined as an "alternative" institution within the Basque and Spanish economies, Mondragón is now one of the leading establishments in the Basque industrial, financial, and distribution sectors. In itself this new status makes it difficult for the cooperatives to maintain the sense that they are different from most multinational corporations. Raymond Russell's research on a variety of types of cooperatives (1985)—ranging from taxi drivers' collectives to Israeli *kibbutzim*—reveals that motivation of employees may decline over time as a result of growth and the accompanying dilution of participatory practices. Similarly, Eric Batstone's investigations of French producer cooperatives (1983) reveals that the "frontier spirit" is likely to diminish as they become more secure in funding and in management.

The visibility of the FAGOR brand of home appliances, the presence in most Basque communities of large Eroski supermarkets, the Caja Laboral's move toward becoming a separate institution in its own right, and the rapid multiplication of Mondragón's international "delegations" and factories are among of the clearest signs that the cooperatives have now far exceeded their founders' expectations of financial success, resources, geographic reach, and power. This tremendous expansion has had its effects on organizational character.

The Caja Laboral's mid-1980s plan to expand the MCC cooperatives' capital base and international market penetration while reducing their diversification has now been significantly realized. With the exception of certain co-ops of the old FAGOR regional group in the Mondragón valley, where intercooperative bonds and traditions are still strong, the new sectoral groupings are coming to life as coordinated policymaking and internal communications plans. Rafael Leturia, former vice president of the Automotive Division, told me in 1997, "Part of the difficulty for some long-time workers in parts of FAGOR [Ederlan and Electrónica] is that they have passed through five different co-ops, five different business arrangements, in the course of MCC's development."

For many long-time *socios*, especially in the FAGOR group, there is a sense of not only an unstable organizational structure but also an unstable organizational identity. This problem has motivated the quasi-union KT's opposition to MCC policies and it is evident in KT's "interventions" or public statements at general assembly meetings of the FAGOR group. KT's representatives appeal to strong notions of tradition, local control, and intercooperative solidarity. One representative insisted, "We just can't allow the corporation to become more important than the individual cooperatives that grant it authority."

The three principal divisions in MCC, are financial, distribution, and industrial, with the industrial group being further subdivided into seven production sectors (*agrupaciones*). At the same time, MCC has attempted to enhance the coordination of market strategy at the corporate level, which has been the justification for increasing the influence of both the governing council of the Cooperative Congress and the LKS consultants. Defending this strategy, a young systems engineer at MAIER told me how the co-op in 1992 endorsed MCC:

> The challenge of the Mondragón cooperatives is to fight against all the "holdings" [holding companies based in other nations] that are being introduced in Spain. MAIER has always been part of the Mondragón group but has also been more on its own. Being one of the most powerful companies within the automobile sector, we were a bit more independent than all the rest [of the co-ops in the proposed new *agrupación*]. And this is why there was a fight about whether to join MCC or not. We considered carefully if we could manage on our own. But to do this, a company needs to be very strong and powerful. When you have clients like Peugeot, the name MAIER may sound familiar but not as much as if you talk about MCC. So we decided it would be best to enter MCC [and be part of its new corporate plan].

ULMA, which now consists of five distinct cooperatives, has also developed a corporate strategy that calls for a unified presence in the market, while still encouraging each individual co-op to develop distinct customer and supplier relations. ULMA's "Organizational Project" (1994) includes, in addition to specifications for the distribution of profits, a statement of corporate values (based almost entirely on the Ten Principles of MCC), corporate strategy, prescribed corporate lines of authority, and guidelines for the further development of a consistent "business and cooperative culture" for the group of co-

ops. As explained to me by Iñigo Agirre, then general manager of
ULMA, "The group's Organizational Project is an attempt to blend
corporate and cooperative values, with one eye toward the traditions
of the cooperatives and another on the need for greater competitiveness in the international market. But above all, the plan is designed
to help us succeed as a business."

Like MCC, ULMA experienced a significant economic upturn in
1995–99, has hired numerous contract-based or nonowning employees (though at pay scales typically closer to those for *socios*), and an-
ticipates substantial further growth. Perhaps the greatest difference
between ULMA and MCC, in addition to size and infrastructure, is
ULMA's opposition to the corporate strategy of sectoralization; it
prefers instead to remain a regionally based group of diverse industrial cooperatives. Finally, both corporations have been developing
comprehensive communication plans since the mid-1990s, to deal
with the complexities of information flow and decision making.

Thus the growth of the cooperatives, especially during the phases
of adaptation to the market (1985–90) and sectoralization (1991 on-
ward) has meant far more than "adding more of the same" to existing
structures. Both "organizations of organizations," MCC and ULMA,
offer important lessons about the problems as well as the benefits associated with this growth. Here I consider the issue of growth briefly
in terms of its implications for (a) employee relations within the cooperatives; (b) the organizations themselves, especially as they balance internal and external priorities; and (c) the communities surrounding the original cooperatives.

Changes in employee relations include obvious ones such as a de-
crease in intimate, face-to-face communication as a cooperative employs more and more persons. But even in that apparently simple dimension, the problems can be profound—going far beyond a mere
nostalgia for the early days. During my research at MAIER, the manufacturer of plastic auto parts, I found that most interviewees who
had been with the company more than a few years drew a sharp contrast between the "family"-like experience of work in the past and
the current "corporate" model. *Socios* spoke with much affection for
the days when communication among employees seemed relatively
easy, informal, and spontaneous. They also reminisced about an easier pace of work—not fewer hours so much as "less intense" times
on the job. An administrative assistant in the financial area explained to me, "We used to have much more participation [in the as-

semblies, organs of governance, etc]. And we had more informal talk. Today the informal talk is even more vital to get work done, but it is harder to make it happen because of the large size of the business and the faster pace of work." She later added, "This place *feels* a lot more like a [regular private] corporation and a lot less like a cooperative than it used to. There are many layers of management to go through with a message."

The issue of size has also become manifest in terms of what I would call "hierarchical distance" within the cooperatives. This issue had already surfaced at the time that the most recent research by Whyte and Whyte (1991) and Greenwood and González (1992) had been conducted in the late 1980s. In fact, the problem was recognized as early as the 1974 strike, both in the complaints of some of the strike leaders and in the reflections of Arizmendi. Cofounder Alfonso Gorroñogoitia remarked to me in the summer of 1997, "In an institution as big as MCC, the perception of democracy diminishes. There is a sensation of distance from the source of major decisions. This is the major criticism of representative as opposed to direct democracy."

It gradually became clear to me, especially through informal discussions with *socios* and citizens on the street, that there was a growing perception of a distinct managerial class within the cooperatives. In part, this perception stems from the sheer size of the cooperatives. A more specific contributor to this perception, perhaps, particularly as argued by the spokespersons of KT, was "the break with solidarity" in the form of linking top managers' salaries to the market. Still, I sensed that there was something more behind negative remarks about MCC's "*cúpula*" (cupola): a feeling that the cooperatives had lost touch with the concerns of the working class and the majority of their employees. A representative of KT told me in 1994: "We see that the *cúpula* has been taken over by a bunch of technocrats who are preoccupied with the corporate issues to the neglect of the social ones. Often they seem to be in a class by themselves." In the larger community this distance translated into less cultural "mixing" of employees at top levels in MCC with those of lower levels than in the past. Some lower-level employees complain of no longer being able to bump into some of MCC's top managers at the same bars—in communities where the bar is an important center for social life. I would not overstate this observation, though, because I also witnessed a number of top-level managers practicing "management by walking around"; they were clearly *not* removed from the larger communities in which they lived.

Finally, certain effects on the communities surrounding the cooperatives are important to note. During the years in which the cooperatives have become very important employers in parts of the Basque Country—now accounting for over 50 percent of total employment in the Alto Deba *comarca* (municipal district or county) centered in the town of Mondragón—they have also become very influential in their communities. This influence takes the form of cooperative schools and social projects, but it is also felt in the sheer size and economic clout of the co-ops vis-à-vis other businesses. Perhaps the most important example of this local economic might is Eroski, the supermarket chain. Though I have no quantitative data on the effects of Eroski on traditional family-run markets, numerous people in those markets complained to me of the "Eroski machine" and its dominance of the consumer economy in the area. Eroski's own small neighborhood franchises, named Erosle, began disappearing from Mondragón and the surrounding towns in the early 1990s, bowing to the dominance and centralization of the massive new supermarkets.

Both MCC and ULMA seem to justify their expansion in terms of two principles: first, the need to have a broader capital base so as to compete reasonably with corporate giants within Spain and without; and second, the desire to maintain and generate employment. These are precisely the reasons why both corporations are now engaged in joint ventures, often with noncooperative firms that are at least 51-percent owned by the cooperative corporation. In regard to competitiveness, MCC has consolidated a number of its functions, reducing the range of its activities to compete in several key industrial sectors. One result of pursuing this road to growth has been a reduced capacity for exploring creative new products and services outside the elected sectors. For instance, by choosing to go head-to-head with other suppliers of automobile parts to the major manufacturers, the cooperatives have opted to avoid new products and services whose markets are not already dominated by multinational corporate giants. Some examples of industries not extensively explored are tourism, crafts, sporting goods, real estate, forestry, public works, furniture making, and high technology—computer software and communications.) To probe this matter more deeply would require economic analysis beyond the scope of this book; suffice it to say that MCC's strategy may be simultaneously more aggressive and less

imaginative than it was previously (Huet 1997). This point is difficult to substantiate, though, and I present it as merely a hypothesis.

The second key justification I heard at Mondragón for policies of
growth was a commitment to generate and maintain employment,
especially in the Basque Country proper. In 1997 MCC signed a historic agreement with the Basque Parliament which officially made
the cooperatives a key instrument in achieving the employment
policies of the Department of Justice, Economy, Labor, and Social Security. A similar accord was signed the following year with the government of the neighboring autonomous community of Navarre.
The practical implications of these agreements are still unfolding as
of this writing. The Basque Country agreement does call for MCC to
work systematically and vigorously toward the creation of more than
eight thousand new jobs by the year 2000. Of course, the capacity of
a single organization to generate such new employment remains a
contested issue in economics, with many analysts insisting that only
macro-economic forces and policies (such as monetary programs) can
effectively alter employment patterns on a grand scale (see, e.g.,
Krugman 1997). Nevertheless, both MCC and ULMA have played
important roles in the economies of their communities, and each
corporation tends to express its solidarity with the larger social environment in terms of a commitment to "full employment." That unemployment rates for these communities have frequently been
lower, even in severe economic recessions, than for the Basque
Country or for Spain is often used as a confirmation of the linkage
between cooperative management policies and employment patterns.

The full-employment justification for expansion is particularly interesting because it can be used as a transcendent goal—with a kind
of implicit utilitarian ethic—expressed like this: "Ultimately what
counts is the *existence and preservation* of jobs for us and for our
children; so whatever we can do to achieve that goal is warranted."
As the 1990s wore on, this position seemed reflected more and more
in the editorial position of *TU* magazine as well as the views of many
managers around Mondragón. Given the recessions of the early
1980s and early 1990s, such a stance is quite understandable. Still, it
does locate a chief rationale for the cooperatives largely outside
themselves, and in so doing it can limit attention to internal affairs
such as personnel issues and governance.

Of course we must remember that much of the recent growth of the cooperatives has been outside their wellspring communities and beyond the borders of the Basque Country. And it is important to note *how* the case for employment policy is made. In MCC especially, the argument about expanding employment is offered as an expression of solidarity at the same time that the corporation is reorganizing along sectoral rather than regional lines and is extending itself globally. For some employees and especially those in the quasi-union KT, these corporate messages are in conflict. A representative of KT in FAGOR Electrodomésticos told me in 1994, "We hear MCC talking about its commitment to employment here, but we also see them breaking with the solidarity that defines us and binds us with the community." Regardless of one's perspective on the wisdom of this constellation of policies, their coherence is not self-evident for many *socios*.

Coupled with the full-employment justification for growth, moreover, is an interest in internationalization almost for its own sake (see Ehrensal 1995; Spich 1995). Indeed it is presented in several issues of *TU* as a *value* in itself. Not surprisingly, such discourse has become much more evident at Mondragón since 1992, when the European Union achieved a substantial degree of economic unification. An article in *TU* (Apr. 1995) by a cofounder of the co-ops, Jesús Larrañaga, underscored the importance of internationalization by saying that the co-ops needed to learn from the successes of multinational corporations to adjust their own practices to meet new needs. In his view, MCC could not afford to remain a "medium-sized" organization in a world of giants. For this reason, a "core strategy" of MCC has been described as "ever-expanding investment abroad" (*TU*, Oct. 1995).

From the standpoint of discourse and argumentation, however, much of the formal discussion of internationalization in MCC's corporate documents borders on the tautological or circular. For example, in an article in the October 1995 issue of *TU*, where the cover featured the theme of internationalization, a strategic planner for MCC argued simply for the "obvious" fact that "one of the Basic Objectives of the Corporation is its Internationalization" (5). In the same issue of the magazine, the director of MCC's international operations insisted that "our internationalization is seeking, principally, new opportunities for business that serve to expand existing possibilities to enhance our position with our international clients" (13). The cooperatives' policies and management of growth may not be as reflective as one might expect. Bowing to market forces as they are understood by the cooperatives, MCC and ULMA may not fully appreciate the disadvantages of expansion and the need to counter or at least cope with some of its most negative effects. In an effort to engage the market completely on its own terms, they may be unduly sacrificing the long-valued "buffer zone" between them and the turbulence of the international market.

Solidarity, Equality, and Autonomy

The foregoing discussion of growth as a superordinate value points us naturally toward a consideration of the interconnected internal values of solidarity, equality, and autonomy. Each of these values expresses how individual workers and the cooperatives themselves relate to one another, and each has an important cultural referent in Basque tradition.

Solidaridad has multiple and changing meanings at Mondragón. An engineer at ULMA-Forja defined it this way: "Solidarity can imply sharing knowledge with co-workers, helping people solve problems, or even renouncing certain economic benefits. Economic solidarity, in the broadest sense, means that I stay in a system even though I could be making more money somewhere else."

The most obvious sense of *solidaridad* is camaraderie and cooperation at work, and in this sense, it is roughly equivalent to the English term "cohesion," but with an added dimension of social support. A number of *socios* illustrated this type of solidarity with examples of workers willingness to do something above and beyond the call of mere duty in order to support another, such as volunteering for extra weekend work hours so another employee might spend time with his family or deal with a personal crisis. An administrative assistant in MAPSA of Pamplona told me, "For me, solidarity is to try to put yourself in somebody else's skin and act from that point of view. . . . It is the opposite of individualism." This sense of solidarity is not institutionalized within the Ten Principles of the cooperatives, but employees of the cooperatives, as well as citizens in the larger communities, readily offer examples from their own experience, many of them hastening to add such comments as, "the kind of solidarity we used to see is disappearing, as people get busier and busier and as young people become more focused on their own careers."

The secretary who said this also told me that she thought "complete solidarity is now impossible within the context of the market because the cooperatives are forced to become more hierarchical and efficiency-oriented." (Indeed I noticed a significant speed-up at work and on the street between the spring of 1994 and the summer of 1997.)

Alfonso Gorroñogoitia adds that broader cultural influences from the market and consumer culture have weakened workers' commitments to maintaining the cooperatives as an institution. He offers the powerful piece of evidence that *socios* are likely today to reinvest only the minimum specified by statute, 30 percent, in the collective capital fund of the organization. In the early years of the cooperatives, he recalls, they would vote to "socialize" up to 70 percent of their profits. Today, as Gorroñogoitia complains, "people tend to think of the regular income taxes they pay as already showing evidence of their 'solidarity.' " He adds that the "culture of sacrifice" has greatly deteriorated as the consumer culture has prospered. These cultural shifts have important implications also for consumers' commitments to the cooperatives, and for employees' work motivations.

A second defining feature of the coops is *solidaridad retributiva* or wage solidarity. This aspect of Mondragón's structure, one of the most celebrated, has in recent years become a focal point of debate and criticism. As established in the Ten Principles, the ratio of lowest to highest pay was originally set at 1:3. (The "job grade" or "index" for a particular employee is constructed from a formula that includes the nature and special circumstances of the position, seniority bonuses, merit increments, and other factors. Actually, no *socios* at Mondragón are at the 1.0 pay grade, and taxes reduce further the ratio between lowest and highest paid.) The ratio was widened first from 1:3 to 1:4.5, and later each cooperative was given the power to decide whether to adopt a 1:6 ratio or stick with the 1:4.5 scale (GCM 1989; MCC 1991). Finally, in the watershed decisions of the Third Cooperative Congress of December 1991, an additional change was made to peg the salaries of the top managers (including the president, vice presidents, and some directors) to 70 percent of the current market average for equivalent positions in the noncooperative private sector. This move was unprecedented in the history of the coops. In the proceedings of the congress this change was justified in terms of "external competition" and the need to "avoid the risks of demotivation derived from [individuals'] comparisons with businesses in the market environment" (MCC 1991, 1:53). As of this writing, some co-ops in the old FAGOR regional group are still adhering to pre-1992 scales.

This last change proved to have not only material implications for the top managers involved (they number about 30 in MCC), but also for the collective social understanding of the practices of solidarity. In 1994 an employee in FAGOR Electrodomésticos (also an activist in the quasi-union KT) asserted, "The change in policy over wages represents a break from the tradition of solidarity in the co-ops. Where's the solidarity in this?" This *socio* explained that the change in policy was a problem even if the managers' salaries did *not* rise to 70 percent of market level.

That year Javier Mongelos, then president of MCC, told me the executives' salaries were indeed only about 50 percent of the market average. He expressed frustration and amazement at the continuing debate over the issue and especially at the air of mystery and suspicion surrounding what were publicly available figures, and said that there seemed to be no effective way to assuage the workers' concerns. In his view, the basic foundation of remunerative or wage solidarity had been shaken not because of the 1991 change in partial deference to the market but because a group of workers were conceiving of wage solidarity too narrowly, too technically. I interpret this episode in another report of my research:

> In this instance of a market-oriented change, the symbolic power of
> the change in the minds of some organizational members seemed to
> overshadow the question of actual salaries. From their standpoint,
> the corporation had compromised an internal value, wage solidarity
> [one of the Ten Principles], in bowing to external market standards
> and had thereby undermined a distinctive characteristic of the co-
> ops. On the other hand, defenders of the change (such as the Presi-
> dent) insist that some compromises are necessary for the sheer sur-
> vival of the system (and by implication, its constitutive values).
> This instance is a reminder of how sometimes a single communica-
> tion event (or "message") can deeply affect the climate and course
> of an organization. (Cheney 1997: 76)

In fact, it appears that at the Third Cooperative Congress both supporters and critics of the wage-scale change saw it as a "turning point" in the development of the cooperatives (see Bullis and Bach 1989). In its official statement at the congress, KT declared the change, along with the process of sectoral reorganization, to represent "a qualitative and not merely a quantitative change in the basic character of the co-ops." The official stance of MCC's leadership, especially as embodied in the proceedings of the congress was that these changes in policy reflected necessary and natural developments of corporate strategy. The director of Human Resources for the entire MCC, Jesús Goienetxe, said, in an article in *TU* (Feb. 1992), " 'Internal equity' and 'external competitiveness' are compatible with the basic ideological foundations of the cooperatives."

An especially insightful observation on wage solidarity was offered to me by Alfonso Gorroñogoitia in the summer of 1997. He said that dissatisfactions would be almost inevitable once the *socios* and the organization began to focus on solidarity in terms of income and dividends. "In the beginning, we simply *had* solidarity with one another; it wasn't something that needed to be institutionalized; it was simply understood." But by focusing on the concrete, material, and legalistic aspects, the cooperatives "set themselves up for lasting tension with respect to the issue of solidarity." Outside pressures would pull some salaries upward, and many *socios* would feel disadvantaged and angry as a result. In my interviews the pecuniary sense of *solidaridad* was typically the first one that came to mind.

The principle of intercooperation at Mondragón is meant to emphasize solidarity at the organizational level. There are three dimensions to these interrelations: financial, structural, and social-communal. First, collective funds exist within groups of cooperatives for the purpose of offering financial support to those *cooperativas de base* that are in need. The ULMA group of cooperatives has established a similar system, from which ULMA-Forja benefited during its lean years in the early 1990s. Similarly, MAPSA enjoyed an infusion of funds from MCC after its acquisition and transformation into a cooperative in 1991–92. But intercooperative assistance often goes far beyond the simple transfer of funds, including as well "the human resources and everything else necessary to help deal with the problems that a co-op or the group may have," as a former president of MAIER told me.

For instance, in MAPSA's conversion—in about five years' time—from a noncooperative and failing manufacturing firm to a modestly profitable co-op, the intervention of MCC provided not only money but also tremendous technical and social help. Top directors were transferred in from better-established co-ops in the MCC system, and there were temporary exchanges of personnel with long-time members of the FAGOR group. In addition, numerous MAPSA employees have attended philosophical and technical training seminars in MCC's Otalora Training Center. And, as of the summer of 1997, the director of Quality at FAGOR-Ederlan, an automotive co-op where Total Participative Management had been employed first in the mid-1990s, was still making frequent trips to MAPSA to design a new program of TPM in the form of a team-based restructuring of the entire cooperative. The first elected president of MAPSA, Joaquin Jímeno (a labor organizer and former union steward), admitted that the change to a cooperative generated mixed emotions in him and other employees because of the new stress on solidarity. "There is a lot happening at once," he said. "On the one hand, supervisors and directors will not have the same kind of definitive authority they had before. And there will be more sharing of information. On the other hand, we're entering into relationships with a different kind of cooperation we don't fully understand and that is directing us on how to change."

MCC's Third Cooperative Congress also established new centralized accounts to support educational and "promotional" projects of the cooperatives (such as more vigorous international marketing efforts and collective investments in new technologies). Actual expenditures are determined by the general council of the Cooperative Congress. These accounts represent a further official commitment to intercooperative solidarity.

Though financial "intercooperation" is meant as an instrument of solidarity among individual cooperatives, it carries implications for their autonomy. Cooperatives that are the strongest in their sectoral groups can resent the beneficiaries of their sound financial position. Indeed, self-protection was one of the chief reasons for MAIER's hesitation in joining MCC in 1992, according to a number of my interviewees. The former president of the cooperative, José Ignacio Gandarias, related to me in 1994 that MAIER's stance regarding full participation in MCC was critical because of the co-op's negative history with a regional group of co-ops. Many at MAIER felt little in common with the other co-ops in their group, and MAIER found it draining to try to coordinate with what it regarded as weaker firms.

Solidarity, then, can be seen as a threat to autonomy for the co-op that is repeatedly asked to share its resources. An engineer at MAIER told me, "We are the leaders [in our *agrupación*], so naturally people want us to share our benefits. If we are on top of the group and another co-op is way at the bottom, we should help them out. But, of course, many people do not understand this." By 1998, MAIER had established itself as a group within MCC, having created its own technology research center and having acquired factories in other parts of Spain.

As we have already seen, the transformation from an emphasis on regional groupings of cooperatives to an emphasis on function and market niche—what I have called "sectoral reorganization"—became an issue in the case of both the old FAGOR group in the Mondragón Valley and the ULMA co-ops in the Oñati Valley to the north. This 1991 policy shift stimulated the emergence of KT as an oppositional voice within FAGOR and caused the subsequent departure of the ULMA group from MCC.

For KT, the issues of FAGOR's identity, solidarity, and autonomy as a group of cooperatives are highly emotional matters that relate to equality as an important (though unwritten) principle of the cooperatives' tradition. In an interview in 1994, two of KT's representatives, Mila Larrañaga and José Angel Echebarría, described the issue:

> We think today that we are changing the fundamental pillars of cooperativism. We do not want to break with the *grupo comarcal* [of FAGOR]. Frankly, we do not see the [competitive] advantages that MCC is suggesting. What we see is an MCC that is losing the philosophical principles on which the cooperatives were founded. These are the principles that we use as points of reference: the right to vote, solidarity, equality, and everything that involves direct participation of the members.

They explained that KT was founded in 1982–83 precisely because the cooperatives were developing in a way that violated some of their very foundational principles.

As of the summer of 1997, the controversy surrounding the FAGOR breakup continued, as shown in KT's repeated *intervenciones* in general assembly meetings. At the same time, MCC's corporate management was continuing with plans to strengthen the ties within the sectoral groupings, especially in terms of strategic planning and the flow of communication. MCC's director of Human Resources, Jesús Goienetxe, explained to me in 1997 that "the *agrupaciones* [by sector] are forming very slowly, simply because they do not have established ties of solidarity or coordinated projects. But this is changing." He concluded: "The new divisions and groupings were originally created more as a managerial concept than an organizational one. In the end I think these two new structures will be very important to the entire organization of the cooperatives."

For ULMA, the question of links among a group of co-ops based in the same valley became pivotal in 1991–92, contributing greatly to the cooperatives' vote to support their own group project over full entrance into the MCC corporate structure. Although ULMA retains strong ties to the Caja Laboral bank, participates significantly in the Lagun Aro social security system, and is a coarchitect of the new Mondragón University, it has had since 1992 a completely distinct corporate decision-making structure. Now five co-ops in all, ULMA includes, besides Forja, the co-ops of Construction, Packaging, Warehousing Systems, and Special Building Materials. As a group and as a cooperative corporation, ULMA is based on many of the same principles as MCC; indeed, ULMA identifies itself as part of the larger "Mondragón tradition" in such corporate documents as the annual report.

In the words of its founding president, José Antonio Ugarte, ULMA chose not so much to vote *against* the project of MCC but to vote *for* its own project. The three features that distinguish ULMA from MCC, besides the obvious differences in scale and support services, are its emphasis on community or *comarcal* solidarity, its refusal (at least so far) to link top managers' salaries to the market, and its official stance in opposition to "excessive centralization and hierarchy" in MCC. Ugarte explained further:

> MCC as a big group is going to have to change or to set aside things that have until today been real assets of the cooperatives: the power of decision at a base level. A *socio* says: I have a vote in the assembly, which means that together with my co-workers we can make decisions; that legally we are allowed to make decisions. In this way, one can feel the "political owner" of a decision. Now, with a cooperative integrated into an *agrupación*, and that into a division; with such complex structures, orders, strategic planning, etc., things can become very complicated. Members are saying, "Now the locus of decision is too far away. I really don't know *who* is de-

ciding about my cooperative. Decisions are being made by someone who is not at all from my cooperative—who belongs to the *cúpula*."

ULMA is trying to assert what it sees as the cooperative values of solidarity, equality, and autonomy. However, it became clear to me that coupled with the sense of autonomy is a strong interest in asserting and controlling its own "project."

Beyond issues of restructuring, a change in the nature of employment options with the co-ops is taking place in both MCC and ULMA. Within the cooperatives, the proportions of *eventuales*, or employees who are not worker-owners, and *socios temporales*, or worker-owners with fixed-terms commitments from the firms, have been steadily rising. Non-*socios* typically make around 80 percent of the salaries of worker-owners, although the gap varies from co-op to co-op and appears to be smaller in ULMA than in MCC. In addition, of course, non-*socios* usually receive no dividends. Temporary *socios* are usually hired for a three-year term, beyond which time they may either be let go or become full-fledged worker-owners. At the end of 1998 there were about three hundred temporary *socios* in MCC. (This new category of employee is specifically permitted under a revised Basque cooperative law of 1993.) From the standpoint of MCC, both of these new types of employees afford greater flexibility in hiring and firing as well as greater ease of movement of personnel among the co-ops. Founder José María Ormaechea justified the policy this way in a February 1996 issue of *TU*: "Flexibility or adaptation" demands "the modification of certain premises that were originally considered essential and inviolable values in the cooperatives" (9). But a long-time *socio* and member of the Otalora Training Center explained to me that this shift in policy was already causing tremendous tension between different classes of employees and undermining the principle of solidarity both in a remunerative sense and a social sense. I should mention, however, that the proportions of owning to nonowning employees are continually fluctuating. For example, as a result of the strong economic upturn of 1997–98, MCC took on many of its nonowning employees as full members. Interesting, it was *socios* rather than contracted workers who reported less job satisfaction in an early 1999 survey. Only in the category of job security were worker-owners more positive than nonowners (*TU*, Feb. 1999).

Observing the worldwide trend toward more temporary, contingent, and even part-time employees, sociologist Vicki Smith (1997) describes the growing prevalence of "noninvolved workers and flexible firms." She notes that the move to loosen ties between employees and employing organizations runs counter to worker expectations of greater participation within teams. At Mondragón and in other organizations with a strong tradition of collaboration or solidarity among employees, such a tension may be especially difficult to handle, in a way threatening effectiveness as well as the social integrity of the firm.

In addition to its importance in the workplace, *solidaridad* has significance for Basque culture. It plays an important role in terms of the cooperatives' dedication of 10 percent of their profits toward community projects, including educational programs—which are conducted exclusively in the Basque language—and also public health and charitable works.

As already suggested, equality or (*igualdad*) also has an important place in the pantheon of Basque values in that there is a common desire to reduce class differences and to emphasize each person's contribution to the larger community. Thus discussions of *solidaridad* in the co-ops frequently lead to considerations of equality, especially in the global sense of common human dignity. From the very beginning of the Mondragón cooperatives, the official rhetoric of the institution has emphasized equality, dignity, and equity in the work experience. For example, in the very first issue of *Cooperación* (Sept. 1960), the notes of Arizmendi that were the forerunner to the now professionally produced house organ *Trabajo y Unión*, mainstream capitalist organizations (including, one assumes, most of the factories in and around Mondragón) were sharply criticized for lacking "equitable participation" and for "not conforming with the exigencies of *human dignity*."

Today, however, the tensions between such a position and the demands of the market are coming into sharp relief. On the one hand is the official rhetoric of the Mondragón cooperatives that all *socios* are basically equal (see especially two of the Ten Principles that concern "sovereignty of labor" and "participation of all workers in the governance of the firm"); on the other is the fact that "this conception does not resonate with member views" which point to "the existence of well-defined hierarchies from the work-floor to the central management offices" (Greenwood and González 1992: 152). Similarly, though there is a persistent cultural *mythos* that emphasizes the equality of the sexes and even frequently characterizes the society as "matriarchal" (de Otazu y Llana 1986), the concentration of decision-making power and technical knowledge is clearly in the hands of men (see Hacker and Elcorobairutia 1987). For the most part, women are still apparently prevented from attaining high managerial positions, even though female membership in the cooperatives is now over 40 percent of the total work force (see Berger and Clamp 1983; Harding 1994). We hear the frequent assertion of a common destiny of the various communities and groups of workers in Mondragón and in neighboring communities, yet there is a growing concern among workers, at least, about forms of segregation along lines of class (Kasmir 1996).

Again, we need to attend to multiple influences with respect to the evolution (or devolution) of values in the Mondragón cooperatives. It's not simply the case that the supposedly pure internal social values of the cooperatives are being modified, coopted, or corrupted by external market-oriented concerns. For one thing, various hierarchies based on gender, class, and education preexisted the cooperatives and have left more than mere traces on the work experiences of today's *cooperativistas*. Even when we speak specifically of the impact of changes in the external environment on the Mondragón co-ops, we must recognize that each member or employee brings to the co-ops some of that wider cultural change. He or she comes as a "message" to the organization, "decoded" through the course of decision making and other work activities.

Still, it's crucial to emphasize the tendencies *against* solidarity, equality, and autonomy that accompany the cooperatives' increased interaction with and reference to the market. In her studies of the long-standing cooperative movement in Denmark, management scholar Ann Westenholz concludes:

> One fundamental contradiction [for cooperatives] exists between the economic demands of the capitalist market and the ideas about equality which are found among employees in employee-owned firms. On the one hand, the capitalist market strengthens hierarchy, unequal power distribution, unequal distribution of income, and an unequal distribution of possibilities toward attaining interesting work. On the other hand, ideas about equality strengthen equality in power distribution, income, and the possibility of at-

taining a job in which the workers can realize themselves as human beings. (1982:28)

Productivity, Efficiency, Quality, and Customer Service

These buzzwords of contemporary organizations are regularly used to apply to a broad array of initiatives, including new systems of employee participation. Alan Tuckman explains the evolution of Total Quality Management (TQM) and related programs from their initial concerns in the 1970s with problem solving in the context of quality circles to the current "penetration of concerns with 'customer service' in areas which had previously not recognized the existence of customers" (1995:67). Productivity, efficiency, and quality are all now justified by the unquestioned meeting of customers' wants, as they are seen, construed, and sometimes created by the organization.

Throughout my interviews and observations in the Mondragón cooperatives there were frequent references to these key terms. "Productivity" was commonly defined as sheer output, though occasionally it also referenced profit. And, in one issue of *TU* (Nov. 1991), both productivity and profitability were said to be limited significantly by "personnel costs." "Efficiency" was used in both a general sense, suggesting maximum output with minimum input, and in a specific sense of an efficiency rating for work processes and outputs. "Quality" was used in a vague, ill-defined sense and in specific reference to the standards of the European Foundation for Quality Management's (EFQM). Finally, "customer/consumer/client service" was frequently expressed as a broad cultural value and as an external point of reference for activities of the organization, including decisions about the organization of work. There was no complete agreement on the meaning of any of these terms. "Quality" and "responding to the customer" came the closest to being slogan-like. A few examples will help to illustrate the dynamics of these terms in the official rhetoric and the work practices of the cooperatives.

Within both MCC and ULMA, a much-discussed vision of quality in the 1990s is EFQM's model of total quality. This foundation, a well-funded private association with links to the European Commission of the EU, was founded in 1988 and had over four hundred member firms as of 1995. The foundation takes as its mandate the development of "total quality within the European environment" and it has regularly awarded prizes to private firms for performance according to the criteria associated with the model (in a manner parallel to the Malcolm Baldridge Awards in the United States). Among the largest participating European firms are British Telecom, Fiat, KLM, Nestle, and Volkswagen. The mission statement of the foundation emphasizes the satisfaction of customers, employees, and the society, obtained through policy and strategy, as well as the management of personnel, resources, and processes, and based on leadership that achieves excellence in business results. The model, called Total Quality Management, is depicted through a triangle of client satisfaction, economic efficiency, and organizational functioning, with "continuous improvement" at the center. In 1991, an award was created for firms best living up to the criteria of the EFQM model. The nine criteria are: leadership; people management ("how the organisation releases the full potential of its people to improve its business continuously"); policy and strategy; resources (and their effective use); processes ("the management of all value-adding activities within the organisation"); people satisfaction (referring to employee satisfaction); customer satisfaction; impact on society (including the environment); and business results. These criteria are weighted in such a way that the most important are customer satisfaction (20 percent), business results (15 percent), and processes (14 percent) (see Dale, Cooper, and Wilkinson 1997).

A variety of supporters of this approach at Mondragón stress that the model should not be reduced simply to the usual implementation of TQM. The personnel manager of ULMA-Forja, José Manuel Biain, told me in 1998: "From the standpoint of those who are promoting it, the European model of Total Quality represents a broader philosophical and strategic vision" than just a means of reorganizing work. Many others in MCC and ULMA told me that the European model is becoming a "key point of reference" in organizational restructuring and the development of new or improved programs of participation. An array of interviews and observations made it clear that part of the appeal of the model was its adoption by large multinational firms. Both the government of the Basque Country and the Federation of Worker Cooperatives of the Basque Country are actively promoting the model and urging a variety of private firms to follow it.

Although the implementation of this model of total quality—and, for that matter, the general idea of TQM—is still relatively new for the cooperatives, in important ways the basic concepts associated with the model have become part of the parlance and strategy of both MCC and ULMA. The terms "economic efficiency," "customer satisfaction," and "continuous improvement" (or *Kaizen*, in Japanese, as it was first popularized) are frequently heard in both the cooperatives and the corporations. Often the terms are used together. A number of the cooperatives are practicing an amalgam of these popular trends, usually with a stress on team-based work restructuring, increased responsibility at the level of each individual's job, and tight monitoring of production levels by workers and management—with the unifying theme being closeness to the customer. Numerous publications of MCC emphasize the need to develop "its own model of self-management and quality" (see, for example, *TU* during the years 1995–97, especially July 1995). But it was evident that both the language and the methods of reorganizing involved substantial borrowing of concepts from the experiences of noncooperative multinational corporations. I was repeatedly surprised by the lack of creativity in formulating new programs of participation and productivity, especially considering the rich social tradition and record of ingenuity in the cooperatives. Ironically, the Mondragón cooperatives may be implementing some key features of Japanese-inspired models of "lean production," especially a stress on quick responses to customers and a bare-bones approach to stocking and overhead, at the very moment that such features are being questioned and tempered in Japan itself (Benders 1996). Still, each of the new programs I saw or heard described at Mondragón did have some local features, such as the specific ways management dealt with work teams.

In addition to the significant organizational transformation at MAPSA, the auto parts manufacturing co-op in Pamplona, it has developed new means of governance, operations, and communication. In 1996, as a result of dramatic increases in production, coupled with wage cuts during the slump of the early-to-mid 1990s, MAPSA actually began to show a modest profit. During 1992–97 the number of wheels sold quadrupled to 800,000, with most of the sales going to the world's largest automobile manufacturers. The president of the co-op, Francisco Javier Egea, told me in the summer of 1997: "We now see some successes as the result of our hard work and sacrifice. That's really gratifying, but I emphasize that the profits so far have been only small. We need to look at better means of production." At

MAPSA, a way of finding these has been through implementation of several phases of Total Participative Management (TPM), largely at the direction of one of the largest co-ops in the automotive sector of MCC, FAGOR-Ederlan.

When I first visited MAPSA in February 1994, this program was only in its infancy. There were so many other transition programs underway—including a complete reevaluation of personnel, positions, and salary and wage indexes, according to the specifications of MCC—that efforts at reorganizing production on the shop floor were postponed. (Some of these changes in human resource management had not been completed by the summer of 1997.) Under the old system of production, most employees in the shop knew only one job, and the jobs were organized serially. From a station where a laborer was working with molten aluminum, the material would be transferred to a series of stations for molding and refinement. There were few efforts at job rotation, and several layers of supervision and direction between laborers and top management. In addition, this firm, like its sister companies near Pamplona, was known for a highly authoritarian managerial style. One laborer told me in 1994: "Participation, in the sense that they have in the tradition of the Mondragón cooperatives, was unknown to us." Also, as I have already mentioned, MAPSA suffered a history of protracted labor disputes, centering on wages, benefits, working hours, and employee rights in decision making.

The implementation of TPM at MAPSA followed the introduction and development of a similar program in Ederlan, a large foundry in the village of Aretxabaleta, near Mondragón, that has been part of the system of cooperatives since the early 1960s. When I visited Ederlan in 1994 and talked with managers and employees of the Personnel Department responsible for spearheading TPM, they had been very enthusiastic about its possibilities. The key elements of the program were an increased emphasis on efficiency through the use of work teams and a tightly organized process of intergroup communication, from the level of work processes up to top management. In a document dated May 1993, the management council of Ederlan endorsed a project that would "bring the shop closer to the customer" and the "management closer to the shop." Throughout the development of TPM for Ederlan during 1992–95, a principle theme was unity of purpose with respect to customer service and the attendant transformation of internal relations with an eye toward "constant improvement to serve that customer."

Curiously, by the time I returned in the summer of 1997, Ederlan had essentially abandoned its TPM program internally while its Personnel and Quality departments were aggressively promoting it for MAPSA. A large turnover in top management within both Ederlan and the *agrupación* had stalled the experiment, leaving only traces in the form of interdepartmental management groups that met periodically to discuss problems and potential innovations in production. Although several managers and technicians remain committed to the project, they told me that a new initiative from the top would be required to get the program going again.

The TPM program in MAPSA was being directed in 1997 by experts from Ederlan working together with MAPSA's newly installed top management. The program is based on a careful diagnosis of MAPSA's production processes and the implementation of a model of Total Quality Management (although in this case under the heading of TPM). Elias Pagalday, director of Quality for Ederlan and the chief overseer of TPM's implementation in MAPSA, explained to me the key features of the program, whose overall slogan is "Client Consciousness + Employee Involvement + Profitability of the Firm = A Stable Future." Under that banner, specific areas of work are targeted for the introduction of TPM, including the foundry, mechanization (or calibrating and finishing), painting, and the offices; the thrust of the program is clearly directed at the reorientation of line rather than staff functions.

By 1997 several work areas had already being reorganized according to the principles and techniques of TPM. Tight reporting procedures were being put into place, so that regular information about production output would be available to team leaders, supervisors, and directors. All employees were expected to fill out an array of charts at the end of each shift and to send suggestions upward, as part of the practice of constant improvement (*Hobekuntza*, in Euskara/Euskera). Despite the use of the term "autonomous" to describe their organizational niche and despite the use of the term *auto-gestión* (self-management) in MCC's publications, according to Pagalday the groups would not really be expected to make decisions. Although the formal authority of the supervisor was being diminished, the need for his frequent communication with those above him was reinforced. And a "comprehensive" communication process was being established for regular cross-function meetings at all levels of the firm, including plans to eventually hold weekly meetings between the management council and all workers on each of the three shifts.

One of the cornerstones of the new system was statistical analysis of efficiency and quality. Specifically, a common efficiency index was applied in MAPSA, as in a number of other MCC co-ops, to standardize assessments of production levels. The index is calculated by a five-step process, beginning with the eight hours that a workstation is theoretically in operation for one entire shift. Time is then deducted for such things as start-up time, breaks, machinery maintenance, "micro-stops," and defective pieces. The resulting time period is the actual percentage of time a machine or a workstation is engaged in the production of acceptable products, and overall efficiency is calculated as a proportion of the total eight hours.

From this statistic, in turn, can be calculated an employee's or a work team's "added value"—that is, direct contributions to production and efficiency. It is interesting to note the change in meaning here: ten years ago "added value" (*valor añadido*) was much more likely to refer to the advantages for an employee of working in a cooperative as opposed to a traditional *sociedad anónima* (see the discussions in Greenwood and González 1989, 1992). Though one might say an employer or manager is *always* concerned about an employee's "added value" (and, in fact, has to be so), the "shorthand" reduction of the person through such an expression can divert attention away from the value of the employee for his or her own sake, and also from specific questions of the organization's responsibilities to the employee as part of a broad-based social contract.

In the implementation of TPM and similar programs and in the discourses surrounding them, the attention of the organization and presumably the workers is focused almost exclusively on a single, measurable idea of efficiency and quality. "Because the *Kaizen* system of 'continual improvement' requires a programme of standards which are measurable and reproducible, work tasks become meticulously regulated and enforced in a manner which is indistinguishable from scientific management" (Boje and Winsor 1993: 61). As I talked further with Pagalday and others in MAPSA, it became evident that one risk with such an overwhelming emphasis on this model of participation was that concern for employees' well-being could easily be lost in an obsession with efficiency.

Of course efficiency in the use of the physical resources and labor cannot be ignored; my caution concerns what might be lost in such a narrowed understanding of work processes. There is a simple step from the sort of efficiency index described above, used as a master indicator of organizational success, to the treatment of employees as mere instruments rather than shaping contributors. The pitfalls of relying exclusively on quantitative factors are stated well by economist Shann Turnbull in a comparative analysis of Mondragón and other innovative and democratic organizations: "The use of only price information [in a firm's external and internal relations] as a governance mechanism denies any social or moral concern in the governance of organizations or the impact which their operations may have on individuals and the environment. . . . Qualitative information is required for any efficient, equitable, socially accountable, self-governing, and environmentally nurturing organization" (1994:327). These remarks remind us that in the very construction of what counts as data are embedded important assumptions about values, people, and work. Central managerial concepts of efficiency are often accompanied by a reduction of the personhood of the worker. From within the system, this may seem logical and reasonable, but the force of such dehumanizing tendencies is seldom fully acknowledged or appreciated in the rush to achieve higher levels of production (see, e.g., Ezzamel and Willmott 1998).

The two top managers in MAPSA said they shared my concern about the potential loss of social energy in the firm, and wanted to see what they could do to establish a "broader base" of participation. As of late 1998, MAPSA was continuing to create "autonomous groups," aimed at reducing the distance between "indirect" and "direct" involvement in production processes and increasing "the assumption of responsibilities for work processes at the lowest hierarchical levels of the organization possible" (from an internal document on *Grupos Autónomos*, 1997). María Jesús Zabaleta, director of Finance and interim director of Personnel, expressed the hope that work teams could make some of their own decisions about how best to maximize production—for example, in the control of stocks and in safety and hygiene. Also, she noted that the "culture" of the younger *socio* and non-*socio* alike was amenable to the development of programs like TPM because these highly trained employees were "enthusiastic about participating in and seeing the concrete results." MAPSA's general manager, Juan Ramón Iñurria, emphasized his de-

sire that, despite the overwhelming emphasis on efficiency and customer service in the TPM process, MAPSA would have "space for
participation with concern for the social values that make it a cooperative." In this respect, he hoped to see active involvement on the
part of both older employees, who have been accustomed to a hierarchical and rigid system of work in the old noncooperative MAPSA,
and younger recruits.

But questioning about plans for the further training of MAPSA's
personnel indicated that my concerns about the the social dimensions of the program being overrun by emphasis on efficiency were
warranted. Within the context of TPM, the only types of training
being planned for are technical in nature, even though the multipha-
sic model for the program's implementation specifically cites attention to job satisfaction. Similarly, through repeated questioning
about MAIER's version of *Hobekuntza*, I found that managers and
elected leaders had delayed considering that the idea of continuous
improvement might be applied to the social as well as physical dimensions of work. At my urging, in 1994, the cooperative did take a
step toward widening the scope of *Hobekuntza*, especially through
the auspices of the Personnel Department, adding hygiene and safety
to the list of concerns for which employees were expected to be alert
and to make suggestions.

What is taking place at Mondragón in the implementation of new
programs to boost productivity has many parallels elsewhere. As
Fairhurst and Wendt have observed in their extensive research on the
implementation of TQM and similar programs, the employee-
oriented dimensions of the larger "quality" philosophy often become
lost in the rush toward implementation in the interest of speeding up
production (Fairhurst 1993; Wendt 1994). These two organizational
communication scholars explain: "Although Deming [1986] calls for
teams, there is very little concern [in most cases of TQM implemen-
tation] for how they function as a *social unit* and a *decision-making
body* within a larger organizational context" (Fairhurst and Wendt
1993: 443, emphasis mine).

Of course, within the boundaries of a single corporation we may
find diverse ways of putting into practice ideas of teamwork and collaboration, and great variability in the level of worker control. For example, in MAIER, famous now for *Hobekuntza* in the Basque Country and beyond (Vázquez 1994), important modifications in the

structure of the program were being made in 1997–98. The director of Training and Development, Julen Iturbe, explained in July 1997 that the system of "mini-factories," where workers in a particular product line were also responsible for relations with their suppliers and customers, was found to be unwieldy, organizationally and for the workers. In 1994 and again in 1997, a major complaint of employees was that the degree of "self-management" required by this system was intensifying work and causing more stress. By the summer of 1997, the complex system of *Hobetaldes* (improvement groups), including both actual work teams and standing committees, was also being revised in order to make communication "more fluid." Finally, in June and July of 1998, two lengthy articles in *TU* magazine argued for a linkage of the term "self-management" to the broader social vision of the co-ops. Whether these changes allay concerns about the continuing speed-up in work processes remains to be seen.

Of the five ULMA cooperatives, Construction has moved furthest toward team-based restructuring for purposes of continuous improvement. Asier Agirregomezkorta, the facilitator of continuous improvement, noted that in the first two years of implementation the program has functioned largely as an "ascending form," with suggestions about such things as safety and hygiene transmitted by workers to a technical assistant or manager. During the second phase of the program, as it was taking shape by mid-1998, there would be an emphasis on "descending *Hobekuntza*." In this form, continuous improvement would involve the creation of *Hobetaldes* (quality circles, or problem-solving groups) to address the performance of machines and other technologies. ULMA-Forja hopes to employ this type of system as well in the further development of its own quality program, *Forjando Futuro* (future forging).

In all of these new programs for quality and participation we see common structural elements: reduction in importance of first-line supervision; use of functional work teams and cross-functional problem-solving groups; creation of tighter information-based relationships between top management and employees at lower levels of the organization; bringing lower-level employees closer to the customer in a variety of ways; creation of new channels for suggestions from below; and development of sophisticated analyses of production based on frequent reporting from various areas of production. Now let us consider what all of this means for participation by employees.

Participation, Communication, and Information

Noting the "sheer breadth" of the term "participation," John Dickson (1979) reminds us that its meaning in any given case should not be simply assumed. How productivity, efficiency, and quality are measured has significant effects on the meanings of participation. And such measurements are determined to some extent by the overarching goals and assumptions of a particular vision of TQM or any other program. Furthermore, Wilkinson and Willmott (1995a) stress that both the local organizational culture and the prevailing managerial wisdom of the time will influence heavily the shape and texture of any program for increased productivity and participation.

Thus it is crucial to consider the framing of employee participation programs in assessing their practical, social, or ethical dimensions (see Fairhurst and Sarr 1996). Fairhurst (1993) found that in major U.S. corporations framing factors such as overarching labels and the presentation of "possible futures" greatly affected the course of program development and the ways employees would ultimately come to understand the program (see also Deetz 1992).

Until recently, Mondragón has been rather exceptional among the large corporations of North America and western Europe for its special attention to the merits of employee participation as a value *in itself* that has both political and social significance (see Cheney et al. 1998; Schiller 1991; Seibold and Shea in press). Is the range of meanings for "participation" now becoming just as narrow there as elsewhere?

For the purposes of this discussion, I have grouped together the terms "participation," "communication," and "information" because they so commonly occurred together during interviews. "Participation" was construed in a variety of ways, although the prevailing managerial use of the concept has made little reference to broad decision-making contributions. The idea of participation for production's sake was clearly being pushed at the MCC-sponsored Symposium on the Future of Participation at Mondragón in March 1997 (MCC 1997a).

In most of my interviews, communication was treated as both a value and something made problematic by the sheer growth of the cooperatives and the acceleration of the pace of work. Information also was regarded as a value, but it was viewed more as a resource or a tool in larger processes of communication and participation.

As shown clearly in the case of MAPSA, a chief component to many new systems of participation is the development of standardized production and efficiency data that is generated by the work team or group and regularly communicated upward. In MAIER's *Hobekuntza*, all data with respect to improvements in production are transmitted to a panel in each work area, to the governing council, to a central bulletin board, and through quarterly company-wide meetings. This process of publicizing and sharing information is seen as critical to a larger circular process of improvement in which "suggestions" and "reflection" are ongoing. In every quality program I witnessed or heard about, employees were strongly encouraged to make suggestions for improving production, by individual employees or work teams or both. In MAIER, with the most developed of such programs, improvement was expected at both the level of the shop floor and through a second-level improvement group that was cross-functional and similar in practice to a quality circle. In each of the three programs on which I concentrated my attention—MAIER's *Hobekuntza*, MAPSA's TPM and ULMA-Forja's *Forjando Futuro*—closer connections were being established between the management team and the shop floor. Usually this took the form of more frequent company-wide meetings or meetings between managers and employees in particular work areas. In fact, this development casts a shadow of uncertainty over the future functioning of the principal governing organs of the co-ops, in that the councils may be sidestepped through the development of stronger connections between management and work teams.

In all of these systems, as I observed them, the idea of communication was focused at the group and intergroup levels and the idea of information was applied chiefly to the vertical (up *and* down) flow of specific data. "Fluid communication" was often explicitly desired of the governing organs of each cooperative, in the sense that the governing council was expected to "go along" with the recommendations of the management council, and the social council was expected to offer input in a way that would "cooperate" with the other two bodies. Thus "fluid communication" often appeared to be another term for "coordination and consent" without the disruption of disputes over the basic direction of the firm. Although most *socios* I interviewed felt that communication was a higher-order value than information, they saw information as necessary to effective participation and as a key component of vertical coordination in the organization. Over the years that I examined the cooperatives, 1992 to 1999, it seemed to me that there was a growing emphasis on "cooperation without debate," at least in the formal meetings of governing bodies of the cooperatives I studied. "Conflict" was therefore treated largely as a sign of "flawed consensus" and organizational "ineffectiveness," rather than being seen as evidence of perhaps legitimate disagreements over policy.

"Information" generally referred to both the data necessary to do a job—such as the specifications for machine maintenance or the latest production targets—and the data transmitted upward through charts and graphs of production processes. Whyte and Whyte (1991) observe in their analysis of the cooperatives through the 1980s that there was already by 1990 a strong concern about "information overload" on the part of many employees. With the increasing complexity of the cooperatives, and especially with the requirement that employees at all levels and in all departments have relevant customer or client information, I found a genuine ambivalence toward the very idea of "information." On the one hand, *socios* emphasize a need for substantial information to do their jobs effectively; also, they consider the basic data on the firm's performance to be "collective property" (and not just something to be revealed periodically, say, in the annual general assembly meetings). But many employees complained to me that they were "drowning" or "asphyxiating" with the volume of job-relevant information they received under new programs of participation (see also De Cock 1998). This view was expressed especially in MAIER, which between 1991 and 1997 was reorganized as six "mini-factories," each with their own responsibility for maintaining relations with suppliers and clients. I found similar complaints in ULMA-Forja and MAPSA. In each of these cooperatives, the work force has been put on four shifts or "turns" in recent years to increase production and handle greater international client demand. The result is that many employees are now working on Saturdays or even Sundays, something that was extremely rare in the cooperatives before the late 1980s. Many of the employees I interviewed in these firms showed a kind of burnout, in that they did not want to attend extra meetings after work (such as the *charlas* or chats discussed in Chapter 2) to receive more information or participate in problem-solving sessions aimed at enhancing production. At ULMA-Forja, employees' enthusiasm for such after-work meetings was obviously flagging. An employee in MAPSA's machine maintenance area said to me, pointing to the top of his head, "I have enough information and enough *participation* already."

As I discussed briefly in Chapter 2, both MCC and ULMA are now developing extensive new communication plans, recognizing the problems associated with increased size and complexity and the dynamics of new participation programs. Neither of these emerging plans, however, seems to place much emphasis on lateral communication—except in the sense of a high degree of coordination among the governing organs of each cooperative. MCC's plan is surprisingly unidirectional, even depicting the flow of communication as basically from the corporate center to the rest of the organization (MCC, internal document on communication). On the positive side, there is an explicit recognition in MCC's draft communication plan of the need for greater "fluidity" and clarity in the decisions, directives, and information that are channeled from top management to the entire system of cooperatives. Also the plan mentions the lack of definition and identity in the *agrupaciones*, something to be remedied in part by clarifying their roles as mediating units in the processes of communication within the corporation as a whole. One of the architects of the plan, Jesús Goienetxe, reminded me by e-mail in 1998 that the plan represents only "a first step toward dealing with the challenges of improving communication in a large and growing corporation."

In ULMA, the comprehensive communication plan is less developed as of this writing, but it is also seen as less pressing due to the physical proximity of the cooperatives in one valley and because of their comparatively small scale (twelve hundred employees, as opposed to 42,000 in MCC). However, the general manager of Forja, Fernando Recalde, stressed to me in 1994 and again in 1997 the need to make communication as "transparent" as possible, not only within the five individual cooperatives of ULMA but also within the larger corporation or group. "The identities of each cooperative and of the group as a whole need to play a part in the communication process as well as being reinforced by it," he added.

In both MCC and ULMA I heard frequent acknowledgment of the deterioration of informal group relations, a cultural change attributed mainly to the general speedup in lifestyle, but also to the specific work demands within the cooperatives. The July 1994 issue of *TU* included an article that highlighted the need for fluid communication in all directions: "descending, ascending and horizontal" (11). However, in my conversations in both systems, I sensed that most leaders and managers were at a loss about how to revitalize what ought to be (and once was) a spontaneous and vital part of the co-ops' social dynamics. The need to provide more forums at work for the informal exchange of ideas and building of relationships seemed to be crucial at the level of individual cooperatives, where there was in every case I studied a "sense of distance between the shop and the offices." The gap was also apparent at the level of sectors in the case of MCC and the level of the group or corporation in the instance of ULMA. Thus the evolution of the two communication plans, and particularly their allowance for the creative exploration of new ways to revitalize daily work interaction in the cooperatives, will be important to watch in the coming decade.

As I suggested at the beginning of this section, the meanings of "communication" and "information" in the cooperatives today should be placed under the larger umbrella of "participation." The transformation in meaning for this, perhaps the central term and idea of the cooperatives, is evident particularly in issues of *Trabajo y Unión* since 1992, the year of European economic unification. The corporate house organ of MCC casts "participation" as being mainly "for productivity" (June 1996); as an "internal mine of efficiency" (Oct. 1996); in terms of "structured democracy" (Dec. 1996); and for "competitive advantage" (Apr. 1997). As already mentioned in Chapter 1, this view contrasts with a traditional perspective on participation within the cooperatives—perhaps best expressed today by workers and managers who are strongly identified with the early phases of the cooperatives—which embraces not only the "one person, one vote" idea for governance but also the broader notion that employees collectively can guide the course of a firm's development.

Thus we have a case where participation is simultaneously greater and less than what existed before. MCC's resident sociologist, Mikel Lezamiz, insisted to me in the summer of 1997: "We are finally moving beyond Taylorism to see what it really means for employees to participate at the level of their daily jobs." Indeed, the move away from assembly-line technologies in co-ops of the FAGOR group attested to this. José Ignacio Gandarias, then president of MAIER, told me in 1994 of his desire to involve more and more employees of the cooperative in the cooperative's program of *Hobekuntza*: "Up until now, the level of real participation in the business has been around 60–70 percent, in terms of people who can get involved in a direct way [in some part of the management of the firm]. But now we want to involve more and more people." María Luisa Orueta, then president of ULMA-Forja, explained similarly in 1994 that "we need a form of cooperativism today that maintains some of the solidarity of the past with a new awareness of the client. And this must apply to all employees of the cooperative."

In making sense of these developments at Mondragón, we do well to recall Paul Bernstein's (1976) three criteria for assessing employee participation programs: *the real extent of influence by employees, the range of issues over which influence is exercised, and the highest level which real influence by employees is capable of reaching.* Although most of the formal participation programs in the cooperatives are still too new to evaluate comprehensively—for example, the notion of teamwork at the level of work process has been only partially and unevenly realized—it's clear that they do vary along these three dimensions and that perhaps few of them merit high marks on all three counts. Their evolution will therefore be important to monitor, particularly as even more waves of educated and independent-minded *socios* and non-*socios* are socialized into quality-and-customer-oriented programs.

The position of members of KT and other critics is that the cooperatives have sold out their established model of participation for a much narrower interpretation of the concept. One of KT's representatives said to me: "We [in KT] are trying to revive the very tradition of participation in the cooperatives, by promoting discussion, debate and confrontation. But our position is not well understood by the *cúpula* because they have their *plan* for how participation should be trained and developed in the cooperatives." Many other employees, though perhaps not as critical of management policies as KT members, nevertheless lamented the fact of diminished participation through the general assemblies and other organs (especially the social councils of a number of cooperatives), attributing this decline in "political" participation to a complex of factors that included not only the thrust of new programs of employee participation but also a deterioration of democratic practices generally and the pressures of a faster pace of life for everyone. "There simply isn't time to participate in *that* way," declared one press operator in the foundry part of ULMA-Forja. "We [longtime *socios*] don't have the energy, and the younger generation doesn't have the desire." But presumably the same employees could find time to issue suggestions for improvement of production, as many employees in the foundry section of

ULMA-Forja were already doing in 1997 (principally through the use of suggestion boards and conversations with peers or immediate supervisors).

These two broad perspectives on the future of participation in the Mondragón cooperatives—one largely optimistic, the other mainly pessimistic—become clearer when we consider the two extended quotations below. The first is from my 1997 interview with Jesús Goienetxe, director of Human Resources for MCC. After relating the successes of the reengineering of MCC's co-op Irizar, in which large teams of employees see the entire production process through and bottom-up communication is strongly encouraged, Goienetxe reflected on the meaning of participation this way:

> With regard to participation, we are all really worried. But why? Not because there isn't a consensus in this culture about the importance of participation. Everybody around here admits to the importance of participation. But what we are betting on is just a concept of participation that has been with us from the beginning of the cooperatives. Looking at the present situation, I do not believe that with respect to the practice of participation we are worse off than we were in the beginning. We are entering a new phase of participation, where it is centered in daily work activities. In fact, nowadays people have the means, education, and culture that are in some ways far superior to what we had twenty, thirty, or forty years ago. But that cultural and technical knowledge has to be translated into an everyday practice of participation.

This view is shared by many managers and elected representatives in the Mondragón cooperatives today. It is cast as a kind of "realism" as well as an "opportunity" for widespread participation in work processes, where all employees are united in purpose through a consistent focus on the customer. As management researcher Gideon Kunda (1992) explains, what many participation programs are seeking is a complete "incorporation" of the person into the customer-service culture of the organization, but largely on management's terms.

At the same time, there are those in the cooperatives who argue that however efficient and profitable such a perspective on participation may be, it does represent a departure from the fundamental values of the cooperatives to such an extent that their long-term future may be jeopardized. Such critics usually blame what they see as the excessive importation of market-oriented ideas. Felix Ormaechea, director of the confederation of education cooperatives associated with MCC, put the matter this way in a 1994 interview:

> I have my own opinion about the *crisis* of the group [MCC]. . . . The issue is very complex, and I wish I could say something more positive about the present circumstances or adapt my own thinking to what's going on. However, I believe that the future of the cooperatives will never be a happy one if we renounce our values like participation, solidarity, and consensus decision making. . . . Capitalism as a system prioritizes certain values. It values possessions—but not for the sake of survival or life. If because of money and the market, I have to stop being a creator—stop being truly free—then I and the cooperatives are changing for the worse. And, this is what some of the cooperatives' leaders are doing today. They are subtly trying to sell a concept of "participation" that goes against my principles. But I think it is not the economic outcome alone that should measure the success of the whole process but also the fact that I have *participated* in it, shared in its execution, and felt like a person through these activities.

These contrasting views of the future of employee participation and workplace democracy within the MCC cooperatives can be understood further in terms of the distinction between de jure and de facto models of participation (Lucas 1992). A de jure perspective recognizes the rights and capacities of employees to participate, but it does not necessarily establish the structures or processes by which participation can take place in any meaningful way. A de facto perspective sees participation as occurring, perhaps in various ways, in the course of experience at work, but it does not necessarily emphasize the legal or political aspects of participation as a rights-oriented concept. Put another way, a de jure perspective recognizes explicitly the importance of participation but may not make it happen, while a de facto perspective acknowledges the reality of participation without necessarily reflecting on it or institutionalizing it.

This distinction can be used to examine both the optimistic and pessimistic views of participation at Mondragón. From the optimistic managerial standpoint, critics of new programs of participation are too focused on a strictly de jure understanding of workplace democracy, with an overemphasis on the rights to make decisions to govern the firm and too little attention to everyday work practices. For many critics of the cooperatives' experimentation with TPM, *Kaizen*, and TQM, on the other hand, the promoters of the new programs are themselves being uncreative in their implementation of new forms of participation, adopting a strict interpretation that derives from the larger market without allowing for the full development of de facto participation.

Quite curiously, Lucas's distinction can also be used in a different way from the standpoint of both supporters of new programs of participation and detractors. Advocates of new forms of participation would charge that old-time *socios* have become preoccupied with an outdated model of participation that is unduly vote-centered and unrealistic about options for individual workers to shape cooperative or corporate policy. Critics would counter that the new programs focus the attention of the employee too much on the restricted domain of his or her job and on the satisfaction of the customer. Holders of either position, however, should be prepared for the fact, as Derber and Schwartz (1983) explained so well in their analysis of "post-Taylorist" models of participation in factory regimes, that the renewed emphasis on participation and democracy, however limited in scope, may result in greater *demands* for participation at all levels of corporate activities. That is, a new program of participation may prime the pump for employee insistence on being part of all the important decisions and core activities of the firm (see also McArdle et al. 1995). Such a tendency may even be accentuated if employees begin to think of themselves as true "consumers" of management programs, asserting rights to reject, modify, or take control of those initiatives. In this way, employees might try to bring the organization in line with their own personal values and preferences (Galbraith 1978).

Thus, in contrast to those who stress the "pacifying" effects of new programs of participation (see Braverman 1974; Burawoy 1979; Grenier 1988), we might expect the unexpected, especially in a cultural context such as Mondragón which so values democracy and participation. Laurie Graham (1993, 1995) has found various forms of resistance by U.S. employees to new TQM-style programs in a Japanese transplant, ranging from refusal to participate in the morning ritual of group calisthenics to outright sabotage.

Ultimately, it may be that the clash of cooperative and corporate meanings for "participation" will result in a new expression of worker participation that appears in settings other than traditional governing bodies and shop-floor employee involvement, where informal groups and even formally recognized unions could play important roles (McKinlay and P. Taylor 1996). That new participation programs at Mondragón are each developing with some distinctive features suggests that the hegemony of a single view of customer-driven participation should not be declared prematurely.

In reviewing the meanings of participation in different organizations, Marcel Bolle de Bal (1990) explains that one must always consider the point of view, whether that of the employee, the union, the employing organization, the customer, or the "macro-institutions" of the larger society. For the worker, Bolle de Bal indicates, participation can have the following types of meanings: *ideological* (recognition, for example), *economic* (ownership), *psychological* (job enrichment), *organizational* (delegation), and *sociological* (integration). However, with at least four of these dimensions there are potential dysfunctions or distortions of the process for the employee. Ideologically, the employee can feel or be manipulated. Economically, the costs of participation may be too great in time and energy. Psychologically, the employee may experience the stress of new responsibilities. And sociologically, there may be alienation, especially if the form of participation is contrived or too narrowly constructed. All of these benefits and problems may coexist in a single organization, as it attempts to engineer an efficient form of democracy or participation.

The Future of Mondragón, and of Cooperativism

What do the foregoing observations suggest for the future of democracy and other core social values within the Mondragón cooperatives? Though my report is mixed, I do not wish to rest on an ambivalent posture that offers no useful indicators. I would like to stress five points.

1. There are large sets of advantages and disadvantages to the "marketization" of employee participation, such as we find developing at Mondragón today. These are summarized below to bring into sharp relief a number of the points made earlier in this chapter and to bring into the discussion a few others.

The advantages include:

- an acknowledged realism about pressures from the market;
- greater responsiveness to the perceived needs of the customer/consumer/client;
- increased competitiveness of the organization;
- unity of objective and language [mission] for all employees; and
- entrepreneurship at the level of the individual or work team.

Among the disadvantages are:

- subordination of the employee's interests with an overriding emphasis on external and internal markets;
- undermining of opportunities for deeper cooperation, both within and beyond the organization;
- displacement of key social values of the organization in the obsession with efficiency;
- increased responsibility and stress without substantial self-determination for employees; and
- neglect of the role that a large firm can play in promoting social values and in actually shaping the market. (adapted from Cheney 1998: 17)

2. In regard to how employee participation at Mondragón is being reconceptualized and redesigned, I would echo du Gay and Salaman's (1992) oxymoron "controlled de-control," which is to say that there is a tension between authentic efforts to decentralize through greater reliance on work teams and employee entrepreneurialship and the desire to centralize the organization's response to the market and to the customer. After describing in detail the need for new initiatives at the level of work teams and cross-functional problem-solving discussion groups, the general manager of MAIER told me: "What we can't afford is a diversification of opinions inside the cooperative. . . . And if we don't agree on a common goal, the market will kick us out." He concluded, "This [threat] is easier to understand from the point of view of cooperative solidarity than from the standpoint of an *S.A.* [a standard, non-employee-owned corporation]."

Recent accounts of transformations toward team-based and highly participative forms of organization show that recognition of this tension is as important practically as it is analytically. It may be that some presumably "unobtrusive" and ostensibly more collaborative systems of work organization are not as liberating or energizing as once hoped—at least not in the forms in which they are typically implemented (see Barker 1993; Bullis and Tompkins 1989; Papa, Auwal, and Singhal 1995, 1997; Tompkins and Cheney 1985). In many cases, more self-discipline and responsibility can be very oppressive. Efforts toward greater teamwork and collaboration may be undermined by the sheer intensification of work processes (Pollert 1996). The message of "empowerment" and "self-management" can be directly contradicted by consistent surveillance and control from the top (Sewell and Wilkinson 1992). Recent reports of team implementation in factories around the world show tremendous disappointments, including the desire on the part of some stressed-out employees to return to "non-participative" work systems (King 1998). Each case should of course be assessed in terms of its own features—especially the nature of the work, the type of leadership, and the kind of reward system. Still, we may find that the "age of employee empowerment" is marked by a heightened cynicism which further dims the chances for true workplace democracy in the future.

This surprising development calls into question both "evolutionary" models of workplace control and "alternating" models. That is, it may not be that organizations are gradually moving toward less obtrusive or direct measures of control (see Edwards 1979; Tompkins and Cheney 1985) or that a stress on work culture necessarily involves downplaying technical concerns (as Barley and Kunda suggest). Today we may well have a new phase of control over work processes and workers that is simultaneously "soft" and "hard" (Barker and Tompkins 1994), subtle and overbearing (Sewell 1998), entrepreneurial in design and dehumanizing in practice (see A. Friedman 1977; P. Thompson and McHugh 1990).

3. Although the interplay of "internal" and "external" organizational influences in the Mondragón cooperatives is as complex as what we would find in many other large organizations, the present analysis is consistent with industrial relations specialist Irene Goll's (1991) conclusion that where new programs are implemented for production and participation, the nature and implementation of those programs cannot necessarily be explained fully by *outside* pressures. Managerial ideology makes as much difference if not more than the influence of the market. This extremely important point cautions us

to examine carefully the claims of top managers, especially as they imitate what they think others in their industries are doing.

Goll's analysis (1991) follows the "strategic choice perspective" of Kochan, Katz, and McKersie ([1986] 1994), in which they argued that industrial relations are shaped by management's key choices within the firm, despite the announced importance of concerns such as globalization. There are parallels to this perspective in the related field of marketing, where organizational strategies are often based more on how the organization wishes to be seen (as part of the "right crowd") than on real responses to signals from customers (see, e.g., Christensen 1997).

My observations of the Mondragón cooperatives suggest that managerial emulation of noncooperative multinational corporations is to a great extent shaping the implementation of employee participation programs. Wholesale borrowing of terminology, procedures, and programs from other firms can undermine the achievements of a long history of workplace democracy in the co-ops. As of this writing, the prevailing managerial interpretation of "neo-cooperativism" appears to be crowding out more political, legal, and decision-making-oriented concepts of "participation." Participation at Mondragón is becoming more of a demand from above and outside than it is being maintained as a right or even a privilege for employees.

Yet, as I explain further in the following two chapters, the flow of influence is by no means one-way or in isolation from larger socioeconomic trends. For the importation of the consumer metaphor into the cooperatives comes not only through the managers but also through new waves of *socios* and other employees. The transformation of the citizen and the employee through the lens of the consumer is part of a much larger societal process. It would be misleading to suggest that this shift in perspective is simply being handed down to employees from their managers.

4. We should revisit the theory of cooperative "degeneration" in light of this study. As discussed in Chapter 1, the debate over the inevitability of the decay of a cooperative (or other kind of alternative organization) has been broadened in recent years to consider not only economic factors such as investment and wages but also social factors such as loyalty to a common set of values. The next step in the development of this research would be to consider fully the complex interplay of economic and social factors, including the ways in which forces that are usually thought to be strictly economic in na-

ture actually have strong social dimensions. This has been a key point of my analysis, as I have tried to show how the very metaphors and interpretations of "the market" and "the consumer" are employed in policy decisions and in the shaping of participatory practices.

There are several factors to keep in mind as we watch Mondragón, including the responses of individual members to changes in the organizational structure (T. Harrison 1992, 1994), and the expressed desires of younger members with respect to participation (see Stryjan 1994); the development of alternative expressions of democracy, including further efforts at unionization (see Rosner 1984); the relationship between understandings of participation and democratic process within the cooperatives and those in the larger social and political culture (see Greenberg 1981, 1986; Pateman 1970); and, of course, the cooperatives' process of self-reflection on the future of workplace democracy (see Cornforth 1995).

5. I would say that the "social question" presented at the beginning of this book can now be somewhat reformulated. In the ways that the Mondragón cooperatives seem to be developing, they offer even more lessons for other organizations and other societies than previously recognized. We can consider three options for conclusions from my analysis: (a) We could insist that current trends, such as the vigorous emphasis on efficiently serving the consumer, are not substantially changing the cooperatives; that both the co-ops and the larger society in which they are embedded remain largely the same as they were, say, before 1980. From this perspective, management and economic trends are simply "washing over" the Mondragón co-ops, without causing social change at a profound social level. (b) We could argue that the discourses and activities associated with the customer-driven firm and heightened efficiency are simply trends that have been appropriated or coopted, and then refashioned in distinctive ways. We could say that the Mondragón co-ops are using programs like TQM in distinctively Basque-like or Mondragón-like ways, and thus preserving a substantial degree of cultural and organizational autonomy. This process might be compared to the appropriation of traditionally left-wing symbols by right-wing parties ("social revolution"), and vice versa ("personal responsibility"), as has been quite evident in U.S. politics since about 1980. (c) A third conclusion would be that the widespread adoption of popular market-focused

discourses and programs at Mondragón signals a fundamental transformation in what the cooperatives are.

The question, for Mondragón, is not "Can they keep their core social values intact?" but "Do they want to?" When we find advertisements in major magazines for the Mondragón Cooperative Corporation (MCC 1996) that do not mention the *cooperative* nature of the corporation, we are led to challenge the wisdom of the cooperatives' departure from advocating their social values—externally, in this case, but also internally (see the account in Whyte 1991, of a controversy over just such an issue in FAGOR, back in 1986). Put another way, to what extent are the traditional cooperative values going to be maintained in light of new and more vigorous engagement of the market—not only in sheer economic terms but also with respect to the importation of market-driven ideas? Moving beyond that query, we might naturally wonder about the degree to which the cooperatives could enjoy continued economic success at all without the strong social foundation that brought them to their status as multinational corporations in the first place.

CHAPTER FOUR

Practical Lessons
from Mondragón

Some people believe that a co-op is different. No, we aren't. We are a company just like any other.
—José Antonio Ugarte, 1994

Why Mondragón Is and Isn't Special

For any organization that must survive in a market, outside pressures and how they are treated within the organization will have a huge impact on the shape of the organization's future. The understanding and practice of employee participation and workplace democracy today in the cooperatives are more strongly affected by market-driven ideas than in the past. Today the very idea of the market is more encompassing and more urgent. Despite the cooperatives' strong efforts to reaffirm tradition and capitalize on their special cultural heritage, discourse on the market and marketing now strongly challenges core values and organizational integrity.

This reconfiguration of the organizations and their activities results in short-term advantages and potentially long-term disadvantages. The existence of the cooperatives depends on their ability to make a profit, reliably and demonstrably. Additionally, as economist Melissa Moye (1993) has suggested, some of that very financial success of Mondragón may well derive from the organizations' special qualities as cooperatives. On the one hand, we may conclude that the Utopian visions of many observers of Mondragón were never really the best yardsticks for measuring its social success, even before the current phase of rapid internationalization, efficiency consciousness, and aggressive customer orientation. On the other hand, a rush to reduce Mondragón to the status of "just another corporation" by either its top policymakers or its analysts, might deny its creative social possibilities *and* its long-term business success. It could become a ship without moorings. More generally, giving up on the potential for reformist businesses to transform capitalism into something responsive to a wider array of human values than those currently favored by prevailing market trends could have profoundly negative social implications, even as material success increases.

Taking a close look at the practical dilemmas of Mondragón today helps us better understand the challenges faced especially by organizations that profess values outside the main currents of contemporary institutions, such as a deep commitment to workplace democracy and multiple senses of solidarity. Organizational creativity and diversity ought to be promoted by a "free market," but in practice the workings of the market seem to squeeze organizations toward conformity (V. Thompson 1961). The market is designed to generate a wide variety of choices, and in some arenas such as the local supermarket, this is clearly the case. But does the market at the same time encourage a kind of "regression toward the mean"? That is, do the workings of the market tend to reduce organizational options to a few, both in kind and in number? Let's consider some practical lessons of the Mondragón case for organizations everywhere that would adhere to a core set of social values while successfully engaging the market.

Fostering a Consensus on Values

Some measure of consensus is necessary to sustain a high degree of commitment to the cooperatives on the part of employees, especially in the face of real market challenges and occasional economic downturns. Worker cooperatives ask for more than one type of employee motivation: both a self-interested "investment" and a broader social commitment. In this sense, co-ops bridge Amitai Etzioni's two categories of "pecuniary" and "normative" organizations, (1975), striving for a balance between monetary reward (including literal ownership) and socially inspired vision. The value consensus of an employing organization may be a weakly held or articulated one, as in the case of corporations where a broadly stated mission, such as "quality products" or "customer service," serves as a diluted form of social glue. But some degree of commitment and coordination is essential, except in the most coercive of organizational cultures (Seashore 1954). In the case of Mondragón, if *socios* are going to accept all of the responsibilities associated with the "new workplace," with its faster pace, longer hours, increased demands for daily participation, and more attention to the customer, they will need to strongly identify with the cooperatives and their mission.

My discussions with the director of Training at MAIER in the summer of 1997 revealed that there is real ambivalence on the part of many of the co-ops' employees about the social price of financial success. They are questioning the rapid pace of work and of organizational change, the imperative of "constant improvement," and the burdens associated with maintaining a complex set of customer relations at the level of each "mini-factory" within the larger company. The increased responsibilities as well as gains in pay may ultimately prove insufficient to sustain a high level of individual commitment and group cohesion.

Serious questions are being raised at Mondragón about the maintenance of core values from which the system derived energy for so long. These have partly do to with the larger cultural transformations discussed earlier. The readiness of younger generations to see themselves as consumers and to stress individual careers over allegiance to a particular organization is playing a tremendous role in the changes felt inside the co-ops. As a number of my contacts observed, this problem parallels the challenge faced by the supermarket chain Eroski: today's customers seem less concerned with the nature of the organization offering them products than with just "getting a good buy." This attitude, which is becoming more prevalent among Basques in their twenties, thirties, and forties, poses a threat to cooperativism as a distinct way of doing business. A young systems engineer at MAIER told me in 1994, "Younger generations of *socios* are more likely to see cooperativism in terms of what it can do for them rather than what they can do for it."

Interestingly, Eroski's own promotional activities, including extensive consumer education programs for adults and children, may have a double effect on the communities in which the giant supermarket chain operates: the increase of its own clientele and the reinforcement of the idea that one of the most satisfying means of "participation" today is what Eroski's corporate magazine calls "appropriate consumption" (see Kasmir 1996).

As I was completing this book, I asked about the local culture of the consumer. The director of Consumer Education for Eroski, Arantza Laskurain, pointed to a diversity of projects being conducted by the supermarket chain in this arena, within a program that is now over twenty-five years old. The projects include workshops, environmental campaigns, and literature aimed at a variety of audiences. Above all, Laskurain stressed to me that these educational activities are aimed at "helping the consumer to make his or her own informed decisions." This program of consumer education will be important to watch in the coming decade, not only for measures of its own success, but also in revealing the extent to which Basque citizens are substituting consumption-related activities for more traditional forms of community participation. MCC cofounder Alfonso Gorroñogoitia admitted to me in the summer of 1997 that the consumer movement had "two sides" for the culture around Mondragón: it fueled demands for products and services, thus benefiting the cooperatives directly, but it also contributed to a growing sense of entitlement focused on material acquisition. In this respect, it will be interesting to see if some roles for the political or activist consumer (see Gabriel and Lang 1995; Solomon, Bamossy, and Askegaard 1998) make a strong appearance at Mondragón.

The distinctiveness of the Mondragón co-ops has been grounded for many years in their special structures of participation, their internal financial support systems, their multiple senses of solidarity, their strong ties to local communities, and their "Basqueness." Today, all of these features are being challenged as a result of cultural transformation, internationalization, and new corporate and managerial policies. Whether the organizationally sanctioned substitution of largely corporate values for cooperative ones (with the satisfaction of the client ranked first—see *Trabajo y Unión*, Jan. 1996) can continue to provide the needed cohesion will be answered in the coming decade. What is clear now is that talk of "being a competitive multinational corporation" is coming to dominate formal communications throughout MCC and the individual cooperatives.

These social and economic challenges to the viability of cooperativism are neither new nor unique. In their studies of five co-ops in California in the late 1970s and early 1980s, sociologists Rothschild and Whitt (1986) identify value homogeneity and a social-movement orientation as two of the most important factors facilitating the success of "alternative" organizations. Value homogeneity (or consensus) gives the organization the internal synergy needed to work creatively and cooperatively; social-movement orientation helps to define the organization vis-à-vis the larger society (see Potter [1891] 1987). In this way, a strong sense of identity is important for both internal organizational dynamics and external relations. Each factor is vital to the long-term success of a venture such as a cooperative.

Maintaining a Simultaneously Open and Closed System

The point about consensus and identity flows quite naturally into a broader consideration of the organization as a system. Here I refer specifically to the nature of the "boundaries" of the organization and to how it defines or positions itself with respect to the larger environment. Consciousness about the organizational-environmental relationship is crucial in any type of organization, but it is acutely important for an organization that seeks to define itself to some extent as being different or perhaps better than other organizations around it.

System openness has always been an issue for organizations. Today, with the internationalization of the market and the regular long-distance communications made possible by advances in computer and related technologies, it takes on increased prominence for most large organizations. In the extreme case of "virtual organizations" with no actual headquarters, physical center, or means for regular face-to-face interaction in the organization, questions about the nature of an organization and its boundaries with the environment may be especially difficult.

Typical for-profit corporations exhibit most of their systems awareness through the positioning achieved in advertising and through locating themselves in a market niche. Even in the cases of the most mainstream, hierarchical, and bureaucratic corporations such as IBM, or Coca-Cola, or Nike, there is a balance to be maintained between being "unique" and recognizable and being part of the cultural crowd. Thus large corporations will mimic one another in adopting the latest fad (for example, TQM or a widely publicized mission statement) yet try to add their own twist on a program or a message (Olins 1989). Today's soft drink ads illustrate these dynamics very well, as when Coke, Pepsi, Seven-Up, Sprite, and others participate in the same type of discourse—about thirst, about image, and about style—yet struggle to play off one another in ways that will score points for uniqueness. The basic problem for the organization, in its advertising as well as in its other programmatic activities, is how simultaneously to admit outside influences while staying above the fray. Each organization wishes to participate in the popular discourse about "quality," but to do so in a way that gives the organization a distinctive identity.

Such examples remind us of why social theorist Niklas Luhmann (1990) argues that no system can be fully open lest it lose its very boundaries and identity. There must be an ongoing effort to balance openness—in its extreme form, dissolution of the organization—and "closedness," which prevents the organization from engaging in the larger society. Ultimately, an organization must be both open and closed, to insure a reasonably consistent identity and success.

The sociology of religion offers some useful terms for describing different organizational postures. The categories of "denomination," "sect," and "cult" are frequently employed by analysts of religious organizations to characterize how each of them relates to the larger world. The denomination is a well-established organization whose boundaries are quite open to the larger society; in fact, this organization plays a significant role in that society. The sect, often a budding religious organization, defines itself to some extent as separate from and against mainstream institutions such as denominations. Finally, the cult, as the most closed of the three types, tries to be removed from the larger society to the extent possible. While the denomination enjoys broad external support, it risks having its identity dissolved into the larger pool of society. At the extreme, it can become indistinguishable from other parts of society. The cult, by contrast, has the benefit of a clearly defined identity; yet it may find itself too cut off from the world for purposes of self-maintenance. The sect is often an energetic and well-defined group. Still, as it seeks legitimacy it may become institutionalized in the very way that it dreads (see especially Weber [1968] 1978, on the "routinization of charisma").

For all value-driven organizations, not only religious ones, the choice between being open and being closed is difficult and inescapable. For the Mondragón cooperatives, as for many organizations grounded in an ideology that transcends the organization itself (in this case, cooperativism), the organization's relationship with the environment is very much a two-way street. When the organization becomes as established as Mondragón, it both admits outside influences and has a greater capacity for influence itself. The MCC organization has decided to engage market influences, especially in the form of new programs of participation popular elsewhere and in the linkage of some top managers' salaries to those obtainable in private noncooperative firms. At the same time, the organization now enjoys more power and influence itself, as readily shown by the Caja Laboral's increasingly independent attitude and financial practices.

Organizational psychologist Karl Weick (1979) has illustrated that large organizations cannot help but suffer from projection as they relate to their environment. Not only do an organization's perceptions of the environment significantly determine its "responses" to that environment, but also it finds that it "bumps into" elements of the environment the organization itself has come to create. MCC cannot claim a disadvantaged position with respect to cooperative laws and regulations in the Basque Country because, as many of my contacts noted, MCC contributed greatly to the shape of those new laws in 1993. (The laws gave MCC and other cooperative corporations more latitude in employment policies, such as in the hiring of part-time workers temporary workers, and short-term owner-workers.)

For an organization based on an ideology such as cooperativism, there is also the question of "evangelism," where an external justification for cooperativism can be value-driven rather than market-oriented. MCC's principles and those of ULMA call for an evangelistic posture toward the larger world regarding solidarity with all workers who struggle for justice. As occasional articles in the MCC magazine *Trabajo y Unión* (see, e.g., Jan. 1994) indicate, the tradition of reflection on creative and collaborative possibilities for workers in other parts of the world is very much alive at Mondragón. According to one long-term *cooperativista* and frequent contributor to the pages of *TU*, José María Sarasua, the most "advanced forms" of capitalist organizations are simultaneously attuned to the dignity of the person inside the organization and the dignity of the person in the larger society (for example, in the form of solidarity with the aspirations of laborers everywhere).

However, it has been apparent in my recent discussions there that the recent expansion, through the establishment of delegations in other countries, engagement in joint ventures with traditional capitalist corporations, and purchases of noncooperative corporations with no plans for conversion, represents a clear departure from an evangelistic stance toward cooperative ideals. To carry the analogy to religious organizations a bit further, these outposts and holdings of MCC and ULMA in twenty or so nations are not being conceived as "missions." In a group discussion at MCC's Otalora Training Center in July 1997, the director of Public Relations, Iñaki Idiazabal, cautioned about the way this internationalization is being pursued: "It worries us that while we are cooperatives here we seem to be forgetting that we are cooperatives when we go into the outside world. Over time, this problem could have an effect on *internal* solidarity as well, so we have to find a creative solution."

In sum, relations with the environment, particularly for a value-based organization, are at issue almost constantly. Any resolution of the dilemmas posed by those relationships can only be contingent and temporary. Still, the posture an organization takes toward its environment, especially in terms of the values promoted, may well have a shaping influence on its internal affairs. Cohesion or solidarity may well be dependent on how the organization preaches beyond the choir as well as on how it welcomes new ideas. An organization's internal and external affairs thus are intertwined in a number of important ways. Perhaps the best metaphor for these relationships is a "floating equilibrium," which suggests that they must continually be examined and adjusted.

Seeking Leadership and Inspiration

One of the most important paradoxes in any democratic organization or society is that of leadership: the tendency to await inspiration from others (see Stohl and Cheney 1999; compare Kanter 1982). This problem may be seen especially in an organization that has moved beyond its founding phase into a kind of organizational adolescence. The universal "problem of succession" arises when the founders depart for another organization, retire, or die. An organization that depends to some extent on the charisma or exceptional personal qualities of its founders must then strive to install specific and qualified successors while in some way institutionalizing the special qualities of the founders. The problem increases for an organization such as Mondragón, that is built on a value-based ideology in addition to the charisma of its founders.

The year 1996 marked the twentieth anniversary of Don José

María Arizmendiarrieta's death, and *Trabajo y Unión* was full of articles about MCC's history, Arizmendi's formative influence, and "what if?" questions about the state of the cooperatives. The November 1996 issue presented a cover story and several follow-up stories on the principal founder, asking, "What if Don José María were alive today? What kind of message would he leave with us?" The articles speak with a dual voice, celebrating the history of Mondragón cooperativism and emphasizing the need for "realism" and adaptation to changing circumstances. Bringing Don José María into the present as a means of justifying and invigorating current cooperative policy, the editors were also acknowledging the need to recapture some of his rhetorical "magic," admitting that there are doubts about the authenticity of the cooperatives' social commitments in the 1990s. A *TU* editorial leaves the reader with these thoughts:

> It is certain that the times have changed. It has already been some time since we lived in a factory economy. Competitiveness itself pushes us to explore new horizons and to establish new commercial relations. But we do run the risk of extinguishing the spirit of solidarity that gave birth to our organization as a group, in pursuit of the same competitiveness.... Our objective [then] ought to be searching for the highest level of solidarity despite the competitiveness of the world, and not the reverse. ("Don José María, 20 Años Después," *TU*, Nov. 1996: 7)

What is most interesting about this passage is that it sees competitiveness as the principal reason for the cooperatives' drive toward "new horizons," yet at the same time treats it as a secondary, subordinated, role with respect to social solidarity. This vacillation runs throughout the issue and marks much of the informal talk I heard at Mondragón.

From my interviews and conversations with top managers at MCC, however, I found less ambivalence on this issue. They were much more united in stressing that Arizmendi would recognize today the need for a nimble and adaptive set of cooperatives. Many of these leaders emphasized that he would be largely untroubled by the demands of the market and the need to modify their structures and practices. In essence, the policymakers of MCC were telling me that the conception of Mondragón's tradition should be broadened; and they also soft-pedaled cooperativism itself.

The discussion of Don José María's legacy at Mondragón brings into clear view the problem of the current and future sources of inspiration for the cooperatives. At their inception, the cooperatives derived social sustenance and power from the persistence and vision of their leader, from the energies and sacrifices of the cofounders, and from the depth of religious and social commitment associated with the principles of the coops.

Today the Mondragón cooperatives find themselves not only without a charismatic or visionary leader but also without a forceful commitment to their social ideology. Although there is great respect for many of the managers and leaders in the cooperatives of ULMA and MCC, there is also a yearning for "someone who will come to reinvigorate our democratic practices." At the same time, market-driven arguments, specifically the values of efficiency, productivity, and competitiveness, are frequently offered in the official communiques of the cooperatives as reasons for commitment to the cooperatives rather than simply means to longer social goals. Though the above passage from *TU* reveals ambivalence about competitiveness, there can be no doubt about its presentation as a guiding symbol and *mythos*. In one of the clearest images I found in any of MCC's publications, the cover of the April 1994 issue of *TU* depicts a young professional man running hurdles on the globe with the simple but bold title "*Competitividad*."

In this context of competition, "participation" is often being discussed rather strictly as enabling greater productivity (see *TU*, June 1996). But that may prove to be an insufficient form of inspiration and leadership for the next generation of cooperative members and employees, especially as they express their career-mindedness and independence. For Mondragón, as well as for other value-driven organizations, there is a need to renew the social energy that gave rise to the organization. A priest and close friend of Arizmendi's, the late José María Mendizabal, told me in 1994, "If the cooperatives do not return to some of the very values that gave them life in the first place, they may become victims of their own success."

The challenges for leadership and inspiration at Mondragón remind one of Chester Barnard's (1968) three "executive functions." Barnard concluded that for long-term economic and social success, an organization needed a common purpose, a dynamic system of communication, and essential contributions (motivations and energies) from its members. Barnard saw the three as interdependent factors in organizational performance. For example, a common purpose had to be communicated daily as part of employee relations and organizational decision making. And the successful pursuit of that common goal depended upon both its inspirational character and the continued adherence of the members who felt that in some way they "owned" the organization and its objectives.

In any democratic organization "an active community" of members must be centered on the *value* of democracy and devoted to its practice. Jacob and Jacob (1984) explain that "to overcome centrifugal forces . . . collective leadership is critical" (320). Such leadership should be energized by a common vision based on core social values. As political philosopher Daniel Kemmis (1990) puts it, there has to be a commitment to the system that transcends individual interests. Genuine democratic commitment, however, may be circumscribed by a recognition that a system has become corrupt and therefore no longer deserving of one's allegiance. (At that point, the options would be "exit," "voice," "loyalty," or "neglect," with respect to one's stance toward the organization; see Hirschman, 1972.)

We have already seen how the organization on the one hand and the work group, team, or department on the other can function simultaneously as important sources of organizational allegiance (see Barker and Tompkins 1994; C. Scott, Corman, and Cheney 1998). These two domains of loyalty may also operate in opposition to one another (see Tjosvold 1991). In fact, the configuration of identifications or attachments for the individual employee may be quite complex (see Cheney 1983b). From the standpoint of this study, it is crucial that we examine every level for the mission and values which are presumed to deserve the loyalty of members (Cheney 1991). In this respect, current efforts to develop pay-for-performance increments in some co-ops will be important to observe because they often tend to "individualize" employee relations and deemphasize the overall collaborative achievements of the work force (Waddington and Whitston 1996). More broadly, such initiatives can substitute calculating and fleeting relationships for strong social bonds among co-workers (Sennett 1998).

We can see a somewhat contrasting problem in organizations without traditions of democracy that seek to convert to more participative systems of decision making and work activities. MAPSA of Pamplona, one of the three co-ops explored in detail here, shows how difficult it can be to shift from a "culture of command" to a "culture of participation" (in the words of the Finance director there). At the

same time that many of the long-standing co-ops of MCC are worried
about how to revive a sense of mission at a broad corporate level,
MAPSA's move into the cooperative fold is blocked to some extent
by vestiges of authoritarianism as well as by the reluctance of many
employees to accept full responsibility in their work areas or to actively engage in the newly created organs of governance. The lack of
a democratic tradition of employee governance and the unfamiliarity
with new participative programs constitute a compound problem.

Leadership must be highlighted both with respect to the mission of
the organization and in terms of team-based restructuring. For the
traditional, hierarchical, and authoritarian firm that would reconfig-
ure itself as a participative enterprise, both types of leadership are
crucial (see Courtright, Fairhurst, and Rogers 1989).

One of the great ironies at Mondragón and in many other organizations is that while they are emphasizing greater individual initiative
at the level of job position and work team, they may not be promoting lofty goals for continued individual identification and commitment with the organization. In the customer culture of today, individual employees are expected to achieve fulfillment upon satisfying
consumers' desires (even "delighting" the customer) (Oakland 1989).
But the images of customer service and market competitiveness in
and by themselves may prove insufficient for the kind of long-term
motivation needed to sustain an enterprise such as the cooperatives
of Mondragón. *Socios* might come to think of themselves as "owners" only in the most limited sense of the term. It may well be that a
broader vision of workplace democracy must be promoted at the
highest levels of an alternative organization in order for more focused and ideologically narrow programs of employee participation
to flourish.

Conserving a Common Mission

How much should the mission of value-based organizations be
adapted in the interests of competition and other changing circumstances? At what point will the organization have changed so much
that it ceases to be, in essence, the same organization?

Any organization, but especially a democratic one, is going to experience change, even without having to face strong external threats
to its practices and identity. For if the organization takes its democ-

ratic commitments seriously, or even if it simply wants to enlist enthusiastic commitments, it must allow space for new members to influence its development. New members bring with them their own values, preferences, demands, and concepts of how to do business. There will be inevitable generational differences among employees, but also pressures from within the organization to renew and modify its practices—especially as positions of responsibility and policy-making are assumed by younger managers. Each new employee and each new manager will want to "make a mark" on the organization.

If the organization does not update, alter, and renew its mission, it necessarily defines itself as one that values its past more than its present or its future, locking employees and decision making into a predetermined model of organizational identity and activity (Westenholz 1991). But if the organization adapts too much, becoming putty in the hands of each new wave of employees and managers, the break with tradition can signal to its internal and external constituencies that there is nothing fundamental or enduring about its commitments. Most organizations will respond to this problem by changing certain features of their structures or processes while holding others constant, and some change may be mere relabeling (Christensen 1996). Regardless of the approach taken, the organization needs to confront the dialectic of continuity and change. But for the organization that is grounded in core values and seeks to promote them, the need for solutions is more pressing.

At Mondragón this dilemma is becoming acute (see MCC 1994). U.S. labor organizer Mike Miller (1994) observes: "The central challenge facing Mondragón is two-fold. First, how to compete in the new global economy. Second, how to remain true to the values and principles that formed it" (17). Fred Freundlich (1996) summarizes his analysis of permanence and change at Mondragón this way: "While the MCC remains an exemplar of democratic worker ownership, it remains to be seen whether the new policies can both bring greater business success and maintain the group's explicit commitment to the principles and practices of cooperative enterprise" (7). Kasmir (1996) argues that the Mondragón cooperatives never really operated from a strong pro-worker ideology or a socially conscious value base because the co-ops were from the beginning estranged from the working-class politics in the Basque Country and were more enamored of the larger market than the co-ops' official principles would suggest.

The question of the cooperatives' mission surfaced clearly in discussions at the end of my first visit to Mondragón, in March of 1992, prompting me to propose to the Otalora Training Center a long-term study of transformations in values within the co-ops. Despite the tendency of some managers to downplay the importance of outsiders' expectations of Mondragón to be an exemplar of workplace democracy, there can be no doubt that the mission of the organization is a focal point of tensions today within the co-ops.

The most dramatic example of this debate can be found in the challenges of the quasi-union group KT to recent policy changes within MCC. Another is the sharp criticism of MCC's policies of centralization and sectoral reorganization by ULMA. Further evidence of tension came in my interviews at Mondragón, in 1994 and 1997, in which many respondents viewed cooperativism as being "on trial" during the next decade or so of engagement of the global market.

Perhaps the fullest expression of the cooperatives' changing mission, especially as seen from the "inside," can be found in the pages of the December 1996 issue of *Trabajo y Unión*, in a cover story entitled "The Second Generation [of *Cooperativistas*]." The principal article, authored by a professor at Mondragón's Polytechnic College, contrasts "the cooperative sense of yesterday and today." The article takes an optimistic view of the present, arguing that despite the worry over the future of the cooperative spirit, younger *cooperativistas*, in contrast with their elders, are more competent, better educated and trained, more willing to take initiative, more critically minded (but with a sense of humor), more pragmatic, more internationally aware, more environmentally conscious, more inclined to use the language of Euskera, and more likely to find negotiated solutions for economic and political problems. This article, along with several others on the same theme in the issue, is emphatic that the "cooperativism of today" is different from but no less authentic than that of the first few decades of the cooperatives' existence. These upbeat characterizations are clearly responding to a felt need to counter the critiques that the spirit, core values, and mission of the organizations have been lost.

Worker-owners' commitment to the cooperatives and to cooperativism is still fairly strong, but it appears to be declining, especially for new *socios* and for some segments of the veteran work force as well. For example, a survey conducted by the Otalora Training Center in 1991 revealed that just 23 percent of *socios* who responded indicated they would leave the co-ops if a comparable (and presumably higher-paying) position were available in a noncooperative private firm (see Lezamiz, as cited in Moye 1993). In a similar survey, which I conducted within several industrial co-ops in 1994 in collaboration with Otalora, about 40 percent of *socios* expressed serious doubts about the direction of the MCC co-ops and the endurance of their special qualities. Moreover, of the same group of respondents in 1994, a significant proportion of *socios* expressed fears about threats to internal solidarity and internal democratic practice. In the open-ended portion of the survey, one respondent commented: "Every day we seem to be less distinguishable from an S.A. [private noncooperative corporation]. I wonder what the cooperative will look like in five or ten years." This complaint was echoed in many of my interviews, not only in MCC but also to some extent in ULMA.

Organizations that do not change in the face of the collective wishes of newer members may be defined by them as irrelevant and as a result may wither away. A paradox of commitment is that the founding generation of a democratic organization are so committed to their own vision of the organization and its goals that they fail to allow subsequent generations the same shaping input (Stohl and Cheney 1999). But if the younger *socios* do display the values characterized by *TU* and yet can maintain a strong commitment to the distinctiveness of cooperativism, less fear over the cooperatives' future may be warranted than has been thought. If, on the other hand, the younger generations of cooperative members and employees simply aid the importation of a full-blown market orientation by the co-ops, while at the same time limiting their involvement in assertive or "political" forms of participation (Bachrach and Botwinick 1992), the distinction between the cooperatives and their noncooperative competitors may erode still further.

In this respect the experience of Mondragón is instructive for other organizations. No one is well served if the tradition of the organization goes unquestioned. Renewal and modification will be pushed by both internal and external forces, and the organization's ability to manage the dialectic of permanence and change will be crucial to both its social success and its very survival.

The Interdependence of the Social and the Economic

Though the market may appear to be wholly a matter of economic, material forces, further analysis reveals a huge component of human persuasion. The market depends on a high degree of trust and confidence simply to operate, as the 1990s roller coaster of stock prices in a number of exchanges around the world demonstrated well. As I have emphasized, discourse plays a shaping role in economic policy and therefore in bringing into being not only economic but social outcomes. Moreover, in today's popular discourse, social concerns have come to be relabeled and recast in market terms so that they must be defended for their bottom-line results. (Cheney in press–b).

At Mondragón and elsewhere I have observed some curious aspects of the arguments about the social side of enterprise. The President of Mondragón's consortium of educational cooperatives, Hezbide, explained to me in 1994: "I believe it is easy to participate when things are secure, when the boat goes well. Security, stability, and well-being are all the basic elements of participation." But Carlos Zubero, director of Personnel for MAIER, told me in 1994, "The *socios* are largely content these days because of the *anticipos* [salary, technically in the form of an advance, plus dividends] they are earning. So, there's less worry about things such as the performance of the social council or the flow of information." At the same time, both of these respondents believed that much of the financial success of the cooperative could be attributed to its social performance: specifically, to the strong tradition of participation inside the cooperative. What may be taken for granted during "fat" times is the very dimension that helped the organization move to a new level of success.

Of course, in the face of bad economic news, social programs at work often take a hit. Certainly some of the first cutbacks to be made in most organizations today are on "the people side" of things. Not only will personnel budgets shrink (in some organizations from 80 percent of operating costs to as little as 30–40 percent) but organizational initiatives in human resources, public relations, and corporate communications will also be cut. The argument runs basically like this: "While we might be able to afford a lot of social frills if we're doing well on the bottom line, a deteriorating position in the market demands that we eliminate some unnecessary functions." Economist David Gordon (1996) sees this justification as common in U.S. corporations in the 1990s, and he argues more generally that capitalism has thus ceased to be responsive to broad social concerns in its dealings with employees and other stakeholders.

Yet it may well be, as organizational theorist Arnold Tannenbaum's research (1983) suggests, that attention to the social side of organizational life, including especially programs of participation, is critically necessary precisely when the organization cannot manage to make much of a profit. According to Tannenbaum, a strong identification with the organization and its activities both contributes to and results from vigorous employee participation in decision making. Therefore, he reasons, attending to the social sources of employee satisfaction during lean times would help both the employees and the organization (see also Tyson 1979).

The most economically disadvantaged cooperative I observed was MAPSA of Pamplona. So severe did MAPSA's economic crisis become, even after it was purchased by MCC in 1991–92 and converted to a co-op, that *socios* were asked to take cutbacks in salary for 1993–95 of between 15 and 33 percent. The words of one department head in the spring of 1994 capture well the interrelation of economic and social factors at work and just how easily the tide of motivation can change, depending on one's attitude and actual experience.

> To me, the conversion of this organization has been a big change. I went from being a manager in a private company to a director in a cooperative. But, entering the [MCC] cooperatives was the only alternative that we had, and it was indeed the only solution if we wanted the company to survive. So we are thankful we could join. But these last years have been very negative for us, and we have had no benefits [profits and corresponding dividends]. And this year will be negative, too. I would have liked to have entered a cooperative with benefits, not losses. If we had by now moved to being an organization with benefits maybe people's faces wouldn't be so long; they would feel better. . . . We are always saying, "Well, maybe next year, or the following year." But here we have a kind of forced solidarity. We have a drastic reduction of salaries: we are earning up to 33 percent less, and I consider this a form of solidarity. Now, we have all accepted this because, if we didn't, we would have to leave. We are going through a period where it is difficult to say if we are *cooperativistas* or not. . . . We all want to participate, but these times are hard.

These reflections remind us of why the relationship between over-all organizational productivity and job satisfaction is so difficult to evaluate. Indeed, the persistent efforts of the Human Relations Movement in the United States and elsewhere, from roughly 1935 to 1970, produced mixed results in a project aimed at showing a definitive positive correlation between job satisfaction and productivity (Redding, 1972). Advocates of the Human Relations approach tried to establish clearly that the happy worker is the productive worker, chiefly in the interest of increasing productivity but also out of some genuine concern for employees (Gillespie 1991). It is now much clearer that the relationship is complicated by many factors such as type of reward, working conditions, common purpose, the passage of time, and so on (Weisbord 1991).

As the Mondragón cooperatives continue to implement new systems of participation, they are initiating wage increments based on group output. In a number of co-ops, up to 20 percent of a *socio*'s salary may result from a combination of group or team productivity. While in a sense the co-ops have always been based on pay for performance, that linkage has been until now established at the global level of the firm in its relationship to the worker-owner—in terms of dividends paid to *socios* per the firm's overall profits. This move toward team-based pay for performance is still in its experimental phase within MCC, and it is controversial. For example, some long-time *socios* see such a method of financial reward as inimical to values of solidarity and equality, arguing that its short-term positive impact on the performance of some teams will be overshadowed by a longer-term harm to the cohesion of the cooperatives. These critics fear heated competition among different departments. Thus policymakers need to consider just how much of a role should be played by the direct linking of individual pay to team performance (see Lawler, Mohrman, and Ledford 1995).

In the research of Britain's Tavistock Institute (Trist and Banforth 1951; Trist and Murray 1993), some of the earliest studies of work teams, called "socio-technical systems," revealed how complex is the relationship between economic and social factors at work. In the socio-technical model, first pioneered in coal mines in Scandinavia shortly after World War II, workers make important decisions about the implementation and uses of new technologies, among other things. Such a model involves a substantial degree of group autonomy, especially in work redesign and problem solving in production.

The success of these work teams thus depends heavily upon worker motivation and commitment. Further, that commitment derives from an amalgam of social and economic factors (see also Naschold, et al. 1993; Seibold 1995). For example, a strong emphasis on pay for performance, for either the individual or the team, may yield disappointing results for morale and motivation if it is not coupled with genuine opportunities for self-determination on the shop floor. Still, for many employees, there may be little desire for getting involved in decision making (Jain and Giles 1985). In addition, the effects of economic versus social motivations can shift over time, with one type becoming more or less salient than the other, from the perspective of the employee. These complications call for periodic reassessment by the organization.

Enacting Democracy as a Process

The tendency to see democracy mainly in terms of social structures that protect individual rights or guarantee forms of representation is strong in the Western world. Recent opinion polls in the United States suggest that the principal way in which most citizens understand democracy is in terms of protection of their individual freedoms, and in some western European nations there is an emphasis on *rights* of participation (Strauss 1982). Both of these interpretations of democracy rely on institutional guarantees. The bias toward structures of protection and representation is understandable and has a certain practical advantage, for once we have decided on mechanisms for organizing democratic activities—whether in politics or board meetings—it makes sense to try to preserve them through institutionalization. This reasoning is behind the "checks and balances" of the tripartite structure of the federal government of the United States. It also shapes systems of "codetermination" in Germany whereby workers, corporations, and the state enjoy legally protected influence in the formation of industrial policy. The same rationale underlies much of the principled support for organized labor (Freeman and Medoff 1984).

However, when protected by rules, rituals, and the force of habit, the very democratic processes that seemed so vital at the time of an organization's founding can come to undermine the democracy itself. This problem is recognized by "modified-constitutionalists" in the United States and by organizational analysts who have noted how democratic organizations often become encumbered by their own structures—even when those structures were expressly designed to promote democratic participation (Ashcraft 1998; O'Connor 1995; Stohl and Cheney 1999; Walker 1996; Westenholz 1993). There is not only a tendency toward excessive bureaucratization in a long-lived organization, but also loss of novelty to the organization's established means of participation. These can lead to a stifling of participation, as the cherished institutions become either irrelevant or actual obstructions to genuine democratic practice. The tendency for internal organizational processes to become inflexible and lifeless helps to explain the basis for Rothschild and Whitt's judgment "that democratic modes of organization are neither impossible nor inevitable. They are conditional" (1986: 75).

From my observations of the Mondragón cooperatives, I would say that the vitality of its organizational democracy (as opposed to specific programs of participation) rests principally on the following factors, in addition to the much-discussed market pressures: (1) the performance of representative social bodies; (2) the equitable distribution of benefits and losses through individual incentives and collective ownership; (3) education in cooperativism and other core organizational values; (4) the allowance for (and benefit from) internal disagreements and dissent; (5) the presence throughout the organization of an authentic concern for the well-being of individual employees; (6) the use of vital feedback loops within the organizations for purposes of a circular flow of communication; (7) the promotion of cooperative ideals beyond the walls of the organization; and (8) and the degree of openness to negotiating the meaning of organizational democracy.

Except for the points about dissent, feedback, and negotiation of the meaning of organizational democracy, all of these proposed criteria are reflected in MCC's Ten Principles. My criteria are basically consistent also with previous formulations by organizational researchers (e.g., Bernstein 1976; Clegg 1983; Deetz 1995; Gustavsen 1992; Monge and K. Miller 1988; Winnicott 1950). Elsewhere I have defined workplace democracy as

> *a system of governance which truly values individual goals and feelings (e.g., equitable remuneration, the pursuit of enriching work and the right to express oneself) as well as typically organiza-*

tional objectives (e.g., effectiveness and efficiency, reflectively conceived), which actively fosters the connection between those two sets of concerns by encouraging individual contributions to important organizational choices, and which allows for the ongoing modification of the organization's activities and policies by the group. (1995:170–71)

If we apply these eight criteria to the cooperatives of Mondragón, the scorecard produces a mixed evaluation.

1. *The vitality of organized governance within the cooperatives is highly variable across individual co-ops and is challenged by both the routinization of participatory practices and the almost complete centralization of corporate strategic policymaking.* We have seen, both in my discussion of three similarly sized cooperatives and in evidence from the Mondragón system more generally, how the important function of the social councils is often neglected in the individual co-ops. This problem extends as well to the social councils at the level of the *agrupaciones* or sectoral groupings of cooperatives. Further, general assemblies have largely abandoned their deliberative functions in favor of top-down information transfer. Finally, the centralization of corporate policymaking, especially in MCC, has necessarily undermined the authority of the organs of governance in the individual cooperatives. In the words of José Antonio Ugarte, former president of ULMA, "sovereignty" rests at three organizational levels: the individual, one's cooperative (or individual firm), and the system as a whole. Too much privilege at the system level, in Ugarte's view, diminishes sovereignty at the other two levels.

The three most important dimensions of organizational structure are *hierarchy*, referring to the vertical dimensions of authority; *centralization*, referring to powers of coordination; and *formalization*, referring to the degree to which organizational activities are standardized and regulated. Curiously, the Mondragón cooperatives especially within MCC are growing more rigid along these three dimensions, even as their official rhetoric is spotlighting flexibility, innovation, and entrepreneurship. Though tensions in the realm of organizational structure are inevitable, the business trend is, at least on the surface, away from formalization, centralization, and rigid hierarchy.

2. *Though the distribution of benefits and losses in the cooperatives is still comparatively equitable, the linkage of a top group of*

MCC's managers' salaries to the global market in 1991–92 repre-sented not only a material change in remuneration but a huge sym-bolic change in the organization with respect to perceived wage sol-idarity. My interviewees across the cooperatives were divided on the wisdom of the Third Cooperative Congress's decision in December 1991 to link salaries of certain managers in the *cúpula* to market in-dicators (reaching 70 percent of the current and agreed-upon market "value" for the same job in the noncooperative private sector). Those who argued for the change did so solely on the basis of competitive-ness and market pressures. Those who criticized the policy shift couched their arguments entirely in terms of organizational trust and internal solidarity. During my visits in 1994 and 1997, there con-tinued to be fallout from this momentous decision. Also, the contro-versy required MCC's top managers to explain the rationale for the change, including the fact that the twenty-five to thirty top officials covered by the new policy were making on average only about 50 percent of their free-market counterparts.

Similarly, the recent decisions to increase the number of nonown-ing workers in the co-ops and to create a new position of temporary *socio* have been justified solely on the basis of organizational adapt-ability, flexibility, and agility. The idea of a temporary worker-owner would have been unthinkable earlier in the cooperatives' develop-ment; the worker's proprietary relationship with the organization was seen as inherently a permanent one (and not easily severed by the cooperatives). The new policy, too, has enormous implications for equity in salary, benefits, and job security. José Manuel Biain, the personnel director at ULMA-Forja, told me in the summer of 1997, "There is now a new kind of diversity in employment in the cooper-atives that has to be recognized and dealt with. We can't pretend we're all totally equal, yet we must accord all the employees as many rights and benefits as possible."

In sum, both material benefits and the security of one's status within such an organization are central to members' notions of eq-uity and fairness. The symbolic as well as practical monetary effects of a widening of difference within the organization should never be underestimated, especially where a tradition of equality and democ-racy is held sacred.

3. *Although education in the philosophical, social, and practical aspects of cooperativism is still alive in the cooperatives of MCC and ULMA, it appears to be taking a back seat to financial, techni-*

cal, and job-specific forms of training. From the very beginning, the Mondragón cooperatives were exceptional in their emphasis on *formación* (education *and* development of the person—there is no correspondingly rich term in English) in the ideals and practices of cooperativism (see the survey of Spanish cooperatives in Colomer 1995). Over the years, this function has been carried out in four ways: in the early and formative role of the technical education school (established in 1943 and forerunner to the Mondragón University created in 1996–97); through the specific policies of individual cooperatives and persons within them; through special seminars offered (since 1987) at the Otalora Training Center; and through the dissemination of corporate documents such as the Ten Principles, and frequent discussions of their application in articles in the *TU* (see especially the issues in 1995–97). In other research, the crucial role of Mondragón's technical education complex—in both its technical and social dimensions—has been well-documented (Meek and Woodworth 1990). I would say that socialization in the ideals of cooperativism is fading in importance within the cooperatives, being eclipsed by market-driven concerns for greater efficiency, productivity, and technical expertise. Perhaps the best evidence of this decline is that in each of the cooperatives I observed closely—MAPSA, MAIER, and ULMA-Forja—plans for further seminars in cooperative practices were treated as having only secondary importance (at MAPSA and Forja) or not at all (at MAIER). From my own attendance at Otalora's seminars in cooperative management in May 1995, it became plain that they are being utilized only by certain cooperatives and usually only for their newly elected members of the general or governing councils. Here it's important to note also a declining interest on the part of middle-level managers and many employees in participating in more philosophically oriented seminars. The general manager of MAPSA complained to me in 1997: "I haven't witnessed any special concern on the part of new members of the councils to educate themselves in the philosophical domain. Knowing this, we are still trying to see how we can give them that *formación.*"

José María Larrañaga, director of Communications in MCC's Otalora Training Center, said that "within a democratic system . . . the spirit of cooperation cannot be taught but must be learned" (*TU*, Dec. 1996: 15). For such cooperative training efforts to work and be woven into the fabric of an organization such as the Mondragón cooperatives, there must be a desire on the part of the participants themselves as well as commitment of time and resources by top management. What we might call "socialization in cooperation" thus cannot completely sustain itself; yet an alternative organization may not be able to maintain its social integrity without regular attention to training.

4. *It is difficult to assess the extent to which individual dissent is permitted within the Mondragón cooperatives today, but we can observe a tendency to contain strong objections to corporate policy through both formal and informal means of delegitimation.* MCC especially remains steadfast in its opposition to intra-firm unionization, although the organizing activities of KT ("Cooperative Groups") especially within the old FAGOR group are well known through the corporation. Dissenting views have been expressed through occasional articles in *TU* (for instance, articles by KT representatives in 1994), and the January 1998 issue carried the second part of an exchange between Mila Larrañaga, a prominent spokesperson for KT, and another *socio*, Eukeni Olabarrieta, about the future of "cooperativism." The debate was heated, with charges by Larrañaga that the co-ops had become essentially "dehumanizing" and a rebuttal by Olabarrieta that Larrañaga's claim was "inexact and cruel." Furthermore, even the stylized performances of general assemblies allow for "interventions" in the form of prepared statements of opposition to prevailing corporate trends.

As already suggested, the strong movement toward policy centralization, especially within MCC and in deference to the market, is being used as the key justification for limiting "diversity of opinion within the cooperative about the advancement of the business" (as the president of MAIER put it to me in 1994). This view I found to represent something of a consensus among managers and leaders in the cooperatives. The notable exception was ULMA's own independent stance toward MCC.

In reflecting on the tension between unity of corporate strategy and divergence of opinion with the cooperatives, cofounder Alfonso Gorroñogoitia described the resulting mix as a *democradura*—best translated as a hybrid of "democracy" and "dictatorship." This neologism, which he picked up from Israeli visitors familiar with the tradition of *kibbutzim* in their own country, captures the idea that even in an organization committed to democracy there will be the need to appeal to strong authority at the top, from time to time, to resolve differences and to focus energies. At the same time, democracy en-

tails an ongoing "licensing" of specific instances of managerial abso-
lutism by the governed.

5. *A genuine concern for the individual was evident throughout
the cooperatives; however, it was more and more being expressed in
terms of interest in people as a means to an end.* My formal interviews as well as informal conversations at Mondragón were peppered
with references to "the dignity of the person," "equality and equity
in our dealings with one another," "health and safety in the workplace," "rights to meaningful work and to participation in organizational decision making," and "solidarity with other workers and
with the community." These expressions seemed genuine to me. At
the same time, there was a willingness—more evident in 1997 than
in 1994—to couch the person's role in the organization largely in
terms of organizational efficiency. This characterization shows up in
the increasing use of a system of efficiency ratings for individuals
that results in a calculation of the "added value" of their contributions to the organization. It is also visible in numerous *TU* articles
during 1995–99; a 1996 article relays the point well by describing the
development of the corporation and the employees' roles within it as
an "internal mine" for greater efficiency and more successful performance in the market. This phrase, which the article admits to be
borrowed from contemporary Japanese corporate policy, reflects an
important shift in the formal discourse of the Mondragón cooperatives. Whether this formal shift will be accompanied by more fundamental cultural changes can be assessed only with further observation of the day-to-day operations of the new systems of participation.

The history of attempts to implement employee participation programs is fraught with cynicism, doubt, and especially participants'
challenges to the authenticity of the organization's commitments to
ideals of democracy *for the sake of employees.* Authenticity must be
believed as well as practiced; regardless of intentions, even an inac-
curate image of a purely instrumental rationale for increasing participation can serve to undermine such programs. Communicating and
practicing the social as well as economic "logic" of participation
thus represents a fundamental challenge to any organization that
would strive to democratize its work processes.

6. *The provision for dynamic communication feedback loops is of
significant concern for the co-ops, yet corporate communication
plans continue to emphasize top-down flow of information and directives with relatively limited opportunities for the flow of news*

and opinion upward (aside from required reporting on production problems and making suggestions for improving). As mentioned in Chapter 3, many of my interviewees treated "communication" as an important organizational value in itself, and they were often quick to distinguish it from "mere information." This view was as widespread in MCC as in ULMA; in both corporations I found a strong awareness of the need to revitalize various media and channels of communication. One of the ironies I found and pressed upon my interviewees was that written communications such as memos, reports, and forecasts were coming to supplant the dynamic oral interaction so treasured by the Basques and very much a hallmark of the cooperatives' early development. The increased demand on work teams to transmit production and efficiency data upward on a frequent basis is a case in point. My observations of work practices led me to conclude that this shift in emphasis resulted not only from bureaucratization but also from a certain amount of corporate imitation, whereby the cooperatives seemed to be applying systems of communication and decision making from other large corporations (chiefly in the United States, Japan, and western Europe).

One way to address the complexities of communication, especially in the larger cooperatives, would be through the dual linkage of every group, team, or unit with one at the next level of the hierarchy. Within this arrangement, each group would have a functional representative to the next level and one additional "linking pin" whose job it would be to look out especially for problems in communication (see Ackoff 1994; Romme 1997). Organizational communication researcher Cynthia Stohl observes from her extensive research on quality circles (1987, 1995) that one of the most important challenges to any large organization is limitations to intergroup relations which get beyond the team or committee level to "stitch the organization together."

Given the deterioration of the roles of the social councils and the ritualized performance of the general assemblies, group dynamics in work processes and in governance become all the more important. The "neo-cooperativism" discussed earlier in this book obviously privileges team-based collaboration at the level of work processes over what might be termed a more embracing form of participation in decision making at the level of the firm. And, in a way, the challenge to communication practice is increased in an organization that stresses *both* corporate and team loyalty. What gets lost in the process, commonly, is an intermediate level of identification and connection.

7. *The ways in which internationalization is being pursued by the cooperatives generally relegate the promotion of cooperative ideals to participation at international conferences and to occasional special service projects, and exclude such promulgation in the process of acquiring and developing new corporate holdings beyond Mondagón.* This point has already been discussed in Chapter 3 and Chapter 4. But I should add that the decisions being made about corporate expansion into other parts of the world are contingent and can be modified. Given the acknowledgment of an internal corporate contradiction on the part of many of my interviewees—a number of whom were themselves top managers—it may well be that the issue of "conversion" will be revisited within the next few years.

8. *The degree of openness to negotiating the meaning of organizational democracy within the cooperatives seems increasingly tied to the importation of customer-oriented and market-driven concepts into corporate strategizing and participatory practices.* The culturally grounded tradition of discussion, debate, and confrontation is still alive within both MCC and ULMA. In marked contrast to my experiences as a researcher and consultant in U.S. organizations, I found nearly all employees of the cooperatives to be quite open in voicing their criticisms of their supervisors, managers, and elected officials; there was clearly little or no fear of reprisal. A *socio* who dislikes his supervisor may be heard to call that person a "chorizo" (sausage). Still, the growing talk of market demands is dampening discussions of core social values, the ongoing formation of corporate policy, and the cooperatives' relations with their regions.

For many observers at Mondragón and elsewhere, true democracy depends on diversity of opinion. For example, Syed Rahim (1994) invokes Bakhtin's notion of "heteroglossia" (1981) to stress that a sound model of organizational democracy should make space for multiple voices, always distinct, sometimes diverging, and occasionally in conflict. Moreover, even when it structurally involves only two parties (as in traditional labor-management negotiations) dialogue ought to seek actively to incorporate a variety of viewpoints. Though such a model may not be thoroughly applicable to a particular business, it does highlight the social merits of stimulating lively and diverse discussions within the organization, and it may be vital, over the long run, to the innovativeness and economic strength of the firm. This concept offers a useful counterpoint to the centralized strategy of corporations like Mondragón seeking to "speak to the market with a single voice." It may also help them to take more seriously their own internal rhetoric about the benefits of a somewhat decentralized entrepreneurial, empowering, team-based organizational structure.

The current developments in the cooperatives of Mondragón come from multiple sources and they defy easy analysis. Though it would be unfair to say that corporate strategy is responsible for all of the transformations at Mondragón, it would be equally misleading to attribute all of them to external market forces or to broad changes in Basque and Spanish societies. The cooperatives are, especially today, well-established and powerful *agents* in themselves—institutions that are helping to shape the very economic environment that they are also responding to.

Mondragón and the Market

Political theorist Robert Dahl (1985) cautions us to pay close attention to the behavior of corporations in contemporary society, and I would like to build upon the foundation of his analysis to close this chapter. Dahl directly refutes Alexis de Tocqueville's thesis that in equating liberty with equality, democracy could collapse, consequently leveling the entire society into a kind of mass mediocrity. In *A Preface to Economic Democracy* Dahl departs from his earlier stance on the issue (1961) to say that it is not rampant equality but gross inequity in the distribution of material resources and influence—that presently poses the greatest threat to democracy's future. He recommends worker-owned-and-governed cooperatives as one just and viable solution.

There are dangers both in the growing income gap between rich and poor and in a kind of "corporatism" that confines decision making to the interlocking activities of highly structured, resource-rich, and media-savvy institutions (see Held's 1996 outline of corporatism), including multinational cooperative businesses such as Mondragón. As co-ops such as MCC and ULMA proceed with more acquisitions, joint ventures, and strategic alliances, they are at once protecting themselves from market forces and helping to create larger blocs of capital and power. Oligopolistic tendencies within many industries are not surprising, given the immense amount of capital needed to compete in the international market as it is now structured (Derber 1998). Given their starring roles on the world stage, it is in the activities of large corporations that we find both fear and hope, according to Dahl. (See also Gray 1998.)

But at the same time that more types of organizations "speak" about their vision, values, and ethics, we may find that the range of discussion as well as access to it are actually quite narrow. The discussion of values itself may become quite ritualized and detached from active forms of engagement, especially as organizations rush to mimic one another in the use of today's buzzwords in the hope of inspiring their employees on the one hand and their consumers on the other (Christensen and Cheney in press). Though nearly all organizations are now announcing themselves as having "core social values," we may find that most of these are justified for their contribution to the bottom line. The market thus lurks symbolically behind many assertions of "value," especially by business corporations.

Organizations in every sector are appealing to an overarching image of the market as their guiding principle, and that point of reference may limit what is seen as ethically and socially possible given the dictates "it's just business" (Cheney in press–b). As long as the market is used as the primary frame within which to view issues such as the dignity of the human person, an organization's commitment to its employees, corporate social responsibility, environmental preservation, and overall quality of life, there will be a strong temptation to commodify social values and to reduce human labor to the status of a mere instrument (Fairclough 1993). As William Greider poignantly observes, we shouldn't be surprised that markets are basically amoral. After all, he explains, "The essential purpose of deregulation . . . is to free market functions of noneconomic considerations" (1997b: 72). It's not that markets are totally undemocratic or that they always steer clear of moral considerations—many economists see their commitment to the market principle as a moral stance in itself (see M. Friedman 1962)—but rather that the market way of framing issues calls for counterpoint. We need a competing way of "telling our story," expressing who we are, and setting the basic priorities of society (Cooren 1998). This can come from inside the market itself in the form of successful organizations like Mondragón that choose to promote social values of lasting importance.

In the case of Mondragón, there are crucial lessons for all of us. Its story has been inspiring and it is still being told. Part of the strength of its tradition has been in the flourishing of multiple opinions, diverse expressions of democracy, and a commitment to social solidarity. Also, the relationship of employee participation to the wider society has been and continues to be important. How the cooperatives will choose to write their own history, addressing themselves and the world, will depend on how they manage the practical tensions now being experienced there. But above all, perhaps, Mondragón's enduring message to us is that we are more than a market.

Participation and Marketization
at Mondragón and Beyond

Human beings are created for work. Seldom is work created for human beings.
—Christian Berggren, *Alternatives to Lean Production: Work Organization in the Swedish Auto Industry*, 1992

The way out of this apparent paradox—the contrast between an apparent advocacy of empowerment by TQM's promoters, contrasted with the apparent disempowerment stressed by its critics—is to see TQM [and related trends] as, among other things, a mode of legitimating the very commodification of relations both inside the hierarchy as well as, more recently, between [organizations] and individual consumers of services.
—Alan Tuckman, "Ideology, Quality and TQM," 1995

Work in the Age of the Consumer

Recent programs to restructure organizations in the interests of greater efficiency, productivity, and employee involvement are more and more being understood within the framework of "customer responsiveness," "internal markets" and the "new democratic firm" (Halal 1996). The employee is expected to serve the almighty customer while being entrepreneurial and independent in spirit. The programs of Total Quality Management, Total Participative Management, Self-directed Work Teams, and Continuous Improvement all depend to a great extent on a form of "self-management" by which the employee is expected to take on ever greater responsibility for the affairs of his or her sector. Much of the discourse and decision making surrounding customer service serves to grant agency or efficacy—the power to accomplish things on one's own—to the customer much more than to the employee. From this perspective, "becoming a better [more productive] worker is the same as becoming a better self" (du Gay 1996a: 137). And being a "smart consumer," getting "a good buy," serves as a replacement for a wider ideal of citizenship.

Still, at Mondragón and elsewhere we find signs of renewed attention to employee as well as to customer satisfaction. And some managers rightly see the two outcomes as interlinked. Two *socios* of MCC's Otalora Training Center told me in 1997: "Some of the managers are starting to understand that customer service is important but that in order to implement certain strategies along these lines we first have to satisfy our employees. So we need the kind of management and leadership that appeals to employees and that really takes their concerns into account."

The "People Problem" in Organizational Theory and Practice

We can gain a deeper and broader perspective on these important issues by returning to a defining moment in the history of industrial relations. Perhaps the most famous research in the history of the modern organization is the Hawthorne experiments, conducted at the Hawthorne Western Electric Plant near Chicago between 1928 and 1935. These studies, which were commonly interpreted as pointing to the importance of social factors such as the individual attitudes and group solidarity of workers, ushered in what would later be called the Human Relations Movement. In the modern mythology of management, this movement (which held sway in managerial textbooks and in many practices in the middle of the twentieth century) is cast in an antagonistic role with its premier predecessor, Frederick Taylor's Scientific Management (or "Taylorism," as many of his followers came to designate it). The excesses of Tayloristic emphases on production and the technical aspects of workplace reorganization, particularly in their presumption about the inherent distastefulness of work and their dismissal of intuition, needed to be countered with a "softer," more sensitive approach. Thus, the Human Relations Movement, born out of the Hawthorne study's "discovery" that social factors make a difference to people, became the dominant force in thinking about organizations and work, with a host of luminaries linked to the movement.

But despite this movement's humane ethos and despite the repeated attempts to demonstrate conclusively that "the happy worker was in fact the productive worker," the results of Human Relations studies were mixed, often finding only a weak positive correlation between job satisfaction and employee productivity. Further, there was an acknowledged inauthenticity to many of the projects conducted under the mantle of "human relations," in that much of the avowed interest in employees related strictly to productivity. Employee attitudes, values, and even their informal communication could then be construed as "governable" in the pursuit of organizational efficiency (see du Gay 1996b; Jacques 1996; Rose 1990). Thus the Human Relations Movement, as the story is recounted in management textbooks, gave way to other more complex views of the organization, such as those offered by systems theory or the cultural perspective on organizations.

But as Richard Gillespie observes in his fascinating reinterpretation of the Hawthorne studies, "little seems to have changed since Western Electric managers and Elton Mayo confronted similar problems of productivity and worker motivation at Hawthorne" (1991: 269). Gillespie argues that the same basic themes regarding participation and productivity hold sway today, though under the guise of new labels. He explains that while there is much hand-wringing over the excesses of technical control in the workplace—especially the current obsession with automation and computerization—the "best" management practices are in fact seen as those which will eke out a bit more productivity from employees. These practices, entirely in the service of greater productivity, offer few or no options for democracy for its own sake. According to Gillespie, despite all the praise for new initiatives of participation and democracy at work, both the research literature and common practices tend to reinforce managerial authority above all. For Gillespie, the limits to the "managerial revolution" make it hardly a revolution at all.

Gillespie concludes his book by mentioning certain exceptions to the elitism and paternalism of most perspectives on workplace organization. He singles out William Foote Whyte, eminent U.S. sociologist and pioneer researcher of the Mondragón worker cooperatives, for maintaining an interest in genuine participation. For Whyte, as for Gillespie, it's not enough for workers merely to *feel* as though they are participating in the decisions that shape their work experience; they ought to have a real voice in those decisions.

Mondragón offers us a remarkably complete case from which to probe these issues, as Whyte recognized when he first approached the cooperatives with his students in 1978. Here is a system built from the ground up, based on a foundation of social values, and dedicated simultaneously to the individual and the group. Co-op expert Robert Oakeshott says, "What struck me most when I was lucky enough to meet [Arizmendi] was his commitment to the values of freedom as well as to the importance of work and technical skill" (1978: 172). Today that set of cooperatives is contemplating further expansion; in the face of internationalization it is questioning its own "Basqueness"; it is striving to be more productive and more competitive; and it is aiming to reorganize its internal activities around new forms of participation and the master symbol of the customer. Within this sea of change is a strong recognition that Mondragón's cherished traditions of *solidaridad* somehow need to be preserved, lest the people find themselves without the strong cultural foundation that helped breathe life into the co-ops. Indeed, both the peculiarities and the universality of the Mondragón case should by now be apparent to the reader.

Taking a closer look at these highly successful but changing Basque cooperatives helps us to see more clearly what the tradeoffs are while examining the basic question posed at the beginning of this book: How can an economically successful, growing organization maintain its essential value commitments? The Mondragón case is important not only as an instance of workplace democracy in a world of organizations that are not typically democratic but also in terms of how tensions between, for example, globalization and local control are being addressed (Castells 1996). It is not so important to me that my students regularly split on the practical possibility for Mondragón-like organizations in the United States (though there indeed are some important examples). Phrasing the question "Can Mondragón survive—here or there?" tends to divert our attention from the larger question: "What is business about, anyway?" If we see the lessons of Mondragón within the limited parameters of the cooperatives' purity or if we shelve the case as a quaint footnote in our consideration of the array of possible organizational forms, we really miss the broader and more important point. What is happening to the Mondragón system internally while it deals with a more "open" external market tells us a great deal about what options are possible, or thinkable, or discussable for other organizations, not only radically alternative ones but also mainstream ones. We can better see the possible futures by noting what course is being charted by socially inspired organizations that are adjusting to today's market.

The answers offered here are necessarily tentative and incomplete. The struggle is continuous, prone to irony and surprise, and practical solutions to the dilemma are only temporary and partial. One certainty, though, is that a complete surrender of socially responsive values to the demands of sheer consumerism will leave an organization without a core ideology. Such a surrender would also leave employees without a sense of how they might "make a difference" even though they might be celebrated as "entrepreneurs" within the context of newly structured work teams and "profit centers." In this regard, Mondragón's departure from its traditionally evangelistic stance about spreading cooperativism is disturbing. Even more notable has been the cooperatives' shift away from an idea of employee participation that is grounded in the rights of employees to contribute to policymaking. For it is in these two arenas that social values can be examined, articulated, and put forth in dialogue with others. Nevertheless, the freedom from the oppressive assembly-line technologies must be acknowledged and welcomed, as anyone who has ever worked in such rigid and depersonalizing industrial environments would agree.

Thus while in certain senses the Mondragón cooperatives are becoming decidedly less democratic, in other ways they are perhaps becoming more so. The specific answer to "What is happening to workplace democracy at Mondragón?" depends on what we mean by "democracy." The work environments of worker-owners at Mondragón, especially of those in newly restructured team-based organizations such as MCC's Irizar bus manufacturing plant or ULMA Construcción's building materials plant are allowing for more flexibility in the decisions and activities of employees. Thus the resident sociologist at MCC's Otalora Training Center, Mikel Lezamiz, could say, in 1994 and again in 1997, that "many *socios* are experiencing workplace democracy in a more concrete way than they have ever experienced it before." The employees of those firms report moderately high levels of job satisfaction, even as they express concerns about the increased workload that goes hand in hand with more on-the-job responsibilities. In the cooperatives of MAIER, MAPSA and ULMA-Forja, where I concentrated my field research, *socios* expressed cautious optimism about programs to restructure work processes according to the method of semiautonomous work teams.

The Mondragón cooperatives are becoming significantly *less* democratic in one important sense: employee participation is less and less valued either for its own sake or for how it contributes to shaping the policies that affect the cooperatives' work processes and market strategies. Nearly all of my interviewees in 1994 and 1997 spoke of the declining importance of the general assemblies, the increasingly blurred line between the functions of the governing councils and the management councils, and the lack of a role for ombudsman in most cooperatives' social councils (even in cases where the social council was perceived as effective and credible). The great symbolism surrounding voting in the cooperatives is clearly being supplanted by a new stress on participation at the level of one's job. Thus, the domain within which most employees see themselves as having influence is narrowing, and this feeling is acute among the temporary *socios* and the contract-based, nonowning employees.

For better and for worse, the *socios* and non-*socios* of the Mondragón cooperatives are very aware of their role as servants to the consumer. Employees must attend to their role as customers to the cooperatives' corporate suppliers, to the ways in which they are suppliers to outside purchasers, to the means by which departments within the firm are both suppliers and customers for one another, and to the manner in which the work process is rationalized as the achievement of external customer satisfaction. The relationship with the "customer" is coming to be privileged over employee relations and the employee's relationship to the cooperative itself. In the co-ops, as well as in the larger communities, this movement is described as "inevitable," "natural," "strategic," "necessary," and "just good business."

Constraints on and Possibilities for Participation Today

The currently popular images of the market and the consumer are being celebrated more than ever before. What happens when the production process and the people in it become redefined as "market," "customers," and "profit centers"? In a sense, these trends represent a natural extension of capitalistic ways of thinking—an expansion of "marketization." Yet these developments may mean even more "severance" or alienation at work and in the community (see Sayer

1991), as more and more social concerns are translated and thereby subordinated in the language of the market.

In such a society as the one we find prevailing in the industrialized world, the commodity, the thing, is no longer something "held in the hand" and then exchanged for another; it is no longer even simply an object transformed by layers of use, exchange, and symbolic meanings; it is no longer even just a service offered in the market. Rather, "commodity" becomes a social and economic concept that is applied to the creator or user of the "thing" itself. "Marx himself noted the effects of commodification in language: referring to people as 'hands' in industrial contexts" (Fairclough 1992: 207). Today we might say that the process of commodification has come to influence how we see not only products, services, and work processes but also the values associated with those.

Marx ([1865–72] 1977) recognized also that even the most abstract ideas, principles, and sacred symbols could be subject to a kind of commodification, where their market value became determined not so much by their use value or other kinds of meaning but rather by their currency of exchange. In this way, ethics itself can become a commodity that is "exchanged," with monetary value ascribed it to by one organization or another that is trying to "sell" itself as ethical. Commodification thus "contains" both meaning and value.

But how do we respond to the presumably well-meaning advertising campaigns of Benetton that feature power images of suffering people as a chief representation of the clothing manufacturer in the marketplace (compare Fialka 1997; Tinic 1997)? We may welcome this development if we see the organization promoting an awareness of pressing social issues. Still, there's a risk that those same issues are being packaged, reduced, and ultimately trivialized within the frame of a marketing strategy.

The effects of placing social values within a market context are not wholly predictable, however, because of the capacity for interpretive diversity and symbolic transformation (think again of changes in the symbol of "the consumer" over the course of the twentieth century). There will always be surprises in the appropriation of symbols by business and consumer culture, especially as some entrepreneurially minded individuals and organizations test the bounds of what is possible—even in a highly constrained marketing genre such as personals ads (compare Coupland 1996; Featherstone 1991). Yet there is a tendency for a value that is marketed to lose the sense that it stands for something apart from market calculations.

The "loss of value" for a symbol in the marketplace is exacerbated by a culture of communications that demands repetition and results in overuse (Baudrillard 1983). This is exactly the predicament faced by the corporate social responsibility movement today: the more it is talked about and the more crowded the bandwagon, the harder it becomes for "social responsibility" to retain a core of well-defined meaning around a set of lauded practices. As every business claims to be socially responsible and seeks to gain approval from professional associations, in a sense no business will be socially responsible. Or, at least, it will become very difficult to sort out authentic or deep commitments to the ideology from those that simply adopt the slogan for momentary convenience.

As employees are seen largely in terms of their "added value" (du Gay 1996a), have we really succeeded in commodifying the employee? As "internal customers" do employees ordinarily enjoy a fraction of the rights that external customers are said to have? Or do cynicism and opposition still exist behind this apparently sweeping trend?

Though capitalist exploitation of workers has been well documented since Marx's time, we can observe something new about the forms of alienation now appearing in the workplaces of industrialized society—what might be termed *commodified empowerment*. Talk of employees as "instruments" or "resources" is all around us, despite claims about an enlightened new workplace. Morally speaking, such terminology makes policies toward their "disposability" all the more thinkable (see Cheney and Carroll 1997; Conrad and Poole 1997), even while those who create the policies are laughing at Dilbert and other cartoons that bitingly portray the down sides of work life at the turn of the twenty-first century.

Despite genuine attempts to stimulate entrepreneurship inside the organization, including healthy competition between the "profit centers" that constitute what used to be departments or functions of the organization, the infusion of market language and ways of thinking into work activities seems to be reducing the freedom and significance of the worker and manager. The prevalence of such discourse and the consequent new pressures on employees are limiting options for imagining what organizations could be or should be.

We should recognize the ambiguities of key terms such as "participation," "quality," and "customer service," while understanding also the tendencies toward consolidation of meaning that may be quite restrictive. Communication theorist Dennis Mumby (1997) has recently explained that the concept of *hegemony* should be thought of neither as an unstoppable force that renders all individuals and organizations as cultural dupes nor an open-ended process of negotiation where subordinate groups simply remake meanings and activities as they wish (compare Clegg 1988; Gramsci [1929–30] 1971; Lukes 1974). Rather, forms of dominance and resistance are in dialectical tension with one another, and these relationships are neither stable nor wholly predictable.

The use of language in capitalism and in other institutions of our society can be slippery, as recent appropriations of the language of marketing by nearly all professions and sectors have shown (see Hall 1982; Mouffe 1992). In theory, linguistic and symbolic transformations are limitless; the creative power of language and visual imagery offers the creator of a message a remarkable array of options. For instance, "teamwork" is defined and practiced in dramatically different ways in various national, cultural, and organizational contexts. Japanese corporations' typical emphasis on the team as representing the corporation as a whole is in marked contrast to the common stress within some Swedish corporations on the autonomy of the group in production processes. And even within nations or in single industries we find an array of different practices under a single popular heading like "quality." The ambiguity itself serves as a strategic resource for policy-makers and managers (Eisenberg 1984). As a recent study of how employees understand and use corporate mission statements shows, the interpretations of "sacred" symbols within the organization may also be widely disparate and have varying implications for decision making and action (Fairhurst, Jordan, and Neuwirth 1997). In the transformation of one plantation-style agricultural organization to a worker co-op in Papua New Guinea in the 1980s, employees actually *quit* working after being designated as "owners" because they felt they were therefore no longer obliged as laborers (Bull 1998). On the shop floor, managerial initiatives and prescriptions will occasionally be transformed in ways that that provide workers greater space for action, as when bonus plans and other incentive pay schemes are used by employees to reorganize work flow to allow for more break time (see Collinson 1992; Lamphere 1995). Consider as well cases where employees in customer service training are demanding their own rights as customers by refusing to "buy" programs (see Gedye 1998). Here are examples of how a less powerful group can appropriate a term from the more powerful, thereby reversing or undermining its meaning (see Foucault 1978; Hayden 1998; Kingfisher 1996). It should not be assumed that organizationally sanctioned symbols, such as "core values," necessarily hold sway over the thoughts and practices of all or most organizational members.

But it is also true that at any given moment in the development of an institution or a society there are real limits to "polysemy" or to multiple or shifting interpretations (see Condit 1989). A kind of "discursive closure" or limitation on debate may occur, where alternatives to the prevailing viewpoint or terminology may be suppressed or not even thought about (Deetz 1992). These limits are to some extent determined by the material and symbolic resources at the disposal of any group that would travel against the prevailing winds of interpretation (Cloud 1996). Also, the abilities of people to persuade one another to accept this or that "paradigm" for, say, reorienting management policy, will be associated significantly with the prestige and popularity of the "gurus" who are promoting a particular approach (for example, TQM, Reengineering, *Kaizen*, and so forth). We should recognize the concentrated efforts of big business associations in spreading the word that the "free market"—as they define it—is the natural state of affairs. "Freedom" may be one of the most powerful and ambiguous terms in the U.S. cultural vocabulary, yet it is clear today that "freedom from governmental regulation" has the upper hand in political discourse over "freedom to organize workers."

The powerful image of "free trade" carries with it a sense of inevitability. So compelling is the metaphor that it actively discourages reflection. In the push for the North American Free Trade Agreement (NAFTA) in early 1994, only one member of the U.S. Senate could admit to having read the entire document (Nader and Wallach 1996). The phrase "rising tide that lifts all boats" continues to be employed by U.S. government and corporate heads to argue for the liberalization of trade and capital flows, thereby masking the elements of such treaties that actually serve to protect the interests of multinational companies. Such language deters questioning. Thus various groups of social activists around the world are trying to shift the discussion from *free* trade to *fair* trade.

At Mondragón the "received wisdom" of prominent management consultants and writers is often accepted virtually without question. From a number of managers I interviewed there, I heard comments along the lines of this one: "Well, what choice do we have than to adopt the best management programs of today?" But when I questioned them further on the meaning of "best," they usually pointed to the most popular books on organizations in the United States (such as *The Machine That Changed the World* by Womack, Jones, and Roos), to the managerial program exports of Japan (such as *Kaizen*), to the best-known management consultants worldwide (such as Peter Drucker), and to "the way everyone is talking about these things in America."

In informal conversations as well as formal interviews at Mondragón, there was almost always a tinge of ambivalence toward the three industrial giants—the United States, Germany, and Japan. My contacts essentially told me: "We have to *emulate* you, but we really don't want to be *like* you." But this two-sided stance seldom provoked a deep questioning of the management paradigms in currency in the industrialized world. There was, in fact, a surprising lack of trust in the wisdom of Mondragón's own extraordinary experience as a guide for future corporate policy. Despite the profound tradition of "solidarity" in the cooperatives, they were moving more and more toward a reconceptualization of the internal affairs of the organizations in largely market terms.

When I next visit Mondragón, I would not be surprised to hear description of different departments of a cooperative as "suppliers" and "customers." Indeed, MAIER seemed already to be using such language as it sought in the mid-1990s to mirror its external relations with customers with an image of "an internal market." This image may have certain merits, especially in terms of stressing everyone's accountability, but it is sorely limited in representing the broader purposes associated with work and with working together. The market metaphor needs competition!

To be sure, the precise local understandings of popular concepts such as the consumer, quality, and the market remain to be explored further in the cooperatives. I would not want to suggest that the appropriation of currently popular terms has obliterated Mondragón's distinctive cultural heritage. Nor would I want to imply a total convergence of meaning for the terms "efficiency" and "quality," any more than I would argue that "solidarity" has ceased to have multiple senses. Interesting and creative uses of terms such as "customer service" may well surprise both managers and analysts of the co-ops like me. Still, it's quite clear to me that the adoption of dominant managerial trends from outside the cooperatives, and specifically the recasting of "participation" in customer-oriented terms, represents far more than a superficial change in "talk." The marketization of Mondragón represents a profound organizational transformation.

In general, the market-oriented transformation of the workplace has probably reduced the space for the operation of intrinsic motivation. The parameters for legitimate meanings and practices of "participation" seem to be narrowing. When we say that employee participation is not of value for its own sake or even that it is a privilege, we are in effect placing the locus of control and motivation outside the boundaries of the organization. Yet most new programs of productivity, quality, and participation emphasize the *gains* in autonomy and self-determination for the individual employee. In the words of one of the strongest advocates of Total Quality Management, the concern is "with moving the focus of control from outside the individual to within; the objective being to make everyone accountable for their own performance, and to get them committed to attaining quality in a highly motivated fashion" (Oakland 1989: 26). But such employee empowerment has a big price tag in loss of independence.

In organizations from Mondragón co-ops to universities to city government, I have found that employees do have a strong sense of contradiction; at least they feel that there's something disingenuous about an organization demanding more "participation" in the form of work intensification while lauding the "entrepreneurial" possibilities in a specific job or on a work team. The contradiction becomes even more pronounced with the demand for increased upward reporting (production figures), downward surveillance (production targets), and peer group pressure, within and between work teams. Sociologist Graham Sewell (1998) speaks of "chimerical" control in today's organization: we find some unexpected bedfellows, given the hype for the New Workplace (U.S. Department of Labor 1994). Intensive monitoring of work behavior does not fit well with an ideology of "entrepreneurship" at the level of one's job unless we interpret the current trend of team-based organizing as simply another phase in the development of organizational control.

Employees in every sector are becoming deeply suspicious of programs directed at "empowerment," "quality," and "participation" because they recognize that with increased responsibility there is usually a demand for more work. With studies such as Guillermo J. Grenier's (1988), in which a quality circle program in a manufacturing company was revealed to be little more than a well-disguised union-busting effort, we can hardly wonder at the depth and persistence of employees' questioning.

The growth of such questioning at Mondragón, especially among younger professional employees, may call for a revival of participation in a new form. And, ironically, further questioning at the grassroots level may be fueled by new management-developed programs of participation. The December 1996 issue of MCC's magazine *TU* featured the "second generation" of *cooperativistas* and highlighted their entrepreneurial and independent spirit. Just as it would have been difficult, say, twenty-five years ago, to predict the dominant expressions of consumerism today in the industrialized world, so we cannot be sure than the seeming individualism and careerism of today's *socio* at Mondragón will not evolve into a new and dynamic form of engagement at work and in the community.

As the practical meanings of *participación* continue to evolve at Mondragón, we may see movement from the consumer culture "inward" toward the co-ops and from the programs of the co-ops "outward" toward the larger society (compare Elden 1981; Greenberg 1981; Huspek and Kendall 1991). That is, influences will likely be seen in both directions, as the surrounding society influences the course of the co-ops and the cooperatives' policies have an impact on host communities.

In my own university, a group of staff, faculty, and administrators has been working for more than four years on a "Quality of Worklife" (QWL) program, genuinely aimed at improving material and social working conditions for all campus employees. That project has enjoyed some real successes, such as a new staff sabbatical program. But the effort has also encountered paradoxes like those discussed in this book. One of the most difficult jobs has been to convince employees that the QWL project is not simply about applying pressure "nicely" so that already overworked and underpaid personnel will "give a little more" to the institution. University employees are understandably skeptical of some administrators' efforts to recast the internal affairs of the university in market-oriented terms, making the symbol of "the customer" applicable not only to students (which, by now, is the generally accepted way of labeling them) but also to one another.

From a neo-Weberian perspective, we can see that the market-oriented transformation of organizations tends to preclude systematic, probing, collective reflection on the meaning of work and the purposes of organizations. Weber's ([1968] 1978) incompletely articulated "fourth type" of organization would be one where the basic logic of relations at work is governed principally by a consensus around enduring and important social commitments (Rothschild-Whitt 1979; Satow 1975). Profound collective reflection over the constellation of values that guide our endeavors is what Stephen Kalberg (1980) calls "ethical substantive rationality." Such a conception and practice of work would necessitate thinking beyond the confines of the metaphors of market or customer.

A strong market orientation tends to grant market relations supremacy over other types of social or political analysis. As a logic for employee relations, such an orientation "frees up" workers from thinking about other persons (or, ultimately, themselves) in ways other than as participants in the supplier-customer chain. Just as a home buyer who enlists the services of a real estate agent is urged not to worry about the seller in the transaction, so an employee who is recast as a supplier/customer is implicitly guided away from thinking of his or her colleagues or co-workers as persons. Thus broader social concerns can also be pushed out of view. More generally, workplace democracy is pointed not toward a broader arena of political participation in society (as envisioned by Pateman 1970) but serves merely as a means of momentarily satisfying the customer. Though participation programs at Mondragón and elsewhere may be directed toward increased productivity and efficiency in the ultimate hope of providing more stable employment to the larger community, their design may reduce commitment and sacrifice within that community. How employee participation programs are framed and implemented should thus be monitored with an eye to their broader social implications.

Bureaucratic relations, as described so completely by Weber ([1968] 1978), thus take on a new cast or become legitimized within a new framework of understanding. In Weber's ideal type of "rational legal" organization, the fatal flaw he anticipated was that allegiance to the system itself could overshadow more basic or fundamental concerns about what the organization was doing and what it was for. Adherence to a set of rules, regulations, and standards could become such a preoccupation that a sense of larger purpose would be lost—for the employee and for the organization. The new "enterprise culture" may also largely forsake ethical reflection as it redefines work processes in market-oriented terms and sees broad-level standards for human resource management as a throwback to the days of bureaucratic inefficiency (du Gay 1996b).

In this new phase of bureaucratic development, many work processes are redesigned in terms of entrepreneurship, teamwork, and customer relations (see Edwards 1979). Today we witness a regime of productivity and efficiency that is directed outward toward the market. The organizations may be "flatter" and "post-Fordist" in many cases, but they are strongly bureaucratic in terms of the standardization of work activity under the imperative of ever-increasing "quality" (Boje and Winsor 1993).

In this type of organization, its very rationale, its reason for being, are the presumed needs of the customer and the presumed dictates of the market. This new orientation makes sense in terms of accountability, responsibility, and service. Yet, as we have seen, this trend can take on perverse and unexpected dimensions. For decisions about and by customers are seldom couched in terms other than the satisfaction of immediate wants and short-term goals. As organizations surrender the capacity to define their own internal standards, they lose a measure of integrity. And advocacy of social values and inspiration of the citizen-consumer gets lost in the rush toward ever more efficient production processes.

Even with the intended emphasis on innovation and dynamism within the new management paradigm, many organizational activities tend to be narrowly circumscribed, highly ritualized, and lacking in analysis. The new "nonbureaucratic" organization can thus be just as rigid as the much-criticized bureaucratic one. It can become a system preoccupied with making tiny improvements in its own "service," with little attention to broader purposes. Despite the high-minded talk about "vision," "mission," and "service," it can become just as trapped in systems of its own making.

These are some of the prevailing winds I feel at Mondragón and elsewhere. What, then, are the options available for escaping the constraints of "commodified employee empowerment" and for reasserting core social values in an organization like the Mondragón cooperatives? These are crucial questions in our reflections on the possibility for democratic, humane, and socially conscious work organizations around the world.

Reflections on the Market We Make

The whole matter of organizational values is difficult to grasp and hold because the values themselves are subject to ambiguity, transformation, and contradiction. The more we talk about some value and the means of assessing it, the more we may find ourselves tangled in a web of meaning of our own creation. A fine current example is the idea of "continuous improvement," an imperative for quality that has led many service organizations deliberately to understate quantitative indicators of their own performance so as to give themselves space to "improve" on the scale. Such are the irrationalities, even absurdities, of our seemingly most advanced systems of management.

The value of postmodern skepticism is its reminder that any of our projects, however noble, are likely to encounter some internal contradictions, produce some unexpected outcomes, and perhaps even become victims of their own labeling. This insight is particularly relevant to the domain of organizational values, where the quest for novel expressions of organizations' identities and missions produces a constant flow of messages about "what the organization *is*." Advertising, public relations, and marketing make it difficult even to ask about the "real" or authentic value commitments on the part of the organizations that employ them. It's not that these professions are inherently dishonest but that the business of producing public representations of the organization necessarily leads to a decline in "value" for the most talked-about symbols. This has occurred with the labels "green marketing" and "cutting edge technology."

Still, we would not give up on attempts to make organizations morally accountable, to humanize work, to give life to ideals of employee participation. We know that some businesses treat their employees better than others do. We can tell from experience that some institutions are more democratic than others. Some organizations are committed to social betterment, to the advancement of interests beyond their own aggrandizement.

It's convenient (and somewhat accurate) to say that by being players in an international market the Mondragón cooperatives engage certain pressures and requirements that are beyond their control. In an economic environment where capital as well as trade is being given freer flight, the co-ops are competing with many giant multi-nationals whose agenda does not include strong social commitments. Thus it's not surprising that Mondragón has pursued some of the same strategies as other large corporations to expand its capital base and minimize the effects of more open competition, such as joint ventures, strategic alliances, and acquisitions of factories in developing countries.

I am in no position to assess objectively the full extent of external economic pressures on the Mondragón cooperatives today, but my research does provide a vantage point for commenting on the social direction of the co-ops and especially the tendencies evident in their internal policies and wider discourses. The cooperatives are changing in dramatic ways. Not all of this change can be chalked up to external pressures, especially not in the sense of outside institutions using leverage to force Mondragón in line with practices of noncooperative multinational firms. The co-ops are still functioning largely as employee-owned enterprises, and a number of their socially inspired principles are still practiced. However, the judgment that the cooperatives are employee-*governed* needs to be modified with a complete recognition of the changing ideology and programs of participation there. The value of "participation" is rather systematically being relocated at the level of work production, redefined in terms of "continuous improvement" in production, and redirected toward the reference point of the customer.

The full scope of this transformation in one of Mondragón's core values is difficult to capture. First, some of the impetus for this change does come from relations with external suppliers and customers, many of whom have become both more demanding and more fickle. Second, the trend can be attributed in part to shifts in managerial strategy and programs toward "quality customer service." Third, this change in the culture of participation in the co-ops is consistent with broader cultural changes around Mondragón with the consumer at the center. Therefore, it would be appropriate to say neither that the "environment" (or market) is completely driving the cooperatives to change nor that the co-ops are fully in charge of their own future, but rather that a complex of influences has made certain values dominant there today.

Though this study has examined a wide range of values under pressure and in flux at Mondragón, the focus has clearly been on work-place democracy and employee participation. I chose these twin emphases for two reasons: to look closely at the democratic performance of a celebrated case and to consider the ambiguities and ironies surrounding the term "participation" as a means of observing the role of the employee in today's new workplace. The case of Mondragón, along with a host of other current examples, suggests that employee participation is a big symbolic umbrella under which we find a variety of types. Often it is employed to emphasize greater demands on and responsibilities of the worker. Sometimes the term becomes a disguise for the perpetuation of autocratic management practices and the introduction of new means of work surveillance. Occasionally it represents a deeper commitment to the capacity of members to determine some of the conditions under which they work. At Mondragón we have seen evidence of all three of these embodiments of participation, and more.

Democracy in the workplace should be assessed on two broad levels: specific opportunities by employees to contribute to the development of business strategy and the ways "participation" itself is open to negotiation by employees. Though we may decide that it's unrealistic in a particular case for all employees to have a shaping influence on corporate or organizational policy, we can say more confidently that everyone ought to have some capacity to affect the conditions and requirements of work. In this pursuit, labor unions, autonomous ombudsmen, and periodic self-assessment all have valuable roles to play—even in the worker-owned and worker-governed cooperative and despite the limitations of any of these measures when institutionalized over time. The right of self-determination at work extends beyond the currently popular notion of "self-management."

Finally, we cannot talk very long about workplace participation or democracy without dealing with the market and the ways we talk about the market. Relationships between the market and democracy are complex in that each can be seen as both supporting and undermining the other (Almond 1991). The Austrian economist Joseph Schumpeter ([1942] 1976) maintained that the market's tendency to break its own constraints would ironically pose the greatest threat to its long-term survival: market expansion would help to promote the very conditions for its reform or dissolution by undermining bonds of trust, commercial relationships, and the stability upon which the market's performance depends. The situation is further complicated by the way we *talk* about the market. Not only do we abstract it from human affairs so as to grant it something of a life of its own, but we also use slogans such as "free trade" in ways that obscure tendencies toward state intervention to help corporations escape the unpredictability of more open competition. As another example, our very use of the term "market globalization" hides the fact that most economies in the world are still overwhelmingly domestic.

The terminology of the market, marketing, and the consumer are dominating boardrooms and everyday decision making in ways that are deeply disturbing. Citizens, employees, and entire institutions are reduced in their social and ethical significance as a result. Also, market discourse can be used to further policies that show utter disregard for people, apart from some minimal and passing instrumental value—for example as "human resources" to be managed.

However, "marketspeak" and the relentless pursuit of "customer satisfaction" do suggest some of their own limitations, as revealed in the contradiction between rising corporate profits and CEOs' salaries, on the one hand, and some industries' cutbacks in personnel on the other. The acknowledged glut of production in many sectors is challenging the ethic of unlimited market expansion. Corporate entitlements from government are now being criticized as "corporate welfare." Associations of citizens have been mobilizing against the proposed Multilateral Agreement on Investment, which would further liberalize capital flow and fuel capital speculation. Some communities in the United Kingdom and in the United States have created local currencies, in order to promote principled and close relations between buyers and sellers. And former marketers and advertisers are promoting "buy nothing days" as new forms of consumer expression. These developments are exceptional but nonetheless important, as we contemplate what form the future market may take (see Jermier, Knights, and Nord 1994, on forms of resistance to organizational control).

These chinks in the mortar should be exposed and widened, allowing for more meaningful debates about democracy and the market—to the degree that these are possible in our symbol-saturated world. Within certain limits, there are options for symbolic and practical maneuvering by the consumer and the employee. Even acting within the world of marketization, people will find creative means of self-expression and pursue avenues toward social values. At work, where employees' creative options may well be more limited, we need to consider how new programs of participation are in the long run going to inhibit or inspire forms of resistance or change. Through the implementation of TQM or *Kaizen* certain avenues of employee discretion are widened. With that, there may be an opening to explore from the shop floor upward what meanings "entrepreneurship" and "teamwork" might hold in practice. As we have already seen, some employees are now using the metaphor of "internal markets" to argue strongly for their rights as "customers" of management's policies. Other employees are being more demanding about benefits and services provided by the employer. Also, many corporations are becoming surprised and disturbed by what they see as a less-than-loyal workforce.

Will consumer- and market-driven systems of employee participation simply reduce employees' actual opportunities for self-determination while demanding more and more of them in terms of work responsibility, speed, and output? Or will the organization of the future evolve or break into a variety of forms, with some allowing for more genuine worker autonomy and empowerment? Answering these questions may be one of the most urgent needs for the study of work to come.

WORKS CITED

Ackoff, Russell. 1994. *The Democratic Corporation*. New York: Oxford University Press.

Adams, Scott. 1995. *Ask Me How My Day Went: The 1996 Dilbert Calendar*. Kansas City MO.: Andrews and McMeel.

Adler, Paul S. 1992. "The 'Learning Bureaucracy': New United Motor Manufacturing, Inc." *Research in Organizational Behavior* 15: 111–94.

Adler, Paul S., and Bryan Borys. 1996. "Two Types of Bureaucracy: Enabling and Coercive." *Administrative Science Quarterly* 41: 61–89.

Adler, Paul S., and Robert E. Cole. 1993. "Designed for Learning: A Tale of Two Auto Plants." *Sloan Management Review*, Spring: 85–93.

Adler, G. Stoney, and Phillip K. Tompkins. 1997. "Electronic Performance Monitoring: An Organizational Justice and Concertive Control Perspective." *Management Communication Quarterly* 10: 259–88.

Almond, Gabriel. 1991. "Capitalism and Democracy." *Political Science and Politics* 24: 467–74.

Alvesson, Mats. 1992. "Cultural-Ideological Modes of Management Control: A Theory and a Case Study of a Professional Service Company." *Communication Yearbook* 16: 3–42.

Argyris, Chris. 1998. "Empowerment: The Emperor's New Clothes." *Harvard Business Review*, May–June, 98–107.

Arizmendiarrieta, José María. 1983. *Pensamientos*. Mondragón, Spain: MCC.

Ashcraft, Karen Lee. 1998. "Assessing Alternative(s): Contradiction and Invention in a Feminist Organization." Ph.D. diss., University of Colorado at Boulder.

Azurmendi, Joxe. 1984. *El Hombre Cooperativo: Pensamiento de Arizmendiarrieta*. Mondragón, Spain: Caja Laboral Popular.

Aune, James. 1996. "Inevitability and Perversity: The Loci of Capitalist Arguments about Labor." Paper presented at the annual meeting of the Speech Communication Association, San Diego.

Bachrach, Peter, and Aryeh Botwinick. 1992. *Power and Empowerment: A Radical Theory of Participatory Democracy*. Philadelphia: Temple University Press.

Bailey, W. 1996. "Corporate/Commercial Speech and the Marketplace First Amendment—Whose Right Was It, Anyway?" *Southern Communication Journal* 61: 122–38.

Bakhtin, Mikhail M. 1981. *The Dialogic Imagination*. Trans. M. Holquist and C. Emerson; ed. M. Holquist. Austin: University of Texas Press.

Banta, Martha. 1993. *Taylored Lives: Narrative Productions in the Age of Taylor, Veblen, and Ford*. Chicago: University of Chicago Press.

Barker, James. 1993. "Tightening the Iron Cage: Concertive Control in the Self-managing Organization." *Administrative Science Quarterly* 38: 408–37.

Barker, James R., and George Cheney. 1994. "The Concept and Practices of Discipline in Contemporary Organizational Life." *Communication Monographs* 61: 19–43.

Barker, James R., and Phillip K. Tompkins. 1994. "Identification in the Self-managing Organization." *Human Communication Research* 21: 223–40.

Barlett, Donald L., and James B. Steele. 1998. "Corporate Welfare." *Time*, 9 November, 18–21.

Barley, Stephen R., and Gideon Kunda. 1992. "Design and Devotion: Surges of Rational and Normative Ideologies of Control in Managerial Discourse." *Administrative Science Quarterly* 37: 363–99.

Barnard, Chester I. [1938] 1968. *The Functions of the Executive* (30th anniv. ed.). Cambridge: Harvard University Press.

Batstone, Eric. 1983. "Organization and Orientation: A Life Cycle Model of French Cooperatives." *Economic and Industrial Democracy* 4: 139–61.

Baudrillard, Jean. 1983. *In the Shadow of Silent Majorities*. New York: Semiotext(e).

——. 1996. *The System of Objects*. Trans. J. Benedict. London: Verso.

Belk, Russell W., Melanie Wallendorf, and John F. Sherry, Jr. 1991. "The Sacred and the Profane in Consumer Behavior: Theodicy on the Odyssey." *Highways and Byways of the Association for Consumer Research*.

Benders, Jos. 1996. "Leaving Lean? Recent Changes in the Production Organization of Some Japanese Plants." *Economic and Industrial Democracy* 17: 9–38.

Bennett, Amanda. 1990. *The Death of the Organization Man*. New York: Morrow.

Berger, Lisa, and Chris Clamp. 1983. "Women Struggle to Overcome Social and Educational Barriers Which Keep Them Out of the Professional Positions of the Mondragón Cooperatives." *Workplace Democracy* 10(4): 6–8.

Berggren, Christian. 1992. *Alternatives to Lean Production: Work Organization in the Swedish Auto Industry*. Ithaca: ILR Press.

——. 1994. "NUMMI vs. Uddevalla." *Sloan Management Review*, Winter: 37–49.

Bernstein, Paul. 1976. "Necessary Elements for Effective Worker Participation in Decision Making." *Journal of Economic Issues* 10: 490–522.

Boje, David M., and Robert D. Winsor. 1993. "The Resurrection of Taylorism: Total Quality Management's Hidden Agenda." *Journal of Organizational Change Management* 6 (4): 57–71.

Bolle de Bal, Marcel. 1990. "Participation: Its Contradictions, Paradoxes and Promises." In *International Handbook of Participation in Organizations, Vol. 1: Organizational Democracy—Taking Stock*, ed. Cornelius J. Lammers and György Széll. Oxford: Oxford University Press.

Bradley, Keith, and Alan Gelb. 1982. "The Replication and Sustainability of the Mondragón Experiment." *British Journal of Industrial Relations* 20: 20–33.

——. 1983. *Cooperation at Work: The Mondragón Experience*. London: Heinemann Educational Books.

Braverman, Harry. 1974. *Labor and Monopoly Capital: The Degradation of Work in the Twentieth Century*. New York and London: Monthly Review Press.

Bull, Allan. 1998. Personal communication. 2 October.

Bullis, Connie, and Betsy Wackernagel Bach. 1989. "Socialization Turning Points: An Examination of Change in Organizational Identification." *Western Journal of Speech Communication* 53: 273–93.

Bullis, Connie A., and Phillip K. Tompkins. 1989. "The Forest Ranger Revisited: A Study of Control Practices and Identification." *Communication Monographs* 56: 287–306.

Burawoy, Michael. 1979. *Manufacturing Consent: Changes in the Labor Process under Monopoly Capitalism*. Chicago: University of Chicago Press.

Burke, Kenneth. 1966. *Language as Symbolic Action*. Berkeley: University of California Press.

——. [1950] 1969. *A Rhetoric of Motives*. Berkeley: University of California Press.

Caja Laboral Popular. 1986. *El Consejo Social: Pasado, Presente y Futuro*. Mondragón, Spain: CLP.

Campbell, Gordon. 1998. "Social Irresponsibility." *New Zealand Listener*, 21 March, 26.

Carey, Alex. 1995. *Taking the Risk Out of Democracy: Propaganda in the U.S. and Australia*. Sydney: University of New South Wales Press.

Castells, Manuel. 1996. *The Rise of Network Society*. Malden, Mass.: Blackwell.

Cheney, George. 1983a. "The Rhetoric of Identification and the Study of Organizational Communication." *Quarterly Journal of Speech* 69: 143–58.

——. 1983b. "On the Various and Changing Meanings of Organizational Membership: A Field Study of Organizational Identification." *Communication Monographs* 50: 342–62.

——. 1991. *Rhetoric in an Organizational Society: Managing Multiple Identities*. Columbia: University of South Carolina Press.

——. 1992. "The Corporate Person (Re) Presents Itself." In *Rhetorical and Critical Approaches to Public Relations*, ed. Elizabeth L. Toth and Robert L. Heath. Hillsdale, N.J.: Erlbaum.

——. 1995. "Democracy in the Workplace: Theory and Practice from the Perspective of Communication." *Journal of Applied Communication Research* 23: 167–200.

——. 1997. "The Many Meanings of 'Solidarity': The Negotiation of Values in the Mondragón Worker Complex under Pressure." In *Case Studies in Organizational Communication 2*, ed. Beverly D. Sypher. New York: Guilford.

——. 1998. "Does Workplace Democracy Have a Future?" *At Work*, May–June, 15–17.

——. In press–a. "Forms of Connection and Severance in and around the Mondragón Workers Cooperatives." In *Communication and Community*, ed. Gregory Shepherd and Eric Rothenbuhler. Albany: SUNY Press.

——. In press–b. "It's the Economy, Stupid! A Rhetorical-Communication Perspective on the Market Today." *Australian Journal of Communication*.

Cheney, George, and James Brancato. 1992. "Scientific Management's Rhetorical Force and Enduring Impact." Working paper, University of Colorado at Boulder.

Cheney, George, and Craig E. Carroll. 1997. "The Person as Object in Discourses in and around Organizations." *Communication Research* 24: 593–630.

Cheney, George, and Lars T. Christensen. In press. "Identity at Issue: Linkages between 'Internal' and 'External' Organizational Communication." In *The New Handbook of Organizational Communication*, ed. Fredric M. Jablin and Linda L. Putnam. Thousand Oaks, Calif.: Sage.

Cheney, George, and Greg Frenette. 1993. "Persuasion and Organization: Values, Logics, and Accounts in Contemporary Corporate Public Discourse." In *The Ethical Nexus*, ed. Charles Conrad. Norwood, N.J.: Ablex.

Cheney, George, Jill J. McMillan, and Roy O. Schwartzman. 1997. "Should We Buy the Student-as-Consumer Metaphor." *Montana Professor* 7 (3): 8–10.

Cheney, George, Joseph Straub, Laura Speirs-Glebe, Cynthia Stohl, Dan De Gooyer, Jr., Susan Whalen, Kathy Garvin-Doxas, and David Carlone. 1998. "Democracy, Participation, and Communication at Work: A Multidisciplinary Review." In *Communication Yearbook 21*, ed. Michael E. Roloff. Thousand Oaks, Calif.: Sage.

Cheney, George, and Steven L. Vibbert. 1987. "Corporate Discourse: Public Relations and Issue Management." In *Handbook of Organizational Communication: An Interdisciplinary Perspective*, ed. Fredric M. Jablin, Linda L. Putnam, Lyman W. Porter, and Karlene H. Roberts. Thousand Oaks, Calif.: Sage.

Cheney, George, and Theodore E. Zorn. 1999. "Is Serving the Customer a Noble Mission or a Misguided Ideology?" *At Work*, Jan.–Feb., 12–14.

Chomsky, Noam. 1994. "Secrets, Lies, and Democracy." In *Interviews with David Barsamian*. Tucson: Odonian Press.

Christensen, Lars T. 1994. "Talking to Ourselves: Management through Auto-communication." *MTC Kontakten*, November (Jubilæmstidsskrift): 32–37.

———. 1995. "The Marketing Culture: Buffering Organizational Identity." *Organization Studies* 16: 651–772.

———. 1996. "Flexibility as Communication: A Deconstruction of the Marketing Discourse of Organizational Change." Working paper no. 4, Odense Universitet, Denmark, Department of Marketing, March.

———. 1997. "Marketing as Auto-communication." *Consumption, Markets, and Culture* 1 (2): 1–31.

Christensen, Lars T., and George Cheney. In press. "When Organizations Talk about Identity: Self-absorption Confronts Lack of Involvement in the Corporate Identity Game." In *The Expressive Organization*, ed. Majken Schultz, Mary Jo Hatch, and Mogens Holten Larsen. Oxford: Oxford University Press.

Clair, Robin P. 1996. "The Political Nature of the Colloquialism, 'A Real Job': Implications for Organizational Socialization." *Communication Monographs* 63: 249–67.

Clay, Eric. 1994. "Toward a Theory of Participation: Neither Democracy nor Equality Is Sufficient for Engagement." *Participatory Communication Research Network Newsletter* 2: 1–8.

Clegg, Stewart. 1983. "Organizational Democracy, Power and Participation." In *International Yearbook of Organizational Democracy, Vol. 1: Organizational Democracy and Political Processes*, ed. Colin Couch and Frank A. Heller. Chichester, England: Wiley.

———. 1988. *Frameworks of Power*. London: Sage.

Cloud, Dana. 1994. "The Materiality of Discourse as Oxymoron: A Challenge to Critical Rhetoric." *Western Journal of Communication* 58: 141–63.

———. 1996. "Fighting for Words: The Limits of Symbolic Power in the Staley Lockout, 1993–1996." Paper presented at the annual meeting of the Speech Communication Association, San Diego, Calif.

Coleman, James A. 1974. *Power and the Structure of Society*. New York: Norton.

Collins, Roger. 1990. *The Basques*. 2d ed. London: Basil Blackwell.

Collinson, David L. 1992. *Managing the Shop Floor: Subjectivity, Masculinity, and Workplace Culture*. Berlin: Walter de Gruyter.

Colomer, Josep C. 1995. "Conflictos Respecto a la Práctica de los Principios y Valores Cooperativos: El Caso de España." In *Anuario de Estudios Cooperativos*. Bilbao: Universidad de Deusto.

Condit, Celeste M. 1989. "The Rhetorical Limits of Polysemy." *Critical Studies in Mass Communication* 6: 103–22.

Conrad, Charles, and Marshall Scott Poole. 1997. "Introduction." Special Issue on Communication in the Age of the Disposable Worker. *Communication Research* 24: 581–92.

Cooren, François. 1998. Personal communication with the author, May.

Cornforth, Chris. 1995. "Patterns of Cooperative Movement: Beyond the Degeneration Thesis." *Economic and Industrial Democracy* 16: 487–524.

Cotton, John L. 1993. *Employee Involvement: Methods for Improving Performance and Work Attitudes*. Newbury Park, Calif.: Sage.

Coupland, Justine. 1996. "Dating Advertisements: Discourses of the Commodified Self." *Discourse and Society* 7: 187–208.

Courtright, John A., Gail T. Fairhurst, and L. Edna Rogers. 1989. "Interaction Patterns in Organic and Mechanistic Systems." *Academy of Management Journal* 32: 773–802.

Cox, Harvey. 1999. "The Market as God." *Atlantic Monthly*, March, 18–23.

Crable, Richard E., and Steven L. Vibbert. 1993. "Mobil's Epideictic Advocacy: Observations of Prometheus-Bound." *Communication Monographs* 4: 380–94.

Cross, Kelvin F., John J. Feather, and Richard L. Lynch. 1994. *Corporate Renaissance: The Art of Reengineering*. Malden, Mass.: Blackwell.

Dachler, H. Peter, and Bernhard Wilpert. 1978. "Conceptual Dimensions and Boundaries of Participation in Organizations: A Critical Evaluation." *Administrative Science Quarterly* 23: 1–39.

Dahl, Robert. 1961. *Who Governs? Democracy and Power in the American City*. New Haven: Yale University Press.

——. 1985. *A Preface to Economic Democracy*. Berkeley: University of California Press.

Dale, Barrie G., Cary L. Cooper, and Adrian Wilkinson. 1997. *Managing Quality and Human Resources: A Guide to Continuous Improvement*. Oxford: Blackwell.

Daly, Herman, and John B. Cobb, Jr. 1994. *For the Common Good*. 2d ed. Boston: Beacon.

Dauncey, Guy. 1998. *After the Crash: The Emergence of the Rainbow Economy*. Suffolk, England: Green Print.

de Azaola, José Miguel. 1988. *El País Vasco*. Madrid: Instituto de Estudios Económicos.

de Certeau, Michel. 1984. *The Practice of Everday Life*. London: University of California Press.

De Cock, Christian. 1998. " 'It Seems to Fill My Head with Ideas': A Few Thoughts on Postmodernism, TQM, and BPR." *Journal of Management Inquiry* 7: 144–53.

Deetz, Stanley. 1992. *Democracy in an Age of Corporate Colonization*. Albany: State University of New York Press.

——. 1995. *Transforming Communication, Transforming Business*. Creskill, N.J.: Hampton.

Deming, W. Edwards. 1986. *Out of the Crisis*. Cambridge: MIT Press.

de Otazu y Llana, Alfonso. 1986. *El Igualitarismo Vasco: Mito y Realidad*. San Sebastián, Spain: Editorial Txertoa.

Derber, Charles. 1998. *Corporation Nation*. New York: St. Martin's.

Derber, Charles, and William Schwartz. 1983. "Toward a Theory of Worker Participation." *Sociological Inquiry* 53: 61–78.

Dickson, John W. 1979. "Values and Rationales of Key Organizational Members for Participation." *Personnel Review* 8: 6–13.

Donnellon, Anne, and Maureen Scully. 1994. "Teams, Performance, and Rewards: Will the Post-bureaucratic Organization Be a Post-meritocratic Organization?" In *Post-bureaucratic Organizational Change*, eds. Charles Heckscher and Anne Donnellon. Thousand Oaks, Calif.: Sage.

Douglas, Mary. 1986. *How Institutions Think.* Syracuse, N.Y.: Syracuse University Press.

Drucker, Peter. 1992. "The New Society of Organizations." *Harvard Business Review*, Sept.–Oct.: 95–104.

du Gay, Paul. 1996a. *Consumption and Identity at Work.* London: Sage.

——. 1996b. "Organizing Identity: Entrepreneurial Governance and Public Management." In *Questions of Cultural Identity*, ed. Stuart Hall and Paul du Gay. London: Sage.

du Gay, Paul, and Graeme Salaman. 1992. "The Culture of the Customer." *Journal of Management Studies* 29: 615–33.

Edelman, Murray. 1985. "Political Language and Political Reality." *PS*, Winter 1985: 10–19.

Edmondson, Brad. 1991. "Remaking a Living." *UTNE Reader*, July–Aug.: 66–75.

Edwards, Richard. 1979. *Contested Terrain: The Transformation of the Workplace in the Twentieth Century.* New York: Basic Books.

Ehrensal, Kenneth N. 1995. "Discourses of Global Competition." *Journal of Organizational Change Management* 8: 5–16.

Eisenberg, Eric M. 1984. "Ambiguity as Strategy in Organizational Communication." *Communication Monographs* 51: 227–42.

Elden, J. Maxwell. 1981. "Political Efficacy at Work: The Connection between More Autonomous Forms of Workplace Organizations and More Participatory Politics." *American Political Science Review* 75: 43–58.

Ellerman, David. 1982. "The Socialization of Entrepreneurship: The Empresarial Division of the Caja Laboral Popular." Working paper, Industrial Cooperatives Association, Boston.

——. 1984. "The Mondragón Cooperative Movement." Working paper, Harvard Business School, Cambridge.

——. 1990. *The Democratic Worker-owned Firm: A New Model for East and West.* Boston: Unwin Hyman.

Estes, Ralph. 1996. *Tyranny of the Bottom Line: Why Corporations Make Good People Do Bad Things.* San Francisco: Berrett-Koehler.

Etzioni, Amitai. 1975. *A Comparative Analysis of Complex Organizations.* Rev. ed. New York: Free Press.

Ewen, Stuart. 1976. *Captains of Consciousness.* New York: McGraw-Hill.

——. 1988. *All Consuming Images.* New York: Basic Books.

Ewing, David. 1977. *Freedom inside the Organization.* New York: Dutton.

Ezzamel, Mahmoud, and Hugh Willmott. 1998. "Accounting for Teamwork: A Critical Study of Group-based Systems of Organizational Control." *Administrative Science Quarterly* 43: 358–96.

Fairclough, Norman. 1992. *Discourse and Social Change.* Cambridge, England: Polity Press.

——. 1993. "Critical Discourse Analysis and Marketization of Public Discourse: The Universities." *Discourse and Society*. 4: 133–68.

Fairhurst, Gail T. 1993. "Echoes of the Vision: When the Rest of the Organization Talks Total Quality." *Management Communication Quarterly* 6: 331–71.

Fairhurst, Gail T., Jerry Monroe Jordan, and Kurt Neuwirth. 1997. "Why Are We Here? Managing the Meaning of an Organizational Mission Statement." *Journal of Applied Communication Research* 25(4): 243–63.

Fairhurst, Gail T., and Robert A. Sarr. 1996. *The Art of Framing*. San Francisco: Jossey-Bass.

Fairhurst, Gail T., and Ronald Wendt. 1993. "The Gap in Total Quality." *Management Communication Quarterly* 6: 441–51.

Featherstone, Mike. 1991. *Consumer Culture and Postmodernism*. London: Sage.

Feldman, Martha, and James G. March. 1981. "Information in Organizations as Signal and Symbol." *Administrative Science Quarterly* 26: 171–86.

Fialka, John. 1997. "Clear Skies Are Goal as Pollution is Turned into a Commodity." *Wall Street Journal*, 3 October, A-1, 4.

Foucault, Michel. 1978. *The History of Sexuality, Vol. 1: An Introduction*. Trans. R. Hurley. New York: Vintage.

——. 1984. *The Foucault Reader*, ed. Paul Rabinow. New York: Pantheon.

Freeman, Richard B., and James L. Medoff. 1984. *What Do Unions Do?* New York: Basic Books.

Freundlich, Fred. 1996. "The Mondragón Cooperatives: Changes and Questions in the Global Economy." *Grassroots Economic Organizing Newsletter*, 20, Jan.–Feb., 7.

Friedman, Andrew. 1977. *Industry and Labor: Class Struggle at Work and Monopoly Capitalism*. London: Macmillan.

Friedman, Milton. 1962. *Capitalism and Freedom*. Chicago: University of Chicago Press.

Gabriel, Yiannis, and Tim Lang. 1995. *The Unmanageable Consumer*. London: Sage.

Galbraith, John Kenneth. 1978. *The New Industrial State*. 3rd ed. Boston: Houghton Mifflin.

Galloway, Chris. 1998. "(Re)Creating Consent: Public Relations, Professionalism and Contagious Thought." Paper presented at the Australian-New Zealand Communication Association annual conference, Hamilton, N.Z., July.

Gedye, Roseann. 1998. "Research Proposal on Market-driven Restructuring in New Zealand's Public Sector." Unpublished paper, University of Waikato, Hamilton, N.Z.

GEO: Grassroots Economic Organizing Newsletter. 1996. Issue 20: "Mondragón: Model or Myth?" Jan.–Feb.

George, William R. 1990. "Internal Marketing and Organizational Behavior: A Partnership in Developing Customer-conscious Employees at Every Level." *Journal of Business Research* 20: 63–78.

Georgiou, Petro. 1981. "The Goal Paradigm and Notes toward a Counter Paradigm." In *Complex Organizations: Critical Perspectives*, ed. M. Zey-Ferrell and M. Aiken. Glenview, Ill: Scott, Foresman.

Gibson-Graham, J. K. 1996. *The End of Capitalism (as we knew it)*. Oxford: Blackwell.

Gillespie, Richard. 1991. *Manufacturing Knowledge: A History of the Hawthorne Experiments*. Cambridge: Cambridge University Press.

Goll, Irene. 1991. "Environment, Corporate Ideology, and Employee Involvement Programs." *Industrial Relations* 30: 138–49.

Gopnik, Adam. 1997. "Trouble at the Tower." *New Yorker*, 4 August, 80.

Gordon, David. 1996. *Fat and Mean: The Corporate Squeeze of Working Americans and the Myth of Managerial "Downsizing."* New York: Martin Kessler Books/Free Press.

Graham, Laurie. 1993. "Inside a Japanese Transplant: A Critical Perspective." *Work and Occupations* 20: 147–73.

——. 1995. *On the Line at Subaru-Isuzu: The Japanese Model and the American Worker*. Ithaca, N.Y.: ILR Press.

Gramsci, Antonio. [1929–30] 1971. *Selections from the Prison Notebooks*. Trans. Q. Hoare and G. Nowell Smith. New York: International.

Gray, John N. 1998. *False Dawn*. New York: New Press.

Greenberg, Edward S. 1981. "Industrial Self-management and Political Attitudes." *American Political Science Review* 75: 29–42.

——. 1986. *Workplace Democracy: The Political Effects of Participation*. Ithaca, N.Y.: Cornell University Press.

Greenwood, Davydd, and José L. González. 1989. *Culturas de FAGOR*. San Sebastián, Spain: Editorial Txertoa.

——. 1992. *Industrial Democracy as Process: Participatory Action Research in the FAGOR Cooperative Group of Mondragón*. Van Gorcum, Netherlands, and Stockholm: Swedish Center for Working Life.

Greider, William. 1997a. *One World, Ready or Not: The Manic Logic of Global Capitalism*. New York: Simon and Schuster.

——. 1997b. "Planet of Pirates: The Manic Logic of Global Capitalism." *Utne Reader*, May–June: 70+.

Grenier, Guillermo J. 1988. *Inhuman Relations: Quality Circles and Antiunionism in American Industry*. Philadelphia: Temple University Press.

Grupo Cooperativo Mondragón (GCM). 1989. *Congreso del Grupo Cooperativo Mondragón: Compendio de Normas Aprobadas*. Mondragón, Spain: GCC.

Gustavsen, Björn. 1992. *Dialogue and Development: Theory of Communication, Action Research, and the Restructuring of Working Life*. Van Gorcum, Assen/Maastricht: Arbetslivscentrum.

Habermas, Jürgen. 1989. "The Public Sphere: An Encyclopedia Article." In *Critical Theory and Society: A Reader*, ed. Stephen E. Bronner and Douglas MacKay Kellner. New York: Routledge.

Hacker, Sally L., and Clara Elcorobairutia. 1987. "Women Workers in the Mondragón Systen of Industrial Cooperatives." *Gender and Society* 1: 358–79.

Halal, William E. 1996. *The New Management: Democracy and Enterprise Are Transforming Organizations*. San Francisco: Berrett-Koehler.

Hall, Stuart. 1982. "The Rediscovery of 'Ideology': Return of the Repressed in Media Studies." In ed. Michael Gurevitch, Tony Bennett, James Curran, and Janet Woolacott. *Culture, Society, and the Media*, New York: Methuen.

Hansmann, Henry. 1990. "When Does Worker Ownership Work? ESOPs, Law Firms, Codetermination, and Economic Democracy." *Yale Law Journal* 99: 1749–816.

Harding, Sandra. 1994. Unpublished notes on Mondragón. June.

——. 1998. "The Decline of the Mondragón Cooperatives." *Australian Journal of Social Issues* 33(1): 59–76.

Harrison, Bennett. 1994. *Lean and Mean: Why Large Coporations Will Continue to Dominate the Global Economy*. New York: Guilford.

Harrison, Teresa M. 1992. "Designing the Post-bureaucratic Organization: Toward Egalitarian Organizational Structure." *Australian Journal of Communication* 19(2): 14–29.

——. 1994. "Communication and Interdependence in Democratic Organizations." In *Communication Yearbook 17*, ed. Stanley Deetz. Thousand Oaks, Calif.: Sage.

Hartman, Lee. 1997. "What is a Co-op?" Working paper, Neighborhood Food Co-op, Carbondale, Ill.

Hawken, Paul. 1993. *The Ecology of Commerce: A Declaration of Sustainability*. New York: HarperCollins.

Hayden, Sara. 1998. "Reversing the Discourse of Sexology: Margaret Higgins Sanger's 'What Every Girl Should Know!' Working paper, University of Montana–Missoula.

Heckscher, Charles, and Anne Donnellon, eds. 1994. *The Post-bureaucratic Organization: New Perspectives on Organizational Change*. Thousand Oaks, Calif.: Sage.

Held, David. 1996. *Models of Democracy*. 2ed. Stanford, Calif.: Stanford University Press.

Hirschman, A. O. 1972. *Exit, Voice, and Loyalty: Responses to Decline in Firms, Organizations, and States*. Cambridge: Harvard University Press.

Holloway, Bruce. 1998. "Jobless Good for Business: Economist." *Waikato Times*, 6 August, 3.

Huet, Timothy. 1997. "Can Coops Go Global? Mondragón is Trying." *Dollars and Sense*, Nov.–Dec.: 16–19.

Humphries, Maria. 1998. "For the Common Good? New Zealanders Comply with Quality Standards." *Organisation Science* 9 (6): 738–49.

Huspek, Michael, and Kathleen Kendall. 1991. "On Withholding Political Voice: An Analysis of the Political Vocabulary of a 'Non-political' Speech Community." *Quarterly Journal of Speech* 77: 1–19.

International Cooperative Alliance. 1996. *Statement on the Cooperative Identity*. Madrid: Confederación Española de Cooperativas de Trabajo Asociado.

Ituarte, Patxi. 1994. "Notes on the Religious Context for the Cooperatives." Unpublished paper. Oñati, Spain, March.

Jacob, Betty M., and Phillip E. Jacob. 1984. "Values and the Active Community." In *International Perspectives on Organizational Democracy, Vol. 2,* ed. Bernhard Wilpert and Arndt Sorge. Chichester, England: John Wiley.

Jacques, Roy. 1996. *Manufacturing the Employee: Management Knowledge from the 19th to the 20th Centuries.* Thousand Oaks, Calif.: Sage.

Jain, Hem C., and Anthony Giles. 1985. "Workers' Participation in Western Europe: Implications for North America." *Relations Industrielles* 40: 747–775.

Jermier, John M., David Knights, and Walter R. Nord, eds. 1994. *Resistance and Power in Organizations.* London: Routledge.

Kalberg, Stephen. 1980. "Max Weber's Types of Rationality: Cornerstones for the Analysis of Rationalization Processes in History." *American Journal of Sociology* 85: 1145–79.

Kanter, Rosabeth Moss. 1982. "Dilemmas of Managing Participation." *Organizational Dynamics* 11(1): 5–27.

Kasmir, Sharryn. 1996. *The Myth of Mondragón: Cooperatives, Politics, and Working-class Life in a Basque Town.* Albany: State University of New York Press.

Keat, Russell. 1991. "Consumer Sovereignty and the Integrity of Practices." In *Enterprise Culture,* ed. Russell Keat and Nicholas Abercrombie. London: Routledge.

Kemmis, Daniel. 1990. *Community and the Politics of Place.* Norman: University of Oklahoma Press.

Kerfoot, Deborah, and David Knights. 1995. "Empowering the Quality Worker: The Seduction and Contradiction of the Total Quality Phenomenon." In *Making Quality Critical: New Perspectives on Organizational Change,* ed. Adrian Wilkinson and Hugh Willmott. London: Routledge.

King, Ralph T. 1998. "Levi's Factory Workers Are Assigned to Teams, and Morale Takes a Hit." *Wall Street Journal,* 20 May, A-1.

Kingfisher, Catherine Pélissier. 1996. "Women on Welfare: Conversational Sites of Acquiescence and Dissent." *Discourse and Society* 7: 531–58.

Klingel, Sally. 1993. *From Revolution to Evolution: Development of the Social Councils at Mondragón.* Master's thesis, Cornell University.

Knights, David, and Hugh C. Willmott. 1987. "Organizational Culture as Management Strategy: A Critique and Illustration from the Financial Services Industry." *International Studies of Management and Organization* 17: 40–63.

Kochan, Thomas A., Harry C. Katz, and Robert B. McKersie. [1986] 1994. *The Transformation of American Industrial Relations.* Ithaca, N.Y.: ILR Press.

Kochan, Thomas A., and Russell D. Lansbury. 1997. "Lean Production and Changing Employment Relations in the International Auto Industry." *Economic and Industrial Democracy* 18: 597–620.

Kohn, Alfie. 1986. *No Contest: The Case against Competition.* Boston: Houghton Mifflin.

Korten, David C. 1995. *When Corporations Rule the World.*

———. 1999. *The Post-corporate world.* San Francisco: Berrett-Koehler. San Francisco: Berrett-Koehler and Kumarian Press.

Krugman, Paul. 1997. *Pop Internationalism*. Cambridge: MIT Press.

Kunda, Gideon. 1992. *Engineering Culture: Control and Commitment in a High-tech Corporation*. Philadelphia: Temple University Press.

Kuttner, Robert. 1997. *Everything for Sale: The Virtues and Limits of Markets*. New York: Knopf.

Lamphere, Louise. 1995. "Bringing the Family to Work: Women's Culture on the Shop Floor." *Feminist Studies* 11: 519–40.

Lane, Robert E. 1991. *The Market Experience*. Cambridge: Cambridge University Press.

Langley, Monica. 1998. "Nuns' Zeal for Profits Shapes Hospital Chain, Wins Wall Street Fans." *Wall Street Journal*, 7 January, A-1.

Laufer, Romain, and Catherine Paradeise. 1990. *Marketing Democracy: Public Opinion and Media Formation in Democratic Societies*. New Brunswick, N.J.: Transaction Books.

Lawler, Edward E., Susan A. Mohrman, and Gerald E. Ledford. 1995. *Creating High-performance Organizations*. San Francisco: Jossey Bass.

Leitch, Shirley, and David Neilson. In press. "Bringing Publics into Public Relations: New Theoretical Frameworks for Practice." In *Handbook of Public Relations*, ed. Robert L. Heath and Gabriel Vasquez. Thousand Oaks, Calif: Sage.

Livesey, Sharon. 1999. "McDonald's and the Environmental Defense Fund: A Case Study of a Green Alliance." *Journal of Business Communication* 36 (1): 5–39.

Long, Mike. 1996. "The Mondragón Cooperative Federation: A Model for Our Times?" *Libertarian Labor Review*, Winter: 19–36.

Lucas, Antonio. 1992. "Mondragón." In *Concise Encyclopedia of Participation and Cooperative Management*, ed. György Széll. Berlin: Walter de Gruyter.

——. 1994. "Industrial Democracy in Spain: The Case of Worker Cooperatives." In *Participation, Organizational Effectiveness and Quality of Worklife in the Year 2000*, ed. University of Piraeus, Litsa Nicolaou-Smokovitis, and György Széll. Frankfurt: Peter Lang.

Luhmann, Niklas. 1990. *Essays on Self-reference*. New York: Columbia University Press.

Lukes, Steven. 1974. *Power: A Radical View*. London: Macmillan.

MacLeod, Greg. 1997. *From Mondragón to America*. Sydney, Nova Scotia: UCCB Press.

Mancomunidad de Alto Deba. 1994. "Orientaciones Estratégicas para el Desarrollo de la Comarca de Alto Deba." Mondragón: MAD.

Mansbridge, Jane. 1983. *Beyond Adversary Democracy*. Chicago: University of Chicago Press.

Markham, Annette. 1996. "Designing Discourse: A Critical Analysis of Strategic Ambiguity and Workplace Control." *Management Communication Quarterly* 9: 389–421.

Martin, Terry. 1994. Conversation with the author. Mondragón, Spain, March.

Marx, Karl. [1865–72] 1977. *Capital, Volume 1*. Trans. Ben Fowkes. New York: Vintage.

Mathews, J. A. 1989. *The Age of Democracy: The Politics of Post-Fordism.* Melbourne: Oxford University Press.

McArdle, Louise, Michael Rowlinson, Stephen Procter, John Hassard, and Paul Forrester. 1995. "Total Quality Management and Participation: Employee Empowerment or Enhancement of Exploitation?" In *Making Quality Critical: New Perspectives on Organizational Change,* ed. Adrian Wilkinson and High Willmott. London: Routledge.

McCloskey, Donald (now Deidre). 1985. *The Rhetoric of Economics.* Madison: University of Wisconsin Press.

———. 1994. *Knowledge and Persuasion in Economics.* Cambridge: Cambridge University Press.

McDonald, Paul, and Jeffrey Gandz. 1992. "Getting Value from Shared Values." *Organizational Dynamics* 20(3): 64–77.

McGee, Michael Calvin. 1980. "The Ideograph: A Link between Rhetoric and Ideology. *Quarterly Journal of Speech.* 66: 1–16.

McKinlay, Alan, and Phil Taylor. 1996. "Power, Surveillance and Resistance: Inside the 'Factory of the Future.' " In *The New Workplace and Trade Unionism,* ed. Peter Ackers, Chris Smith, and Paul Smith. London: Routledge.

McMillan, Jill, and George Cheney. 1996. "The Student as Consumer: Implications and Limitations of a Metaphor." *Communication Education* 45: 1–15.

Meek, Christopher B., and Warner P. Woodworth. 1990. "Technical Training and Enterprise: Mondragón's Educational System and Its Implications for Other Cooperatives." *Economic and Industrial Democracy* 11: 505–28.

Meyer, John W., and Brian Rowan. 1977. "Institutionalized Organizations: Formal Structure as Myth and Ceremony." *American Journal of Sociology* 83: 340–63.

Michels, Robert D. [1915] 1962. *Political Parties: A Sociological Study of the Oligarchical Tendencies of Modern Democracy.* New York: Free Press.

Miller, Mike. 1994. "Mondragón: A Report from the Cooperative." Working paper, Organize Training Center, San Francisco.

Mondragón Corporación Cooperativa (MCC). 1985. "Creación del Congreso Cooperativo." Unpublished corporate document. Mondragón, Spain: MCC.

———. 1988. *España y la Comunidad Europea: Aspectos Relevantes del Cooperativismo.* Mondragón, Spain: MCC.

———. 1991. *Congreso de la Corporación MCC.* Unpublished corporate document. Mondragón, Spain: MCC.

———. 1994. *Corporate Profile, 1994.* Mondragón, Spain: MCC.

———. 1996. "Mondragón Corporación Cooperativa: Primera Corporación Empresarial del País Vasco." Advertisement. *Expansión,* 3 May, 7.

———. 1997a. *International Symposium on Employee Participation: Proceedings.* Mondragón, Spain: MCC.

———. 1997b. *Mondragón: Cuarenta Años de Historia Cooperativa.* Mondragón, Spain: MCC.

———. 1998. *Informe Anual, 1997.* Mondragón, Spain: MCC.

Monge, Peter R., and Katherine I. Miller. 1988. "Participative Processes in Organizations." In *Handbook of Organizational Communication*, ed. Gerald M. Goldhaber and George A. Barnett. Norwood, N.J.: Ablex.

Moody, Kim. 1997. *Workers in a Lean World*. London: Verso.

Morris, David. 1992. "The Mondragón System: Cooperation at Work." Working paper, Institute for Local Self-Reliance, Washington, D.C.

Morrison, Roy. 1991. *We Build the Road as We Travel*. Philadelphia: New Society.

Mouffe, Chantal. 1992. "Feminism, Citizenship, and Radical Democratic Politics." In *Feminists Theorize the Political*, ed. Judith Butler and Joan W. Scott. London: Routledge.

Moye, Melissa A. 1993. "Mondragón: Adapting Co-operative Structures to Meet the Demands of a Changing Environment." *Economic and Industrial Democracy* 14: 251–276.

Mumby, Dennis K. 1997. "The Problem of Heglmony: Rereading Gramsci for Organizational Studies." *Western Journal of Communication* 61: 343–75.

Nader, Ralph, and Lori Wallach. 1996. "GATT, NAFTA, and the Subversion of the Democratic Process." In *The Case against the Global Economy*, ed. Jerry Mander and Edward Goldsmith. San Francisco: Sierra Club.

Naschold, F., R. E. Cole, B. Gustavsen, and H. van Beinum. 1993. *Constructing the New Industrial Society*. Van Gorcum, Netherlands: Swedish Center for Working Life.

Oakeshott, Robert. 1978. *The Case for Workers' Co-ops*. London: Routledge.

Oakland, John S. 1989. *Total Quality Management*. London: Heinemann.

O'Connor, Ellen Swanberg. 1995. "Paradoxes of Participation: Textual Analysis and Organizational Change." *Organizational Studies* 16(5): 769–803.

Olins, Wally. 1989. *Corporate Identity: Making Business Strategy Visible through Design*. London: Thames and Hudson.

Ormaechea, José María. 1991. *La Experiencia Cooperativa de Mondragón*. Mondragón, Spain: MCC.

Papa, Michael J., Mohammad A. Auwal, and Arvind Singhal. 1995. "Dialectic of Control and Emancipation in Organizing for Social Change: A Multitheoretical Study of the Grameen Bank in Bangladesh." *Communication Theory* 5: 189–223.

——. 1997. "Organizing for Social Change within Concertive Control Systems: Member Identification, Empowerment, and the Masking of Discipline." *Communication Monographs*. 64: 219–249.

Parker, Mike. 1993. "Industrial Relations Myth and Shop-floor Reality." In *Industrial Democracy in America: The Ambiguous Promise*, ed. Nelson Lichtenstein. Cambridge: Cambridge University Press.

Patemen, Carole. 1970. *Participation and Democratic Theory*. Cambridge: Cambridge University Press.

Polanyi, Karl. [1944] 1957. *The Great Transformation: The Political and Economic Origins of Our Time*. Boston: Beacon.

Pollert, Anna. 1996. " 'Team Work' on the Assembly Line: Contradictions and the Dynamics of Union Resilence." In *The New Workplace and Trade Unionism*, ed. Peter Ackers, Chris Smith, and Paul Smith. London: Routledge.

Potter, Beatrice. [1891] 1987. *The Co-operative Movement in Great Britain.* Aldershot, England: Gower.

Putnam, Robert. 1993. *Making Democracy Work.* Princeton, N.J.: Princeton University Press.

Rahim, Syed A. 1994. "Participatory Communication as a Dialogic Process." In *Participatory Communication: Working for Change and Development,* ed. Shirley A. White, K. Sadanandan Nair, and Joseph Ascroft. New Delhi: Sage.

Redding, W. Charles. 1972. *Communication within the Organization: An Interpretive View of Theory and Research.* New York: Industrial Communication Council.

Riggs, Fred. 1979. "Introduction: Shifting Meanings of the Term 'Bureaucracy'." *International Social Science Journal* 31: 563–584.

Romme, A. Georges L. 1997. "Work, Authority, and Participation: The Scenario of Circular Organizing." *Journal of Organizational Change Management* 10: 156–166.

Roper, Juliet. 1996. "Takeovers Legislation in New Zealand: A Critical Discourse Analysis." Working paper, University of Waikato, Department of Management Communication, Hamilton, N.Z., May.

———. 1998. "Political Communication: Mapping the Pathways of Discursive Interaction." Working paper, University of Waikato, Department of Management Communication, Hamilton, N.Z., October.

Rose, Nikolas. 1990. *Governing the Soul: The Shaping of the Private Self.* London: Routledge.

Rosenthal, Peggy. 1984. *Words and Values: Some Leading Words and Where They Lead Us.* New York: Oxford University Press.

Rosner, Menachem. 1984. "A Search for 'Coping Strategies' or Forecasts of Cooperative 'Degeneration'." *Economic and Industrial Democracy* 5: 391–399.

Rothschild, Joyce, and J. Allen Whitt. 1986. *The Cooperative Workplace: Potentials and Dilemmas of Organizational Democracy and Participation.* New York: Cambridge University Press.

Rothschild-Whitt, Joyce. 1979. "The Collectivist Organization: An Alternative to Rational-Bureaucratic Models." *American Sociological Review* 44: 509–527.

Rule, James B. 1998. "Markets, in Their Place." *Dissent,* Winter: 29–35.

Russell, Raymond. 1985. *Employee Ownership.* Albany: State University of New York Press.

Samuelson, Robert J. 1996. *The Good Life and Its Discontents.* New York: Vintage.

Satow, Roberta L. 1975. "Value-rational Authority and Professional Organizations: Weber's Missing Type." *Administrative Science Quarterly* 20: 526–31.

Sayer, Derek. 1991. *Capitalism and Modernity: An Excursus on Marx and Weber.* London and New York: Routledge.

Schiller, Bernt. 1991. "Workplace Democracy: The Dual Roots of Worker Participation." In *Managing Modern Capitalism: Industrial Renewal and Workplace Democracy in the United States and Western Europe,* ed. D. Hancock, J. Logue, and B. Schiller. New York: Praeger.

Schumpeter, Joseph A. [1942] 1976. *Capitalism, Socialism, and Democracy.* New York: Harper and Row.

Schwartzman, Helen. 1989. *The Meeting.* New York: Plenum.

Scott, Craig R., Steven R. Corman, and George Cheney. 1998. "Development of a Structurational Model of Identification in the Organization." *Communication Theory* 8: 298–336.

Scott, William G., and David K. Hart. 1979. *Organizational America.* Boston: Houghton Mifflin.

Searle, John R. 1969. *Speech Acts.* Cambridge: Cambridge University Press.

Seashore, Stanley. 1954. *Group Cohesiveness in the Industrial Work Group.* Ann Arbor: Institute for Social Research, University of Michigan.

Seibold, David R. 1995. "Developing the 'Team' in a Team Managed Organization: Group Facilitation in a New-design Plant." In *Innovations in Group Facilitating Techniques: Case Studies of Applications in Naturalistic Settings,* ed. Lawrence Frey. Creskill, N.J.: Hampton.

Seibold, David R., and B. Christine Shea. In press. "Participation and Decision Making." In *The New Handbook of Organizational Communication,* ed. Fredric M. Jablin and Linda L. Putnam. Thousand Oaks, Calif.: Sage.

Sennett, Richard. 1998. *The Corrosion of Character: The Personal Consequences of Work in the New Capitalism.* New York: Norton.

Sewell, Graham. 1998. "The Discipline of Teams: The Control of Team-based Industrial Work through Electronic and Peer Surveillance." *Administrative Science Quarterly* 43: 397–428.

Sewell, Graham, and Adrian Wilkinson. 1992. "Someone to Watch over Me: Surveillance, Discipline and the Just-in-Time Labour Process." *Sociology* 26: 271–89.

Simon, Herbert A. 1976. *Administrative Behavior.* 3d ed. New York: Free Press.

Sklar, Holly. 1995. *Chaos or Community? Seeking Solutions, Not Scapegoats, for Bad Economics.* Boston: South End.

Smith, Adam. [1776] 1986. *The Wealth of Nations.* London: Penguin.

Smith, Kerri. 1995. "Employee Empowerment? Don't Insult Our Intelligence, Cynical Worker Tell Pollsters." *Missoulian,* 26 November, F-3.

Smith, Vicki. 1997. "New Forms of Work Organization." *Annual Review of Sociology* 23: 315–39.

Solomon, Michael, Gary Bamossy, and Søren Askegaard. 1998. *Consumer Behavior: A European Perspective.* Englewood Cliffs, N.J.: Prentice-Hall.

Soros, George. 1997. "The Capitalist Threat." *Atlantic Monthly,* February, 45–58.

Spich, Robert S. 1995. "Globalization Folklore: Problems of Myth and Ideology in Discourse on Globalization." *Journal of Organizational Change Management* 8: 6–29.

Steingard, David S., and Dale E. Fitzgibbons. 1993. "A Postmodern Deconstruction of Total Quality." *Journal of Organizational Change Management* 6: 27–42.

Stohl, Cynthia. 1986. "The Role of Memorable Messages in the Process of Organizational Socialization." *Communication Quarterly* 34: 231–49.

———. 1987. "Bridging the Parallel Organization: A Study of Quality Circle Effectiveness." In *Communication Yearbook 10*, ed. M. L. McLaughlin. Newbury Park, Calif.: Sage.

———. 1993. "European Managers' Interpretations of Participation." *Human Communication Research* 20: 97–131.

———. 1995. *Organizational Communication: Connectedness in Action.* Newbury Park, Calif.: Sage.

Stohl, Cynthia, and George Cheney. 1999. "Participatory Processes/Paradoxical Practices." Paper presented at the annual meeting of the International Communication Association, San Francisco, May.

Strauss, George. 1982. "Workers' Participation in Management: An International Perspective." *Research in Organizational Behavior* 4: 173–265.

Stryjan, Yohanan. 1994. "Understanding Cooperatives: The Reproduction Perspective." *Annals of Public and Cooperative Economics* 65: 59–79.

Tannenbaum, Arnold S. 1983. "Employee-owned Companies." *Research in Organizational Behavior* 5: 235–68.

———. 1986. "Controversies about Control and Democracy in Organizations." In *International Yearbook of Organizational Democracy, Volume 3: The Organizational Practice of Democracy*, ed. R. N. Stern and S. McCarthy. Chichester, England, and New York: Wiley.

Taylor, Frederick. [1911] 1967. *The Principles of Scientific Management.* New York: Norton.

Taylor, Peter Leigh. 1994. "The Rhetorical Construction of Efficiency: Restructuring and Industrial Democracy in Mondragón, Spain." *Sociological Forum* 9:459–89.

Teune, H. 1988. *Growth.* Thousand Oaks, Calif.: Sage.

Thomas, Henk, and Chris Logan. 1982. *Mondragón: An Economic Analysis.* London: Allen & Unwin.

Thompson, Paul, and David McHugh. 1990. *Work Organizations: A Critical Introduction.* London: Macmillan.

Thompson, Victor. 1961. *Modern Organization.* New York: Knopf.

Tinic, Serra A. 1997. "United Colors and Untied Meanings: Benetton and the Commodification of Social Issues." *Journal of Communication* 47: 3–25.

Tjosvold, Dean. 1991. *Team Organization: An Enduring Competitive Advantage.* Sussex, England: Wiley.

Tompkins, Phillip K. 1987. "Translating Organizational Theory: Symbolism over Substance." In *Handbook of Organizational Communication: An Interdisciplinary Perspective*, ed Fredric M. Jablin, Linda L. Putnam, Lyman W. Porter, and Karlene H. Roberts. Thousand Oaks, Calif.: Sage.

Tompkins, Philip K., and George Cheney. 1985. "Communication and Unobtrusive Control in Contemporary Organizations." In *Organizational Communication: Traditional Themes and New Directions*, ed. Robert D. McPhee and P. K. Tompkins. Thousand Oaks, Calif.: Sage.

Trist, Eric, and K. Banforth. 1951. "Some Social and Psychological Consequences of the Longwall Method of Coal Getting." *Human Relations* 4: 3–38.

Trist, Eric, and H. Murray. 1993. *The Social Engagement of Social Science, Vol. 2: The Socio-Technical Perspective*. Philadelphia: University of Pennsylvania Press.

Tsiganou, Helen. 1991. *Worker Participation Schemes: The Experience of Capitalist and Plan-based Societies*. Westport, Conn.: Greenwood.

Tuckman, Alan. 1995. "Ideology, Quality and TQM." In *Making Quality Critical: New Perspectives on Organizational Change*, ed. Adrian Wilkinson and Hugh Willmott. London: Routledge.

Turnbull, Shann. 1994. "Stakeholder Democracy: Redesigning the Governance of Firms and Bureaucracies." *The Journal of SocioEconomics* 23: 321–360.

Tyson, Laura D. 1979. "Incentives, Income Sharing, and Institutional Innovation in the Yugoslav Self-managed Firm. *Journal of Comparative Economics* 3: 285–301.

Uchitelle, Louis. 1997. "Global Good Times, Meet the Global Glut." *New York Times*, 16 November, F-3.

Uchitelle, Louis, and N. R. Kleinfield and Associates. 1996. "The Downsizing of America" (special series). *New York Times*, 3–9 March.

ULMA. 1994. *Proyecto Organizativo Grupo ULMA*. Unpublished corporate document. Oñati, Spain: Grupo ULMA.

———. 1998. *Informe Anual, 1997*. Oñati, Spain: Grupo ULMA

Uribe-Echebarria, Agustín. 1981. *Burocracia o Participación: Un Ensayo sobre Organización y las Cooperativas de Mondragón*. Bilbao: Gráficas Oro.

U.S. Department of Labor. 1994. *Road to High-performance Workplaces*. Washington, D.C.: Office of the American Workplace, U.S. Department of Labor.

Vanek, Jaroslav. 1975. Introduction. In *Self-Management: The Economic Liberation of Man*, ed. Jaroslav Vanek. Harmondsworth, England: Penguin.

———. 1977. *The Labor Managed Economy*. Ithaca, N.Y.: Cornell University Press.

Vázquez, Alfonso. 1994. *La Sorprendente Vía de MAIER hacia la Competitividad Total*. Bilbao: Sociedad para la Promoción y Reconversión Industrial.

Viggiani, Frances A. 1997. "Democratic Hierarchies in the Workplace: Structural Dilemmas and Organizational Action." *Economic and Industrial Democracy* 18: 231–60.

Vincent, Barbara. 1996. "The Religious Ideology of the New Zealand Business Roundtable: Underlying Values and Ethic." Master's thesis, Massey University, Palmerston North, N.Z.

Waddington, Jeremy, and Whitston, Colin. 1996. "Empowerment Versus Intensification: Union Perspectives of Change in the Workplace." In *The New Workplace and Trade Unionism*, ed. Peter Ackers, Chris Smith, and Paul Smith. London: Routledge.

Walker, Juanie. 1996. "Embracing Paradox as a Means to Democratization in Organizations." Paper presented at the annual meeting of the Speech Communication Association, San Diego.

Webb, Sydney, and Beatrice (Potter) Webb. 1897. *Industrial Democracy*. London: Longmans, Green.

Weber, Max. [1968] 1978. *Economy and Society*. 2 vols. Trans. Gunther Roth and Claus Wittich. Berkeley: University of California Press.

Weick, Karl. 1979. *The Social Psychology of Organizing*. 2d ed. Reading, Mass.: Addison-Wesley.

Weisbord, Marvin. 1991. *Productive Workplaces: Organizing and Managing for Dignity, Meaning, and Community*. San Francisco: Jossey-Bass.

Welch, Denis. 1998. "Our Market, Which Art in Heaven." *New Zealand Listener*, 11 July, 25.

Wendt, Ronald F. 1994. "Learning to Walk the Talk: A Critical Tale of the Micropolitics at a Total Quality University." *Management Communication Quarterly* 8(1): 5–45.

Werhane, Patricia H. 1991. *Adam Smith and His Legacy for Modern Capitalism*. New York: Oxford University Press.

Westenholz, Ann. 1982. "Alternative Possibilities in the Sphere of Production: Experiments with Producer Cooperatives." *Acta Sociologica* 25: 25–31.

——. 1991. "Democracy as 'Organizational Divorce' and How Post Modern Democracy Is Stifled by Unity and Majority." *Economic and Industrial Democracy* 12: 173–86.

——. 1993. "Paradoxical Thinking and Change in the Frames of Reference." *Organizational Studies* 14: 37–58.

Wexler, Philip. 1990. "Citizenship in the Semiotic Society." In *Theories of Modernity and Postmodernity*, ed. Bryan S. Turner. London: Sage.

White, Gregory L. 1998. "For GM, a Hard Line on Strike Has Become a Matter of Necessity." *Wall Street Journal*, 12 June, A1, 4.

White, Harrison C. 1981. "Where Do Markets Come From?" *American Journal of Sociology* 87: 517–47.

White, James Boyd. 1984. *When Words Lose Their Meaning*. Chicago: University of Chicago Press.

Whyte, William Foote. 1991. "Learning from Mondragón." In *International Handbook of Participation in Organizations, Vol. 2: Ownership and Participation*, ed. Raymond Russell and Veljko Rus. Oxford: Oxford University Press.

Whyte, William F., and Kathleen K. 1991. *Making Mondragón: The Growth and Dynamics of the Worker Cooperative Complex*. 2d ed., rev. Ithaca, N.Y.: ILR Press.

Wilkinson, Adrian, Graham Godfrey, and Nick Marchington. 1997. "Bouquets, Brickbats, and Blinkers: Total Quality Management and Employee Involvement in Practice." *Organization Studies* 18: 799–819.

Wilkinson, Adrian, and Hugh Wilmott. 1995. "Introduction." In *Making Quality Critical: New Perspectives on Organizational Change*, ed. Adrian Wilkinson and Hugh Willmott. London: Routledge.

Williams, Raymond. 1980. "Advertising: The Magic System." In *Problems in Material Culture*, ed. Raymond Williams. London: Verso.

Wilms, Wellford W. 1996. *Restoring Prosperity: How Workers and Managers are Forging a New Culture of Cooperation.* New York: Times Business/Random House.

Winnicott, D. W. 1950. "Thoughts on the Meaning of the Word 'Democracy'." *Human Relations* 4: 171–85.

Womack, James P., Daniel T. Jones, and Daniel Roos. 1990. *The Machine That Changed the World.* New York: Rawson/Simon and Schuster.

Worthy, James C. 1957. "Management's Approach to Human Relations." In *Research in Industrial Relations,* ed. Industrial Relations Research Associates. New York: Harper and Brothers.

Wren, Daniel A. 1987. *The Evolution of Management Thought.* New York: Wiley.

Yates, Ronald E. 1996. "Backfire: Study—Employee 'Empowerment' Efforts are Failing." *New York Times,* 7 January, F-1.

Young, Ed. 1989. "On the Naming of the Rose: Interests and Multiple Meanings as Elements of Organizational Culture." *Organization Studies* 10(2): 187–206.

INDEX

ABOUT THE AUTHOR

George Cheney (Ph.D., Purdue University, 1985) is Professor in the Department of Communication at the University of Utah. Also, he is Adjunct Professor in the Department of Management Communication at the University of Waikato, Hamilton, New Zealand. He previously taught at the universities of Illinois, Colorado, and Montana. Cheney specializes in the area of organizational communication and has published extensively on such topics as organizational identification and commitment, power in organizations, public relations and marketing, business ethics, and workplace democracy. Recognized both for his teaching and for his research, Cheney has lectured and consulted in the United States, western Europe, Latin America, and Australasia. He is a past chair of the Organizational Communication Division of the National Communication Association.